A Probus Guide to
Subcontract Project Management & Control

Progress Payments

Quentin W. Fleming
Quentin J. Fleming

PROBUS PUBLISHING COMPANY
Chicago, Illinois

Library of Congress Cataloging in Publication Data Available

ISBN 1-55738-283-2

Printed in the United States of America

IPC

1   2   3   4   5   6   7   8   9   0

Table of Contents

List of Figures

Introduction

September 14, 1988: I was walking down the hall minding my own business when my vice president (of materiel) stopped me. He had just left a meeting and did not like what he had seen. He asked that I get myself "involved" with the management of progress payments to our subcontractors. He also asked that I look into both the unclassified areas, as well as some of our isolated, special project areas. I saluted, and with that brief encounter, received a new assignment which would last almost three years, until I took an early retirement from the Northrop Corporation.

Although I wouldn't admit it publicly, it had been two decades since I had last worked with progress payments, and, there were likely a couple of changes which had happened in that period. Therefore, my first action had to be to research of all the written material I could find on the subject.

I immediately reviewed the Federal Acquisition Regulation (FAR) and the Department of Defense (DOD-FAR) supplement, not exactly light reading. I looked up the subject in our company policy and procedural documents, also exciting reading. I read the progress payment terms and condition provisions in our prime and principle subcontracts.

After obtaining a list of all the subcontracts which had progress payment provisions, I then interviewed some thirty or so buyers who had the responsibility for administering these subcontracts. It was not a pretty sight. Somehow the buyers, and we had some excellent buyers, had almost totally relinquished their roles and responsibilities for the administration of progress payments to the finance department. The evolution had been subtle, and had taken place gradually over several years. Someone, some twelve or more years earlier (we couldn't trace the exact year), had made the decision to "pay first," and then ask the buyers to review and "approve" the invoices after the fact. The concept was legally proper, but it just wasn't working. The buying community could never quite get interested in taking charge of something after all of the decisions (to pay or not to pay) had been made by someone else for them.

Then, before I had had a chance to formulate any plan of action, we got the dreaded word: "The customer was coming." Yes, we would have the honor, the pleasure of a formal Contractor Operations Review (COR) in mid-October, in less than three weeks! The visit would cover a review of all of our systems and procedures, including our procurement system and our progress payments to subcontractors. We needed a quick fix of some type to get through this exercise. Progress payment administration was acknowledged to be our weakest activity.

I quickly structured a brief progress payment training outline and asked for help. And I got the best kind of help possible—multi-functional professional help from each of the various functions involved in the subcontract management processes.

The law department prepared an overview of the Federal Acquisition Regulations (FAR) as related to progress payments. The financial audit department covered the pre-subcontract award survey requirements, and their audit activities. Accounts payable reviewed the processing of supplier invoices, and the problems therein. Materiel business management covered the pre-award and post-award management of a subcontract, including the administration of progress payments.

With the vice president (of materiel) introducing each session, we ran the total materiel department and other key functions through our sessions. And with the help of a most cooperative customer (and they do exist), we got a "green" approval of our procurement system review.

Now it was time to stand back and make an objective assessment of our progress payment procedures. We needed to make certain permanent improvements in the overall progress payment methods. Although many firms have devised and use very precise formulas for evaluating each and every line of the process payment invoice, that approach seemed to us to be overly complicated, and likely to miss the main goal. Our main mission was subcontract management, and progress payment administration was just one part of that process.

We elected to make three fundamental changes in the way we managed our progress payments: (1) place the buyer and the buyer's immediate manager in a position to review and approve (or reject) all payments before they were made; (2) obtain and display a *cost* plan from all suppliers, to allow for a comparison with each request for progress payment against the supplier's own projections; (3) obtain a *schedule* plan from all suppliers, a Gantt chart, one in which we could link their physical (earned value) performance to all payments being made to them. With these three changes in place we felt we could stay on top of our progress payments, keep the risks of loss to a minimum, and not overly burden our suppliers with reporting requirements.

The first change which needed to be made was to get the buyer, and the buyer's immediate manager, into the approval cycle *before* any progress payments were made. They had to feel it was their decision to pay or not to pay. Back in "Business 101" we called this issue one of having commensurate "authority" and "responsibility," but sometimes we do forget the basics.

Next we had to provide the necessary "tools" to our buyers so that they could make intelligent decisions, to approve or to reject an invoice, based on the cost and schedule performance of the suppliers. However, most of our subcontracts were firm fixed-price (FFP) type subcontracts, and suppliers who receive FFP type contracts do not take kindly to oversight, in any form. Rightly or wrongly, many suppliers flatly refused to supply their performance plans against which they could be monitored. But our vice president and most senior subcontract management held tight. They supported the fundamental principle of requiring supplier performance plans as a pre-condition to the granting of progress payment terms in any subcontract. Without a supplier's cost and schedule plan in place to give us assurance that they could repay all payments, they would get no progress payments. It was as simple as that.

In June of 1989 we issued a new procedure requiring a Gantt chart prepared by the supplier on all procurements which contained progress payment provisions. Thus, we had put in place a simple "earned value" management approach which linked supplier physical performance measurement with the approval of their progress payments—yes, even on firm fixed-price (FFP) type subcontracts.

The real significance of our new procedural change was not known for more than a year and a half later. In January of 1991, the Navy canceled the A-12 Avenger program which has an alleged over payment of some $1.35 billion to the contractors. There are post mortems and lessons learned and lawsuits underway at this time on the A-12. The final results may not be known for years.

Suffice it to say that we were quite pleased to have in place a simple procedure which "linked" the progress payment process to a supplier's physical performance, in the summer of 1989.

Quentin W. Fleming
Tustin, California

Acknowledgements

Several individuals contributed their time and expertise to this manuscript, and we want to express our appreciation. Two in particular helped us with the full document, one a leading expert in progress payments and the other a founder and leader in earned value performance measurement.

M.G. (Bud) Rudisill, division financial specialist, for the Northrop Corporation, Aircraft Division, was "the" expert on the subject of progress payments. He gave us constructive suggestions and helped in our initial training sessions. **Robert R. Kemps** is currently in charge of Humphreys & Associates' Washington, D.C. office. Prior to retirement from the Government he was with the Department of Defense where he was instrumental in establishing the earned value concept at the DOD, and later with the Department of Energy. Both of these gentlemen read every word and gave us invaluable comments on the manuscript.

From the field of progress payments we also had valuable support from: **William Wescott**, manager of accounts receivable for a large aerospace company in the Los Angeles area; and **David Robertson**, with the Defense Logistics Agency, Cameron Station, Alexandria, Virginia.

From the performance measurement field we had **Joseph R. Houser**, a program manager for management systems with IBM, the Federal Sector Division in Bethesda, Maryland. Joe is also the current president of the Performance Management Association (PMA), and was the past chairperson of the management systems subcommittee of the National Security Industrial Association (NSIA).

Additional people who lent their expertise were: **John O'Neil**, president of Micro-Frame Technologies, Inc, of Ontario, California, a company which provides program management software for earned value measurement, and **Harry I. Sparrow**, president of Decision Planning Corporation, of Costa Mesa, California, a firm which consults to management in C/SCSC.

Our special thanks to each of you for your comments, contributions, and support.

Disclaimer

Our attorney, **Sheldon J. Fleming**, has advised us to include a disclaimer to this book, or else he could be providing us with his professional legal services at the expense of his more lucrative (and paying) clients.

What is contained in this book are personal opinions on a very complex and rapidly changing technical subject of progress payments. These opinions are based on our collective experiences in this industry. These opinions should not be considered as representing legal advice, or financial accounting advice, for these can only come to you from a qualified attorney or an accountant of your choice.

Whenever contemplating a business arrangement which has areas of uncertainty, it is always a wise practice to do so under the guidance of a trusted and professional attorney or certified public accountant.

Chapter 1

Some Background
on Progress Payments

One of the major challenges facing all prime contractors is managing the risks of contract performance: the cost, schedule, and technical risks. With the progressively larger share of contract dollars now going outside of prime contractors down to their subcontracting base, many prime contractors are now looking outward at their suppliers to share some of the "glory" of the risks of contract performance.

There are a multitude of ways to minimize prime contractor performance risks, one of the more obvious is with the preparation of high quality specifications for a program: system, performance, process, development, procurement—to mention just a few. Another key factor in risk management is the ability to define an airtight statement of work, both for internal budget performance and most particularly for subcontracted (external) supplier performance.

However, many times it is not possible to precisely define either a tight specification or even an adequate statement of work. In these cases the prime contractor may attempt to allot some of their own risks with subcontractors by selecting an appropriate contract type for the occasion—choosing from the two broad families of contract types, either a fixed price or a cost reimbursable contract.

1

The importance of selecting the appropriate type of contractual arrangement for a given subcontract is a critical one for all procurements. Selecting the type of contract should be decided by many factors, perhaps none more important to both parties than the amount of "cost risk" the buyer (the prime contractor) wishes to transfer to the seller (the subcontractor), and conversely, how much of the cost risk the seller is willing to assume. If the prime contractor is willing to retain the risks of cost growth, for whatever reason, then they will likely choose a cost reimbursable type of subcontract.

If, however, it is the buyer's intent to transfer the maximum potential cost risk to the subcontractor, then some type of a fixed price contract would be used, likely a Firm Fixed Price (FFP) subcontract.

Under a FFP type subcontract, a supplier is obligated to assume the complete risk of any resulting cost growth and losses. This is the normal rule, but there is one very important condition, almost an exception, which should be understood. When the subcontract includes a "Progress Payment" clause in the arrangement, there is some likelihood that the cost risk factor *may* well have remained with the prime contractor and did not transfer to the supplier. And although not a widely publicized fact, there is a history of shall we say "unfortunate cost experiences" (called losses) in the industry which have been the direct result of the poor management of progress payments. For example, one of the more obvious ways for a prime contractor to lose money is to make progress payments in advance of the supplier's physical performance, and then have the supplier close its doors.

Proper management of progress payments begins prior to making the subcontract award, and must continue throughout the life of the subcontract. A prime contractor which uses progress payments is particularly vulnerable if its buyers fail to understand the importance of doing the right things both prior to award, and after subcontract award.

Therefore, with progress payments so very common in the government contracting business, and with prime contractors "encouraged" by the government to flow these financial arrangements downward to all their subcontracting team members, the subject and the associated risks of using progress payments must be clearly understood in order to best protect the interests of prime contractors and, of course, the United States Government.

Just What Are Progress Payments

In their simplest form, progress payments may be viewed as a "loan," a temporary interest free loan from a buyer (the prime contractor) to a seller (the subcontractor). They are based on costs incurred by the supplier in the performance of a specific order and are paid directly to the supplier as a stipulated and agreed to percentage of the total costs incurred as defined in the Federal Acquisition Regulation (FAR). The supplier promises to "pay back" the temporary progress payment loan by (1) making contractual deliveries or by completing contractual line items, and (2) allocating some portion of the proceeds of the delivered unit price or completed line item values to liquidate the loan, based on the established subcontract unit price of the articles or services so delivered.

Note that there is an important distinction to be made between the "loan" value (the progress payment rate), and the repayment of the loan (the "liquidation" rate for the progress payments). Progress payments are paid as a percentage of *costs* incurred by a supplier, for example 80 percent of the costs incurred. By contrast, the liquidation of the loan is based on a percentage of the unit *price* of article or service deliveries, which includes the supplier's fee. As such, the loan liquidations will include both the supplier's costs as well as the supplier's profit (i.e., the full subcontract unit values of the delivered articles).

Thus, the delivery of contract units and the completion of line items once started, will result in a dramatic reduction of the outstanding progress payment loan. However, contract deliveries must first happen, and subcontractors must make physical progress in order to liquidate or repay the loan—this sometimes is the very heart of progress payment difficulties. More on the critical issue of making physical progress later.

Progress payments are a form of contract financing to be used on *fixed-price* contracts. The payments cover the period which starts when a supplier begins to incur costs against an authorized order and continues to when the supplier is making unit deliveries or completing contractual tasks. This results in a supplier getting paid based on established unit or line-item task prices. The intent of progress payments is to prevent an "impairment" of the working capital of industrial suppliers doing business under United States Government contracts.

To best illustrate the concept, Figure 1-1 presents the cash flow requirements on a subcontract without progress payments to Hypothetical Engines, Inc. Note that this supplier has had to float over $5 million dollars in costs over a nineteen month span before they start to make contract deliveries and finally receive funds for their efforts. Thus without progress payments to assist in providing working capital, the supplier would likely have to borrow funds to accommodate the order, and the overall cost to the United States Government would be greater than with progress payments included. The savings to the government is the difference between the diminished value of the dollars and the commercial cost of capital that the supplier would have

Figure 1-1.   Payments on Delivery

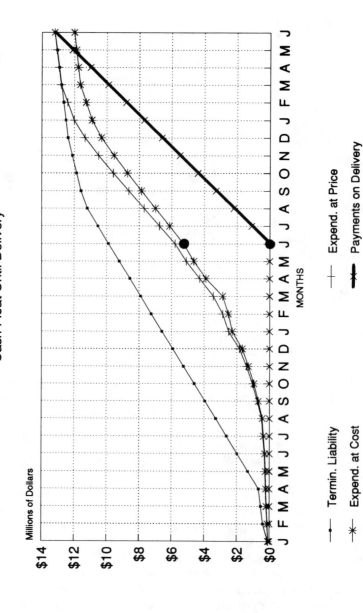

HYPOTHETICAL ENGINES, INC.

-Cash Float Until Delivery-

Millions of Dollars

$14

$12

$10

$8

$6

$4

$2

$0

J F M A M J J A S O N D J F M A M J J A S O N D J F M A M J

MONTHS

— Termin. Liability

* Expend. at Cost

+ Expend. at Price

→ Payments on Delivery

otherwise incurred and passed-on to the government in the price of the articles delivered.

In Figure 1-1, four curves are shown on the chart and each line should be understood. The top line is the "Termination Liability" for the subcontract, which consists of the estimated open commitments for the period shown, plus all costs actually incurred, plus all other estimated costs which would be required to satisfy the obligations of the order including the supplier's profit.

The second line consists of "Expenditures at Price," which represents all incurred costs including estimated supplier profit.

The third line is the "Expenditures at Cost," the same data as the second line but without the supplier's profit. The significance of the cost expenditure curve is that progress payments, if authorized, will be a stated percentage value of this line, for example, 80 percent of costs incurred.

The lower straight diagonal line (the fourth line) is the price value of supplier deliveries, which includes the supplier's costs plus profits, as defined in the subcontract. The supplier deliveries will have importance with progress payments in that some specified dollar portion of all deliveries will go to liquidate progress payment loans.

The concept of progress payments is authorized by the United States Government in their Federal Acquisition Regulation (FAR),[1] and further implemented by various elements of the government, including the Department of Defense, which functions under its DOD-FAR Supplement.[2] All prime contractors who enjoy progress payment provisions in their contracts are encouraged by the government to flow these financial arrangements downward to their subordinate next tier subcontractors as a way of assisting firms associated with a particular contract.

Prime contractors who have progress payment provisions in their contracts will typically have three authorities to further issue such terms downward to their suppliers. First, they have the Federal Acquisition Regulation (FAR) which must be followed, and which are sometimes further modified in the Defense industry by the Defense FAR Supplement (DOD-FAR). Second, the prime contract documents received from the government will contain specific reference to the appropriate FAR and DOD-FAR clauses and will give a prime contractor authority to receive and further issue progress payments downward to their supplier base. Lastly, a given company's internal policies and procedures will authorize the use of progress payments in their procurements and will generally follow the language of the FAR and DOD-FAR provisions which have authorized such activity.

There are four types of progress payments available to industry. The first two are common to firms doing business with the United States Government, and the second two are unique to only the Defense industry:

1. *Customary progress payments* with an *ordinary liquidation rate,* which will be identical to the progress payment rate.[3]

2. *Customary progress payments* with an *alternate liquidation rate (ALR),* which allows a lesser liquidation (repayment) rate than the customary progress payment rate.[4]

3. *Customary flexible progress payments* with an *ordinary liquidation rate.*[5]

4. *Customary flexible progress payments* with an *alternate liquidation rate (ALR).*

From a supplier's standpoint, the four types of progress payments become progressively more attractive as you move from number one to number four. The supplier is able to both retain the loans for a longer period of time prior to repayment, as well as utilize some small portion of their profits as they move from number one to number four. A prime contractor will typically offer suppliers alternative number one, placing the burden upon suppliers to advance to higher levels. To obtain the other types of progress payments, the supplier must first request them, and then must be prepared to meet higher qualification and performance standards. All subcontractor cost data will be subjected to closer scrutiny in order to receive the more attractive flexible progress payment and alternate liquidation terms.

In order to minimize the use (cash flow) of their own funds, a contractor will flow upward to the government (or to a next higher tier contractor) all allowable progress payments paid by them to their lower tier subcontractors. All legitimate and allowable progress payments paid to lower tier subcontractors are fully reimbursable upward at 100 percent of the full (net unliquidated) value of such funds paid. The fact that there could be differing payment rates in effect at the same time between a prime contractor and a subcontractor (e.g., customary/flexible/ordinary/alternate) does not change the reimbursement practice. Therefore, all legitimate payments paid to lower tier suppliers will have no adverse impact on a prime contractor's cash flow, other than the brief time-lag until full reimbursement.

The processing of progress payment activities is accomplished according to a precise, prearranged monthly submittal schedule, as defined in the contractual arrangement between the prime contractor and each subcontractor. Since such reimbursement cycles are monthly, all supplier requests for progress payments must also be monthly and precisely conform to a billing schedule in order for each participant in the process to receive their respective cash payments in a prompt manner.

It is therefore imperative that all suppliers involved in this precise cash flow process submit proper and complete invoices in order to prevent any delays in reimbursement. Should there be any flaws or mathematical errors or simple questions to be answered in a request from a supplier, it is possible (highly likely) that a supplier's request for payment will be delayed by at least thirty days or more until such matters are clarified. Thus, a contractor's cash reimbursement will queue until a subsequent month's payment cycle comes around, and the supplier will be funding its own contract activity without the benefit of the government's financial interest free loan.

Since progress payments are a technique used in United States Government contracting, any progress payment loans used by firms in non-government, purely commercial, or internally financed business endeavors will have no place with which to flow funds for reimbursement by a higher external (government) authority. Thus in these circumstances, if progress payments are used, the private contractor must stand ready to provide all such funding for the deals from their own internal operating funds. Therefore, most private firms who are sensitive to the importance of managing cash-flow, and who isn't these days, will likely set up very stringent procedural controls restricting (limiting) the use of progress payments on all non-government work.

One last point on the use of progress payments. The government defines in FAR what they call their "order of preference" for contract financing. Their preferences as stated are:

1. Private financing without government guarantee.

2. Progress payments based on costs at customary rates.

3. Loan guarantees.

4. Progress payments based on costs with unusual terms.

5. Advance payments.[6]

Thus, the government has stated it would prefer private contractors do their own contract financing and receive funding when they make deliveries of hardware, software, or services. This is the government's stated policy, which is encouraged as long as the circumstances do not call for the use of private funds at unreasonable terms or funds from other agencies of the government. If private contractors are not able to underwrite their activities with reasonable financing terms (and most are not), then customary progress payments are encouraged, including a flow-down to all lower tier subcontractors.

Legal Authorities for Progress Payments

There are two broad legal authorities as defined in the Federal Acquisition Regulation (FAR) which authorize the use of, and specify the rules under which contractors in the Defense, Space, and Energy industries may issue progress payments to their fixed-price suppliers. In addition, the Defense industry has two related authorities defined in the DOD-FAR supplement. The four legal authorities are:

1. FAR SUBPART 32.5: Progress Payments Based on Costs
2. FAR 52.232-13 to 16: Progress Payment Contract Clauses
3. DOD-FAR SUBPART 232.5: Progress Payments Based on Costs
4. DOD-FAR 252-7003 to 7007: DOD Progress Payment Contract Clauses

These four authorities (two FAR and two DOD-FAR) are reviewed and "unofficially" restated in Appendix B to this book. They are described and paraphrased in the appendix in order to better understand the complex regulations which govern the use of progress payments. However, a caution is in order: what is covered in Appendix B is but a brief "unofficial" synopsis of the FAR and DOD-FAR regulations. Those individuals and firms needing more definitive interpretations or a more extensive explanation should refer directly to the government regulations, or to their own legal counsel.[7]

Big versus Small Businesses

There are important distinctions which must be made between a large business, a small business, and a small disadvantaged business in the awarding of progress payments to fixed-price suppliers. It will help to start with a few definitions in order to better understand the subject.

A "large business" is any firm which is a significant contributor in its field and does not meet the definition of being a small business.

A "small business" is any business, including its affiliates, which is independently owned and operated and is not dominant in its field of operation. Such firms typically receive preferred treatment in government contracting matters.

A "small disadvantaged business" is a small business concern that is at least 51 percent unconditionally owned by one or more individuals who are both socially and economically disadvantaged, or a publicly owned business that has at least 51 percent of its stock unconditionally owned by one or more socially and economically disadvantaged individuals and that has its management and daily business controlled by one or more such individuals. This definition also includes economically disadvantaged Indian tribes or native Hawaiian organizations.[8]

If progress payments are included in a prime contract, they are in effect an "entitlement" to a small business and a small disadvantaged business concern. Progress payments *must* be included in any award to a small business, or small disadvantaged business concern, if they are present in the prime contract, are so requested by a small business firm, and the small business concern meets the minimal qualifications for progress payments.

As with any firm hoping to receive progress payments, all small business firms must satisfy certain minimum qualification requirements in order to receive such payments. First, they must demonstrate a financial capability, a fiscal solvency, and a record of reasonable financial stability in order to qualify for the loans. There must be reasonable assurances provided that all progress payment loans will be repaid properly through the performance of the supplier.

Secondly, the small business concern must demonstrate that they have an adequate cost accounting system in place. They must have the ability to segregate one order from another, particularly those which have progress payment provisions.

There are additional "guidelines" involving the use of progress payments to small and small disadvantages business concerns. These are guidelines only, and may be altered if particular circumstances so dictate. Generally, subcontracts to these concerns must exceed $100,000, and the period from the supplier first incurring costs on the order until the first contractual delivery must be four months or more. Small business firms receive a 5 percent higher customary progress payment rate than do large business firms. Small disadvantaged businesses under DOD contracting currently receive a 10 percent higher rate than the current rate set for a large business.

By contrast, progress payments are a "discretionary" flow-down to a large business concern. While the government's policy encourages progress payment flow-down to all suppliers, they may or may not be awarded to a large business supplier, based on the particular circumstances of a given procurement and the best business interests of the buyer's firm. The subcontract's value to large businesses must be $1,000,000 or more, and the period of the supplier incurring its first costs after award until the first contractual delivery (hardware or line-item services) must be six months or longer. Multiple orders to the same large business supplier may be combined to satisfy the $1,000,000 threshold requirement. However, in combining orders to satisfy the threshold requirement, the orders must have certain homogenous characteristics such as the same time period, the same or related contract source, the same FAR rates, etc.

Small businesses have also been given a distinct advantage with their cash flow by virtue of their ability to meet a lower standard in the issue of what must constitute an "incurred cost." Costs incurred for a large business means only those payments actually paid by the supplier at the time it submits a progress payment request (i.e., all bills must have been previously paid by a large business concern). A small business firm is allowed to merely make an accounting accrual in order to qualify its payments for reimbursement.

A summary of the more significant differences in requirements between progress payments to large and small businesses is shown in Figure 1-2.

Nineteen-ninety changes in the DOD-FAR concerning customary flexible progress payments to a small business concern essentially puts small businesses on the same footing as a large contractor if the small business concern desires to go to a flexible progress payment rate. In the past if a buyer awarded progress payments to a small business they would include an Alternate I substitute clause in their contractual agreement which would provide two advantages to the small supplier: (1) cost incurred was defined as merely an accounting accrual, and (2) the supplier received the 5 percent higher customary rate. With the DOD-FAR change, Alternate I is not to be used when the small business concern elects to go to a customary *flexible* progress payment rate. These issues of the proper contract clauses and flexible progress payments will be covered in more detail in the next chapter on pre-award activity.

Lastly, a financial official of any supplier, either large or small, must sign the monthly progress payment invoice to certify the legitimacy of all costs contained in the request.

Who Manages Progress Payments

The government is quite clear on who it expects to hold responsible for managing progress payments for private contractors. In every case it is the buyer—that individual who has procurement authority and has awarded a subcontract—who will be held responsible for the proper administration of progress payments on behalf of the contractor.

There are several reasons for the government's decision to hold the contractor responsible. In the first place, it is the buyer who is the principal person who will make the initial decision as to whether or not progress payments are warranted on a particular procurement. Prior to making an award, it is the buyer who will obtain the appropriate concessions from a supplier. The buyer should incorporate the proper terms and conditions at the

Figure 1-2. Small versus Large Businesses

	Small Business	Large Business
Period from award & initial costs to first delivery:	4 months	6 months
Minimum Value of Subcontract:	$100,000	$1,000,000
Conditions of Award:	Entitlement, if qualified to receive progress payments	Discretionary with Buyer
Progress Payment Rates:	+ 5% Customary Rate + 10% Customary Rate for SDB	Customary rate
Costs Incurred Method:	An Accounting Accrual	Actual Payment of Costs

time of award in order to adequately protect the government's (and the private firm's) best financial interests.

The buyer will frequently receive technical assistance from the company's finance department (sometimes internal audit, price/cost analysis) to assess the "financial health" of each prospective supplier before making an award with progress payments. It is the buyer who must make a final determination as to whether the supplier has an adequate cost accounting system and financial controls in place to be able to properly segregate the costs on various orders—in order to qualify for the progress payment loan.

Sometimes, there is a resistance (often a flat refusal) from a subcontractor to accommodate a private audit from another contractor. This is particularly the case when the prime contractor and subcontractor are competitors in their fields and are sensitive about the sharing of financial information. In these cases, the audit branch of the government may be called on to perform the pre-contract audit. But recognize that government audits do take time, much time. Often a recent government audit report on the subcontractor may be used to satisfy the requirement for a precontract financial assessment.

Also, prior to the awarding of progress payments, it is the buyer who will obtain from a supplier a series of financial profiles (e.g., a termination liability projection, an expenditure curve, etc.) and then subsequently authorize progress payments as a percentage of the supplier's projected incurred costs. The authorized or "net" progress payment amount will increase up to the point when subcontract deliveries begin, then decrease with liquidations consistent with the approved liquidation rate. This critical issue will be covered in detail in the next chapter.

Consideration must be obtained when making an award of progress payments to a supplier. It is reasonable for a buyer to assume that consideration will have been included in any prospective bidder's response, *if* the initial solicitation had notified all prospective bidders that any resulting subcontract award would include progress payments in the order. But, the buyer must always be alert to judge the validity of such compensation.

If a deal is concluded with a supplier (i.e., the negotiations are concluded) and the subcontractor subsequently requests progress payments, the buyer must then obtain and should document for the procurement file the value of the consideration subsequently obtained. Legal consideration may take many forms, such as improved terms and conditions, warranty arrangements, patent rights, rights in data, better deliveries, the point of delivery, etc. However, a general (and safe) rule with which to measure the adequacy of subcontract consideration is through a specific reduction in some percentage of supplier's proposed profit rate. That is a tangible value which everyone can understand.

Firm Fixed-Price (FFP) Subcontracts

The subject of firm fixed-price (FFP) type subcontracting is often a sensitive and sometimes emotional one, both for a prime contractor and for the subcontractor. In theory, under a FFP type arrangement, the offeror promises to assume *all* of the risks of subcontract performance. But that is just theory. The theory often (quite often?) breaks down in actual practice.

For example, the FFP subcontractor is expected to assume all risks of cost growth under a FFP type contract. Yes, that is the theory. However, once a supplier starts to lose money on a given order (for whatever reason), and they sometimes do, there suddenly develops a constant demand from the subcontractor for claims for equitable adjustments, which some people refer to as "get well" requests. Such demands often impede the once cordial relationship between the two parties. And, if the impending loss on a fixed-price order is significant in relation to the overall corporate size of the supplier, the supplier may even ask for a contract "restructuring," or to be relieved from their performance obligations under the order itself. Recent experiences between the Department of Defense and certain major prime contractors have painfully demonstrated this example. Also, whenever a supplier starts to lose money on a given order, there is the ever-present temptation for them to take short-cuts in the quality of the product being provided to their customer.

What once may have been a harmonious alliance, suddenly gets bogged down in a dialogue whereby the supplier will attempt to "make a recovery" on each and every simple query from the prime contractor's organization.

Under a FFP type subcontract, the supplier is also expected to assume all of the risks of schedule performance. Once again, this is just theory. Not infrequently, a late delivery of perhaps a fifty dollar supplier part will hold up an entire production line and result in a late delivery of a million dollar prime contract system. A seemingly minor action by a supplier will sometimes result in a loss (or a penalty) to the prime contractor, but may not impact the subcontractor providing the late delivery. And yet when asked to provide performance monitoring data, most suppliers will unyieldingly object to any attempt to oversee their subcontract schedule performance under the FFP subcontract because "We have assumed all of the risks under this firm fixed-price subcontract and do not need anyone's help—thank you very much." Pragmatic evidence in the industry would seem to suggest otherwise.

What all this means to any prime contractor wishing to avoid undue cost and schedule risks and the potential resulting losses is that *all* subcontracts must be managed after the contract is awarded, even those which are placed under a firm fixed-price (FFP) type subcontract. Unfortunately, empirical evidence suggests that FFP suppliers have historically refused buyer requests for basic performance monitoring information such as a simple funding projections, cost performance plans, schedule plans, etc., without demanding substantial added costs to the subcontract price.

Now enter the issue of "progress payments," which remember is essentially a form of a "loan" from a prime contractor to a subcontractor. When an individual goes to a bank to apply for a loan, a loan application must be dutifully prepared and submitted, and the application reviewed and approved by the lender prior to any loan being granted. Sometimes even collateral assets must be provided for the loan. Rules must be precisely followed or the loan will not be granted.

Likewise, when progress payment "loans" are requested on a given procurement, the subcontractor should reasonably be expected to meet certain minimum qualifications *prior* to the approval of their request. Instead of a loan application, the prospective supplier should be required to produce their cost performance plans and their schedule performance plans in order to provide the prime contractor (and the government) with tangible evidence that such plans do exist, thereby giving them assurances that the progress payment loan will be repaid properly during the term of the subcontract period. Each month, the supplier should be expected to demonstrate to the lender (the buyer) that its cost and schedule subcontract performance is sufficient to warrant an additional progress payment "loan advance" in order for each progress payment invoice to be paid.

Progress payments (loans) thus provide a prime contractor with an "opportunity" to obtain (to require) the appropriate post-award monitoring tools from a supplier, and to do so without adding costs to the procurement package. These basic tools are needed by prime contractors in order to reduce the risks of financial loss, which can be ever present even on firm fixed-price (FFP) type subcontracts.

Progress payments thus allow a prime contractor, acting on behalf of itself and the United States Government, to position itself to be able to monitor the performance of all of their subcontractors, even (particularly) those with FFP type subcontractors.

The tactical (near-term) goal of requiring supplier performance plans is to be able to expose and to avoid surprises in the form of cost overruns and schedule slippages, wherever possible. But on the other hand, a more strategic (longer-term) objective is to isolate through close subcontractor performance measurement, those orders which might have a negotiated profit value which is in excess of the best interests of the United States Government. Sound progress payment management will help to facilitate and achieve these goals.

The subject of progress payments will be explained in more detail in the following chapters. Those things which must be done prior to subcontract award will be covered next, followed by a chapter on post-award subcontract management. Subsequent chapters will provide an analysis of progress payment data and the management of progress payments used in concert with the earned value (C/SCSC) concept.

Endnotes

1. Federal Acquisition Regulation, Subpart 32.5, Progress Payments based on costs.

2. Department of Defense FAR, Subpart 232.5, Progress Payments based on costs.

3. Federal Acquisition Regulation (FAR), 32.503–8.

4. Federal Acquisition Regulation (FAR), 32.503–9.

5. Defense Federal Acquisition Regulation (DOD-FAR), 232.502–1, (S-71).

6. FAR 32.106.

7. Two books which cover the FAR and DOD-FAR in some detail as described in these sections are available for purchase from the Commerce Clearing House, Inc., 4025 W. Peterson Avenue, Chicago, Illinois 60646. They are: (1) *FAR: Federal Acquisition Regulation,* 1991 Edition; (2) *DOD-FAR Supplement,* 1991 Edition, Parts 201–270.

8. See FAR, Part 19, for a complete description of the regulations covering small and small disadvantaged business concerns.

Chapter 2

Pre-Award Activity

The time for a couple to think about a prenuptial agreement is not six months into their marriage. At that point it is too late. Rather, the time to express any such concerns and to work out the details, is prior to their saying "I do."

Likewise, with subcontract management, the time to start worrying about the "post-award" management phase is not after the subcontract has been awarded. Rather, the right time to plan for post-award subcontract management is prior to the execution of the legally binding subcontract. Unfortunately, it does not always happen that way. Too often in being anxious to get started, the award is authorized and then the critical details are worked out along the way. What a price is paid for impatience.

Similarly, there are a number of issues relating specifically to the subject of progress payments which can only be properly addressed prior to the issuance of the subcontract document. Many of these matters are also critical to the formation of a sound contract in which the best interests of both parties are protected, particularly those of the prime contractor.

The Solicitation

One of the issues facing a buyer about to award a new subcontract is which provisions of the prime contract will be flowed downward to the supplier. With the subject of progress payment flow-down, some discretionary latitude is available to the buyer. If the resulting subcontract award will go to a small or to a small disadvantaged supplier, then the buyer *must* provide progress payments to any qualified subcontractor in that category in order to comply with the language of the Federal Acquisition Regulation (FAR). However, if the resulting award is expected to go to a large business concern, then a buyer may, if they so choose, withhold such provisions from the large supplier. However, whichever approach is chosen must be indicated in the solicitation package to all prospective respondents.

Some people in the industry, as a matter of their procurement policy, advocate the restriction of progress payments to only those suppliers which must receive them, that is, a small and small disadvantaged business concern. They take this somewhat unorthodox approach perhaps as a result of having had bad experiences (losses) with progress payments, and thus want to limit the risks associated with providing such loans. However, by restricting the downward flow of progress payments, a prime contractor may be missing an opportunity to secure the lowest possible price for their procurements, recognizing that the interest free money provided to suppliers with the use of progress payments offers an opportunity to them seldom available in a purely commercial environment.

Displayed in Figure 2-1 is a table of solicitation and contract clauses which cover progress payments from the Federal Acquisition Regulation (FAR) and the Defense FAR supplement. Lines (1) or (2) or (3) as shown in the figure should be cited by reference in any solicitation document to notify all prospective suppliers exactly what forms of progress payment funding (if any) will be available in the resulting subcontract award. Line (4) is the actual contract clause from the FAR to be incorporated, also by reference, into the subcontract document itself. Note that in DOD procurements, the DOD-FAR has its own progress payment clause as listed in line (4), plus certain other unique DOD payment clauses as listed in lines (5) through (8).

Some Progress Payment Issues Prior to Awarding the Subcontract

Assessing the Subcontractor's Financial "Health"

It would not do much for the management reputation of a prime contractor for them to authorize the issuance of progress payments to a subcontractor on one day, and then in the next few days to have that same supplier start bankruptcy proceedings. That simply would not play well in the local press, as warm and as understanding as they always are about such things. Instead, it would be far better for the prime contractor to take positive steps to assure that progress payment loans are granted to only those suppliers who are

Figure 2-1. Progress Payment Solicitation and Contract Clauses

	FAR	DOD-FAR
(1) Notice of Progress Payments in RFP	52.232-13	none
(2) Notice of Progress Payments for Small Businesses only	52.232-14	none
(3) Progress Payments not included	52.232-15	none
(4) Progress Payments contract clause -Alternate I Small Businesses -Alternate II Letter Contracts	52.232-16	252.232-7007
(5) Foreign Military Sales	none	252.232-7003
(6) Flexible Progress Payments	none	252.232-7004
(7) Fixed Price Construction Contracts	none	252.232-7005
(8) Architect-Engineering Contracts	none	252.232-7006

financially viable and are likely to repay the funds in an orderly way. An evaluation of the financial well-being of any supplier being considered for progress payments is a necessary prerequisite for all such awards. The supplier must be capable of repaying the progress payment funds that have been advanced to it.

Also, and perhaps of greater importance, the Federal Acquisition Regulation (FAR) specifically requires that the buyer, acting on behalf of the government, take steps to protect the government's interests. To cite the language of the FAR, the buyer is required to be "informed of the contractor's overall operations and financial condition, since difficulties encountered and losses suffered in operations outside the particular progress payment contract may affect adversely the performance of that contract and the liquidation of progress payments."[1] (Note that what the FAR called "contractor," the terms "supplier" and "subcontractor" have been used here).

The financial stability of the supplier must be assessed. What reputation does the supplier enjoy in the industry? Does the supplier have sufficient financial resources to complete this order, or is there a possibility that they will use these funds to "float" other less profitable orders which do not provide progress payments? What is the relative size of the subcontract which provides the progress payment funding in relation to all other orders in the supplier's plant. What is our past relationship with this supplier, if any? A long-term prime contractor/subcontractor relationship can provide valuable assurances that a prospective new order will be performed well.

One issue which can have a significant impact on the risks associated with the advancing of funds to a new supplier is to understand exactly "who," in a legal sense, the subcontractor is. Will your company be dealing with a private firm or public corporation, a sole proprietorship, a partnership, an operating division, a subsidiary, or what? If it is a subsidiary, what is the structural makeup of the ownership? In these days of the acquisition, divesting, and merging of companies being so commonplace, it is important to know precisely with whom one is dealing. Some firms have been acquired then stripped of their assets by the new management, only to leave a shell of the former company. It is wise to be alert to these potential adverse financial realities.

The buyer's obligation is to assure that a current audit of the supplier's financial condition has been performed and is available to support the inclusion of progress payments on any order. Sometimes, private firms who are both a prospective subcontractor and a competitor with the prime in other endeavors will be sensitive about opening their internal books to another private contractor. In such cases, the prime contractor can request a government assist audit to assess the financial condition of the prospective subcontractor. A government audit which has taken place in the past year will be sufficient to meet this requirement. The one drawback about government assist audits is that they take considerable time to get the results. It is far more desirable for the supplier to provide sufficient financial data to enable the buyer to make the assessment without outside government help.

Assessing the Supplier's Ability to "Segregate" and "Control Costs"

A closely related issue to that of requiring a pre-award assessment of the financial well being of a company is the corollary requirement that an assessment be made of the supplier's accounting system and controls prior to actually making the progress payment award. The issue is straightforward: *Does the supplier have the ability to segregate the costs of the order, which has progress payments, from all of their other orders?* The buyer would not want to authorize the issuance of progress payments and then later find that the supplier cannot keep the costs separated from other orders which do not enjoy progress payments. Buyers have the obligation to withhold the authorization of progress payments from a supplier until they have verified that "the contractor's accounting system and controls are adequate for proper administration of progress payments."[2] Suppliers have the obligation to provide adequate financial controls and auditable records to support their activities with government funds.

The buyer can satisfy this requirement with a recent audit, either their own firm's audit or a government assist audit, that has been carefully reviewed and placed in the procurement file.

Allocation of Subcontract Costs to the Appropriate Prime Contract(s)

The buyer must take steps to assure that whatever is being purchased is done so with a proper allocation of costs against the appropriate prime contract, or frequently, prime contracts. The issue is an fundamental one: Who (which prime contract) will pay the bill for the purchased parts or services, and to which production lot or lots will the resulting hardware costs be allocated?

Quite often, in the life cycle of a long-term program or production run, there will be concurrent (and active) multi-year buys for the same deliverable end-items. At any given point in time there may be a half a dozen active prime contracts for the same program's hardware items, or spares, or buys for company inventory. The buyer must take steps to assure that there is a proper segregation of costs to the appropriate prime contract(s) for the items being bought.

The segregation of costs to the appropriate prime contract may be done by the structuring of separate contract line items in a subcontract. Frequently, a buyer will find that one prime contract allows for progress payments while another for the vary same hardware or services may not have progress payment provisions. In such cases, the buyer must take care to structure the subcontract to specify which line items are to be subject to such progress payment provisions, and which are not.

"Consideration" for Progress Payments

When progress payments are included in a procurement, or when the liquidation rate is subsequently changed to provide more attractive interest-free funding to a supplier, the government expects that such terms be supported by some type of legal consideration from a supplier. However, if the procurement was solicited and negotiated with the understanding that customary or flexible progress payments would be included in the resulting order, and/or that an alternate liquidation rate would be later authorized at the appropriate time, then no separate consideration need be obtained.[3]

If, however, the subcontract was awarded, and then progress payments were requested as an afterthought, then some form of legal consideration must be obtained from the supplier, and the results of the consideration so obtained should be documented by the buyer for the procurement file. Likewise, when the alternate liquidation rate is later requested in lieu of the ordinary rate, or the use of flexible progress payments over customary progress payments, then some form of consideration must also be obtained from the subcontractor.

Consideration can take many forms: monetary, more attractive terms and conditions, etc. The importance is that the issue of consideration be thought out by the parties and documented in the procurement file prior to the awarding of the subcontract document.

Progress Payment and Liquidation Rates

The one perpetual characteristic of progress payments is that, much like income tax regulations, the rules are constantly changing. In recent years the customary progress payment rate has gone from 90 percent down to 75 percent, and back up to 80 percent. In July, 1991, the DOD-FAR has changed the rates for contracts issued between July 31, 1991, through March 31, 1992, to: 85 percent for large businesses, 90 percent for small businesses, and 95 percent for small disadvantaged businesses.

Small businesses have normally been allowed a 5 percent more attractive rate. Small disadvantaged businesses have sometimes been given a 5 percent more attractive rate, while at other times they get as much as a 10 percent higher rate. At times the FAR and the DOD-FAR will authorize the same rates, but at other times their rates will be different. The only thing certain about progress payment rates is that they are certain to change. Always check the rates in the contract authorizing subcontractor progress payments.

What may be currently authorized by the FAR or DOD-FAR is only of interest to you in determining what rate to flow down to a supplier. What is paramount to you is what is specifically cited in the prime contract or higher subcontract which is authorizing your use of progress payments to your suppliers. Your prime contract may have been awarded prior to the current rate called out in the FAR or DOD-FAR, in which case you must use only that which is authorized in the prime contract or you will likely be found to have authorized an "unusual" progress payment. Unusual payments will often impact your ability to flow your progress payments upward to a customer for reimbursement, unless you have received prior approval to make such payments by the Government Contracting Officer.

Typically, a buyer will be advised on the correct rates to use by their internal legal counsel, or they may have an administrative group which will guide them in such matters. However, if such groups do not exist, then the buyer should only authorize that rate which is specifically cited in their prime or higher tier subcontract (which gives them the authority to issue payments to their subcontractors).

Criteria for Deliveries and Line Item Completion

All subcontractor progress payment loans must be repaid in full. This will be accomplished with the delivery of items or the satisfaction of specific contractual line items, which will result in a liquidation (or payback) of such loans. Obviously, in order to liquidate the loans with line item satisfaction, each line item specified in the subcontract must be described in sufficient detail so as to unambiguously convey what constitutes a "completion." Also important is the matter of when each line item is scheduled for delivery or completion, and the unit price value.

Thus, each line item in a subcontract with progress payment loans must as a minimum define: the unit price value for each event or part number, when it is due, what unique terms it might carry, and whether only a full delivery of a completed item will qualify to liquidate/satisfy the line item (i.e., partial completions or partial deliveries may not count as a delivery for purposes of liquidation). In short, each line item which constitutes a contractual delivery must in essence be a separate and divisible contractual agreement.

Milestone Payments

There is a certain amount of confusion surrounding the use of the term "milestone payments" when used in conjunction with "progress payments." Technically, neither the FAR nor the DOD-FAR approve the practice of paying costs to a supplier based on achieving a "milestone." The term "milestone payments" connotes the payment of costs based on the supplier meeting a specific program milestone.

However, the concept of making progress payments based on a supplier's attainment of a specific programmatic goal is a sound one under certain conditions, and one which can be consistent with the use of progress payments if the contract is structured properly. Progress payments according to the FAR are to be based on "costs incurred" by the supplier. If one wants to incorporate into a subcontract the achievement of specific programmatic goals, one merely needs to set up the use of customary progress payments based on supplier costs incurred, but with the desired milestones specifically called out as contractual line items. When these milestones are accomplished, they will liquidate the progress payment loans previously paid, which were based on costs incurred.

The use of milestones as specific contractual line items is perhaps more difficult to administer than the delivery of a particular piece of hardware. The buyer must take steps to call out a specific price value and the time frame in which the event is planned to happen, as with any contractual delivery. Also, it is a sound practice to spell out the specific acceptance criteria for each milestone as language in a line item. When accomplished, the line item will be paid, along with the supplier's profit, part of which will go for the liquidation of previously paid progress payments.

There can be a significant disadvantage to a prime contractor who allows payments based on meeting programmatic milestones. The drawback is in the adverse cash flow impact to the prime contractor. Unless both the prime contract and the subcontract "mirror" similar line items and milestone achievements, then the prime contractor will "float" the cash difference between the prior progress payment percentage (perhaps 80 percent) and the full 100 percent costs paid on delivery, plus the supplier's earned profit. And to compound the negative cash impact, the prime contractor's cost category will change from a "supplier progress payment" to a normal "cost incurred." Thus, the reimbursement from the customer is reduced from 100 percent down to the approved progress payment rate for the prime contractor. Indiscriminate use of milestone line items can have as much as a 20 percent adverse impact on a prime contractor's cash flow. More on cash flow in the next chapter on post-award management.

Letter Contracts

There is almost universal agreement among members of the procurement community (both in the government and in the private sector) on the undesirability of the use of letter or temporary "get-started" contracts. And yet, out of necessity, letter contracts do happen.

The FAR allows progress payments to be used in letter contracts and provides a special subclause for incorporation in letter contracts as an addendum to their normal progress payment clause (FAR 52.232-16, Alt.II). Only customary progress payments (no flexible) may be authorized, and only the ordinary liquidation rate (no alternate) may be used until the letter contract is definitized. The maximum dollar ceiling amount of unliquidated progress payments must be specifically called out in the letter contract document. Upon contract definitization, all unliquidated amounts under the letter contract must be superseded by the new definitized contract value, and if a full liquidation of letter contract progress payments does not occur, the supplier is obligated to pay a full liquidation of prior payments upon demand.

United States Government Approval for Progress Payments

Normally there is no requirement to get approval from the government for the use and authorization of progress payments in a subcontract. The one exception will be whenever you deviate from the specific rules for progress payments called out in the FAR or DOD-FAR. FAR 32.502-2 cites five situations which require the government's approval for the use of progress payments. In other words, you must get the Government Contract Finance Office's approval if any of the following conditions exist:

1. Whenever a progress payment rate is authorized which is higher than the customary rate allowed by the FAR or DOD-FAR, as reflected in your prime or higher level authorizing subcontract.

2. Whenever there are deviations authorized from the progress payment terms as specified in FAR Subpart 32.5, or in DOD-FAR Subpart 232.5 in defense subcontracting.

3. Whenever a supplier's financial condition is in question.

4. Whenever a supplier has had an advance payment request or loan guarantee denied for financial reasons in the past twelve months.

5. Whenever progress payments are being authorized for a supplier which is on the government's "Hold-up List."

Getting Cost/Schedule Plans *Before* Issuing The Subcontract

In order to best illustrate the type of information which will be needed in managing the post-award phase (i.e., information which *must* be obtained from a subcontractor prior to making the award), an imaginary or "hypothetical" procurement—with specific terms, conditions, and dollar amounts—will be described below. Of course, such needed post-award information could be obtained from a supplier after the award of the subcontract, but to do so at that time there would be a price to pay, perhaps a substantial price, to get such information from the subcontractor.

Prior to the award of the subcontract, most of the negotiation leverage is on the side of the buyer. Not only does the supplier want the order, but they also would like the order to include the best possible terms, including those allowing for the financing of their costs incurred prior to making any deliveries. Thus, the lure of progress payments allows the prime contractor's buyer to extract concessions from the supplier, and do so without incurring additional costs to the order. In a nutshell, all that is needed is a demonstration that the supplier has both a cost plan and a schedule plan to satisfactorily perform on the prospective order. Not an unreasonable requirement.

For purposes of this illustration, assume a scenario under which we plan to buy twelve (12) fully developed electrical engines from a company called "Hypothetical Engines, Inc." These are large and expensive articles which must be modified slightly and then retested in order to meet our particular procurement specification.

The following contractual provisions will be assumed on this imaginary procurement:

A. We will purchase twelve engines from the supplier.

B. The supplier's cost is established at $1.0 million for each engine.

C. The supplier's profit will be 10 percent on costs.

D. Each unit will thus carry a $1.1 million line item unit price.

E. The total subcontract value will thus be $13.2 million.

F. The subcontract type will be firm fixed-price (FFP).

G. The subcontract period will start in January, and run for thirty months.

H. The first delivery is scheduled for nineteen months after award.

I. One unit will be delivered each month thereafter.

J. Customary progress payments are authorized at an 80 percent rate.

K. Progress payment liquidations are at an ordinary rate of 80 percent.

L. The subcontractor is a large business concern.

The first thing to do in this effort is advise all prospective suppliers in the solicitation notice that progress payments are intended to be included in any resulting award, incorporating the appropriate FAR clause (FAR 52.232-13) in the solicitation document. Also, to help monitor the subcontract's performance after the award, include in the solicitation notice the requirement that the supplier provide both a "cost" plan and a "schedule" plan in order to demonstrate their ability to perform on the resulting subcontract.

Obtain the Subcontractor's "Cost Projection Plan"

The supplier's cost plan must indicate they have a sufficient understanding of the financial requirements needed to perform this order. Obviously, their cost projections must be in concert with their cost/price proposal, which is a separate subject in itself. The solicitation should include language along these lines:

As a precondition to the award of progress payments on any resulting award, all respondents will submit two (2) financial projections profiles to describe their cost plans as follows:

1. *A Termination Liability Profile:* A projection of the supplier's planned open commitments, all obligations and expenditures against this order, together with the estimated earned profit as of a point in time. (Note: this requirement is identical to the termination liability curve the prime contractor provides to the government to support their prime contract).

2. *An Expenditure Profile at the Cost Level:* A projection of the forecasted actual cost expenditures (the costs incurred) as of each month. No supplier profit will be included in these values. This expenditure curve will be used to forecast the progress payment

values for the subcontract, which will be specified as a constant percentage of these projected dollar values.

With the supplier's forecasted expenditures at the cost level (profile 2), it is a simple matter to extrapolate upward or downward to compile a fairly detailed summary of their expected cost plans. With the addition of the supplier's negotiated profit rate, a forecast of their expenditures at the price level can be made. By simply scaling downward the cash requirements for progress payments at the authorized customary progress payment rate can be determined.

Thus, with just these two simple cost profiles (provided by the supplier), and with the aid of any of the various financial spreadsheet software programs available for personal computers, a fairly complete and detailed financial summary can be developed for this subcontract (see Figure 2-2). This financial summary can aid us in the efficient post award monitoring of the subcontractor's cost performance against their own plans. But perhaps of greater importance, selected columns of the data displayed in Figure 2-2 are directly relatable to the line item cost data which will be provided to us in the supplier's Contractor's Request for Progress Payments on FAR Standard Form 1443.

For example, the supplier's forecast of their expenditures at the cost level, as shown in column (E) in Figure 2-2, will be directly relatable to the cost data which will be listed in line 12a, "Total Costs Incurred To Date," on their SF 1443 progress payment invoice.

There are ten columns of data displayed in Figure 2-2, and it is important that each column of information be understood:

Column (A)   Calendar Month: Reflects the full period of performance by month for this subcontract.

Column (B)   Cumulative Unit Deliveries: Reflects the contractual delivery schedule for the twelve engines. This schedule will be incorporated into the subcontract document itself.

Column (C)   Termination Liability Profile: Reflects the Termination Liability forecast as provided by the supplier (profile 1, above). It would be wise to incorporate this profile into the subcontract document in order to set the upper limits of our liability to the supplier at any point in time. (Should the supplier exceed their own projections it could reflect adverse conditions, such as an excessive inventory being produced, or even an overrun, etc.)

Figure 2-2. A Financial Spreadsheet of Progress Payment Data

HYPOTHETICAL ENGINES, INC. (values in $000)

Conditions: 12 units; @ $1M cost; 10% fee; $1.1M price; 80% Progress Payments; 80% Liquidations

(A) Calendar Month	(B) Cum. Unit Delivery	(C) Termin. Liability Profile	(D) Expend. @ Price Profile	(E) Expend. @ Cost Profile	(F) "Gross" Prog.Pmts @ 80%	(G) Unit Del. Price @ 100%	(H) Loan Liquid. @ 80%	(I) Supplier Payment @ 20%	(J) Authorized "Net" Prog.Pmts.
Jan		$100	$92	$84	$67				$67
Feb		$396	$132	$120	$96				$96
Mar		$525	$198	$180	$144				$144
Apr		$659	$238	$216	$173				$173
May		$1,314	$264	$240	$192				$192
Jun		$1,976	$303	$275	$220				$220
Jul		$2,635	$396	$360	$288				$288
Aug		$3,295	$475	$432	$345				$345
Sep		$3,953	$740	$673	$538				$538
Oct		$4,611	$1,043	$948	$759				$759
Nov		$5,270	$1,412	$1,284	$1,027				$1,027
Dec		$5,929	$1,835	$1,668	$1,335				$1,335
Jan		$6,588	$2,508	$2,280	$1,824				$1,824
Feb		$7,243	$2,772	$2,520	$2,016				$2,016
Mar		$7,905	$3,050	$2,773	$2,218				$2,218
Apr		$8,561	$4,290	$3,900	$3,120				$3,120
May		$9,223	$5,108	$4,644	$3,715				$3,715
Jun		$9,882	$5,795	$5,268	$4,215				$4,215
Jul	1	$10,540	$6,745	$6,132	$4,905	$1,100	$880	$220	$4,025
Aug	2	$11,200	$7,696	$6,996	$5,597	$2,200	$1,760	$440	$3,837
Sep	3	$11,592	$8,646	$7,860	$6,288	$3,300	$2,640	$660	$3,648
Oct	4	$11,855	$9,596	$8,724	$6,979	$4,400	$3,520	$880	$3,459
Nov	5	$12,121	$10,507	$9,552	$7,641	$5,500	$4,400	$1,100	$3,241
Dec	6	$12,384	$11,352	$10,320	$8,256	$6,600	$5,280	$1,320	$2,976
Jan	7	$12,513	$12,012	$10,920	$8,736	$7,700	$6,160	$1,540	$2,576
Feb	8	$12,647	$12,408	$11,280	$9,024	$8,800	$7,040	$1,760	$1,984
Mar	9	$12,780	$12,804	$11,640	$9,312	$9,900	$7,920	$1,980	$1,392
Apr	10	$12,913	$12,936	$11,760	$9,408	$11,000	$8,800	$2,200	$608
May	11	$13,043	$13,068	$11,880	$9,504	$12,100	$9,504	$2,596	$0
Jun	12	$13,200	$13,200	$12,000	$9,600	$13,200	$9,600	$3,600	$0

Column (D) Expenditures at Price Profile: Reflects the expenditure curve at the price level, which is derived by taking the projected expenditures at the cost level (E) and adding a forecasted supplier fee (at 10 percent) to bring the total profile up to the expended price level.

Column (E) Expenditure at Cost Profile: Reflects an expenditure projection at the cost level, with no profit. This curve represents the actual costs incurred by the supplier in performance of the contract.

Column (F) "Gross" Progress Payments Profile: Reflects the projected progress payment requirements as a percentage of the forecasted expenditures at cost from column (E).

Note: The "gross" progress payments profile is for informational purposes only. The gross values should never be expended during the subcontract performance period because the supplier will be making contractual schedule deliveries as displayed in column (B), which will have the effect of immediately liquidating the progress payment loans down to a "Net" progress payment value, as shown in column (J).

Column (G) Unit Deliveries at the Contract Price Level: Reflects a projection of the value of contract unit deliveries, which is the price ($1.1 million) times the deliveries forecast as delineated in column (B).

Note: Columns (G), (H), and (I) are needed in order to calculate progress payment requirements from the "Gross" (F) payments down to the "Net" progress payment amounts shown in column (J).

Column (H) Progress Payment Loan Liquidations: Reflects the liquidation of the progress payment loans at the approved "ordinary" rate of 80 percent of the delivery unit price, or 80 percent of column (G).

Column (I) The Payment to the Supplier: Reflects the net amount of payments to the supplier with each contractual delivery. In this case, when the supplier makes a delivery, they get the full unit value as displayed in column (G), less the 80 percent progress payment liquidation as depicted in column (H), for a 20 percent net value payment to the supplier.

Note: In other words, the supplier has delivered an engine to you, and you owe them $1.1 million for it. But, because of prior progress payments, you have already "loaned" the supplier 80 percent of the costs incurred to produce the engine. Under the rules of FAR, 80 percent (or the current liquidation rate) of the price of the unit delivered must go to liquidate the progress payment loan.

Column (J)   The Authorized "Net" Progress Payment Profile: Reflects the "net" progress payment amount, which is what the subcontractor should expect to receive in the form of progress payment loans. This amount is derived by taking the "gross" prog- ress payment amount (F), less the liquidations (H) if started, for a "net" amount as displayed in column (J).

With the data displayed in a spreadsheet, which are based on the two financial profiles provided by the supplier and represented as columns (C) and (E), the next step is to take the data and exhibit it in graphic form to assess the reasonableness of the slope. Figure 2-3 is a graphic display of the data from the financial spreadsheet.

An examination of the Termination Liability curve (C) indicates that this curve appears to be reasonable when compared with the Expenditures at Price (D) curve. You expect to see a T/L curve rise rapidly since it reflects cost requirements based on commitments prior to any cost expenditures. You can also see the "gross" progress payment curve (F) increasing to the point where contract deliveries are scheduled to begin (G), at which time the progress payments start to dramatically decrease to "net" amounts, as shown in the (J) curve. The buyer will want to watch closely the relationship between scheduled versus actual deliveries, as these have a profound impact on the unliquidated (outstanding) progress payment amounts, which represents a risk exposure to the prime contractor and ultimately to the government.

Figure 2-3, the summary of financial projections, is useful in assessing the reasonableness of the supplier's forecast of its financial needs.

However, for purposes of monitoring the supplier's performance and monthly request for progress payments (SF1443), certain of the data may be excluded in order to focus on the two more critical items: the "gross" progress payments, item (F), and the "net" authorized progress payments, item (J). See Figure 2-4 for a display of these two critical financial curves. These two

Figure 2-3. **Progress Payment Data**

HYPOTHETICAL ENGINES, INC.
-Summary of Financial Projections-

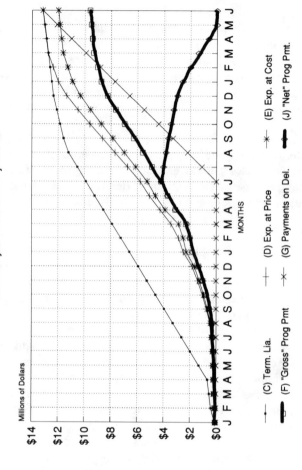

—•— (C) Term. Lia.   —+— (D) Exp. at Price   —*— (E) Exp. at Cost

—■— (F) "Gross" Prog Pmt   —*— (G) Payments on Del.   —◆— (J) "Net" Prog Pmt.

Figure 2-4. **"Net" Progress Payments**

HYPOTHETICAL ENGINES, INC.
-Monitoring "Net" Progress Payments-

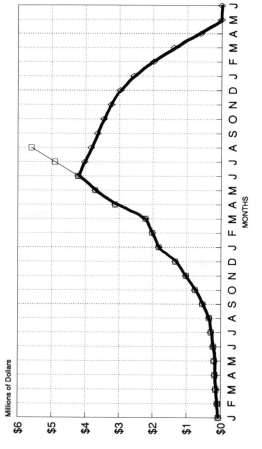

□— (F) "Gross" Prog Pmt   ◆— (J) "Net" Prog Pmt.

curves are vital to the businesslike monitoring of the supplier's performance during the post-award performance phase. The buyer should use the display in Figure 2-4 to "plot" selected data from the supplier's progress payment requests.

Obtain the Supplier's "Schedule Plan"

In concert with obtaining a cost projection plan from the subcontractor, a critical corollary step is to also obtain their schedule performance plan. This plan, in the form of a Gantt Chart, will demonstrate the supplier's understanding and commitment to physically completing the subcontract in the time frame promised. The supplier's definitive schedule plan must initially be provided to support their proposal and then updated each month after the subcontract award. This schedule is vital to a prime contractor's ability to monitor the subcontractor's physical work performance on the order.

The monthly schedule updates will be compared with the supplier's cost performance, as reflected in the monthly progress payment invoice (SF1443) submittals. Since some feel strongly that all requests for additional progress payments should carry some relationship to the actual "physical" work being accomplished, a good initial schedule plan provides perhaps the single best tool needed to verify that the supplier is in fact making satisfactory tangible progress against the order.

As a part of the initial solicitation process, a Gantt Chart (schedule) should be requested from all suppliers. Since this hypothetical order is for twelve units with deliveries starting nineteen months after award and a single unit delivered each month thereafter, we have some idea of what the Gantt Chart should portray at a minimum. We also know that there will be some hardware modification required by the supplier, as well as a requalification test, so these additional tasks should also be displayed on any Gantt Chart.

Figure 2-5 is a hypothetical Gantt Chart, as might be submitted by one of the respondents to our proposal solicitation. Note in this sample format that there are some seventeen discrete tasks listed on the chart, that each task listed must have an estimated weighted value, and that the sum of these weighted values must add up to 100 percent of the full subcontract price. This detail is needed so that the supplier can provide us with their estimated percentage of work completed each month. The tasks listed on any respondent's Gantt Chart will be different for each subcontract, depending upon the makeup of effort and the extent to which there is (nonrecurring) developmental work versus (recurring) production activity.

Figure 2-5. A Gantt Chart to Support Progress Payment Evaluations

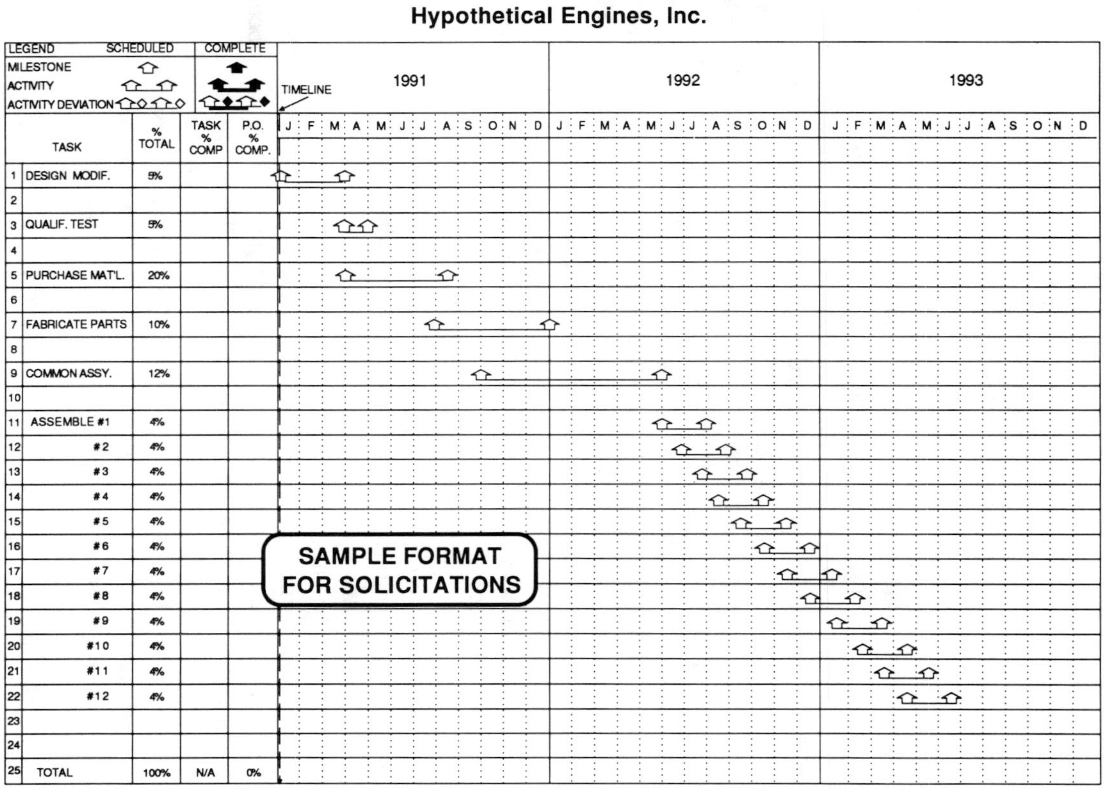

Hypothetical Engines, Inc.

LEGEND		
MILESTONE	SCHEDULED	COMPLETE
ACTIVITY		
ACTIVITY DEVIATION		

TIMELINE

SAMPLE FORMAT FOR SOLICITATIONS

	TASK	% TOTAL	TASK % COMP	P.O. % COMP
1	DESIGN MODIF.	5%		
2				
3	QUALIF. TEST	5%		
4				
5	PURCHASE MATL.	20%		
6				
7	FABRICATE PARTS	10%		
8				
9	COMMON ASSY.	12%		
10				
11	ASSEMBLE #1	4%		
12	#2	4%		
13	#3	4%		
14	#4	4%		
15	#5	4%		
16	#6	4%		
17	#7	4%		
18	#8	4%		
19	#9	4%		
20	#10	4%		
21	#11	4%		
22	#12	4%		
23				
24				
25	TOTAL	100%	N/A	0%

Timeline headings: 1991, 1992, 1993 (J F M A M J J A S O N D)

Three issues are critical to the receipt of an adequate and complete Gantt schedule from the supplier. They are listed below in the solicitation and subcontract clause suggested as follows:

A Gantt Chart (schedule) in the format as shown in (Figure 2-5) is required to support the award of this subcontract, and for the evaluation and processing of each progress payment invoice (SF1443) during the life of this subcontract. The Gantt Chart must have the following data displayed in order to be considered complete: (1) *all* of the tasks necessary to satisfy the subcontract must be listed on the Gantt chart; (2) each task so listed must indicate a performance period as reflected with a bar, placed into a specific time frame to reflect the point where the performance is planned to occur; and (3) each listed task must be assigned a weighted value, the sum of the weighted values must add up to 100 percent of the total value of the subcontract price. A monthly update of the Gantt Chart must be submitted to reflect the percentage completion of the subcontract in order to support the processing of each progress payment request.

By insisting on a schedule plan to evaluate the physical performance against the subcontract, the buyer will have obtained sufficient plans—the supplier's own plans—which can be used to monitor accomplishments during the period of subcontract performance.

The illustration in Figure 2-5 reflects the supplier's initial "baseline" schedule plan through a "Time Now" period prior to starting the subcontract effort (as of January 1, 1991). Note that the supplier has reflected a "zero" Purchase Order percentage complete value at the bottom of the fifth column from the left. As the subcontractor updates their schedule report each month, they will move the "Time Now" line to the right to reflect their performance through a new point in time. They will also reflect their new percentage complete estimate in the fifth column.

These supplier furnished cost and schedule plans should be corroborated by what the buyer observes in periodic visits to the supplier, in program status reviews with the supplier, in reports from the field offices, or through any of the other sources of supplier performance intelligence available to the buyer. By getting a pre-award commitment from the supplier—to report their own cost status in the form of progress payment invoices that will be compared against their own cost profiles and to report their schedule status on a monthly Gantt Chart that will be compared against their initial schedule plan—the buyer will have obtained two vital tools with which to monitor the performance measurement of even firm fixed-price (FFP) subcontractors.

Customary "Flexible" Progress Payments

Originally the subject of "flexible" progress payments was placed in the next chapter of this book, which covers post-award subcontract management. The thinking was that in order to approve flexible progress payments one had to have a definitive price value to run a cash model and determine the flexible rate. However, in 1990, the DOD-FAR clarified the rules governing flexible progress payments. Now, flexible progress payments must be addressed prior to the award of the subcontract in order that "consideration" be obtained for the awarding of flexible progress payments. Thus, the subject was moved into this chapter on pre-award subcontract activity.

Some background on flexible progress payments. In 1981, the Department of Defense adopted major changes in their policy toward assisting contractors by financing their work in process for the period prior to receiving payments for contract deliveries. In earlier years, it had been the DOD practice to allow contractors to submit and receive payments twice per month. Then, the DOD changed their policy to allow only one progress payment reimbursement each month—and that was certainly not good news to the private contractor sector.

However, at this same time, the DOD authorized a new financing concept called "flexible progress payments," an idea which had been considered by the DOD for at least a decade prior to its official release in 1981. For those contractors who could qualify, this new method was a most attractive policy change, allowing for reimbursement of costs up to 100 percent of actual expenses. Flexible progress payments would now be available to those suppliers who requested them, who could meet certain additional criteria requirements specified in the DOD-FAR, and who had a contract with a value of at least $1 million or more. Flexible payments were to be available only for negotiated contracts, not for either formally advertised contracts or on contracts to be performed in their entirety outside of the United States.

All contracts being proposed for flexible payments must be definitized, or at least have a negotiated contract value, in order to allow for the supplier's cost data to be processed through a Department of Defense "Cash Flow Model." The original DOD cash flow model has since been superseded by later cash model versions II, III, IV, and at the time of this writing, cash model V (the current version). The primary difference between these models is the amount of contractor investment required.

Figure 2-6. Applicable Flexible Progress Payment Cash Flow Models

Date of Contract Award	Uniform Rate (%)	Investment (%)	Cash Flow Model
Prior to May 1, 1985	90%	5%	CASH-II
May 1, 1985 to October 18, 1986	80%	15%	CASH-III
October 19, 1986 to October 1, 1988	75%	25%	CASH-IV
After October 1, 1988	80%	20%	CASH-V

The original cash flow model required an investment by contractors in work in process over the life of the contract of not less than 5 percent, which has since been increased to 25 percent. The threshold for changes to an established flex rate are a 2 percent variance (+ or –) to the required 25 percent contractor investment. Figure 2-6 summarizes which Cash Flow model applies to a given contract, based on the date of contract award.[4]

The DOD cash flow models consider such factors as: contract delivery schedules, progress payments to a subcontractor's next tier of subcontractors, liquidation rates, and payment disbursement/reimbursement cycles (referred to as "floats" and "lags"). These latter two very specific terms were new to most people, and were defined by the DOD as:

FLOAT: "The number of days difference between the cost statement date and the time the cost is paid on a cash basis . . ."

LAG: "The length in days between the end of the cost statement date and the progress payment receipt."[5]

Contractors desiring flexible progress payments were encouraged to establish an "advanced agreement" on the proposed floats and lags with their responsible administrative contracting office in the office of the local Defense Plant Representative Office (DPRO).

Any contractor wishing flexible payments must be prepared to submit certified cost or pricing data as defined in FAR 15.804-2 for review by the buyer (or buyer's representative), who must verify the data contained in such projections. Cost data needed for the cash flow model includes actual and projected incurred costs—by cost element, by month—for the duration of the contract period.

The flexible progress payment standards for all lower tier subcontractors are identical to those available to the prime contractor. However, such standards must be established by any subcontractor *independent* of the prime contractor. Thus, flexible payments could be available to a lower tier supplier even if the prime contractor does *not* enjoy them (i.e., the prime contractor did not request and/or meet the flexible standards). The only requirement is that the prime contract must be subject to DOD-FAR regulations and the lower tier supplier must qualify for flexible progress payments on their own merits. Thus, there could be a situation where the prime contractor fails to qualify for flexible payments, but its next tier subcontractor does qualify. This condition would be perfectly proper.

The same FAR 32.5 terms which apply to customary progress payments, for example, liquidation rates, invoicing, etc., also apply to DOD flexible progress payments.

On September 26, 1990, the Deputy Assistant Secretary of Defense for Procurement (Eleanor R. Spector) issued a letter to the contracting representatives of the Army, Navy, Air Force, Defense Logistics Agency, and Defense Contract Audit Agency releasing a new PC-Based Flexible Progress Payment Model.[6] This new model is called "CASHP," and the initial release was version 1.01, carrying a file name of "CASP101.EXE." Effective this date the CASHP PC model became the official cash program to be used for establishing flexible progress payments as required by the Defense Federal Acquisition Regulation Supplement (DOD-FAR) 232.502-1 (S-71) and clause 252.232-7004. Contractors interested in securing flexible progress payments will be wise to obtain a copy of the most current "CASHP" PC computer model.

In Summary

The prime contractor should take steps *prior* to making an award of a sub-contract which contains provisions for progress payments. Certain of these matters cannot be properly addressed after the release of the subcontract. Below are three forecasting plans which should be the minimum obtained from the supplier:

1. A projection of their termination liability requirements.

2. A forecast of their expenditures at the cost level.

3. A Gantt Chart with weighted values for each task, the sum of which will add up to 100 percent of the subcontract value, plus a commitment to update this schedule to support the processing of each request for progress payments.

With these three supplier forecasts, the prime contractor will have the ability to monitor the supplier's performance during the life of the subcontract period.

Please keep in mind that there are differing approaches used by the various prime contractors to minimize their exposure to the risks associated with the use of progress payments. What was described above is but one approach. However, some contractors go so far as to require a subcontractor "performance bond" from any supplier desiring to receive progress payments. Although such practices do reduce the probability of the prime contractor sustaining a loss, the performance bond does add a cost to the total program which some consider to be an excessive program cost. And, of course, the costs of the performance bonds may be ultimately passed on to the government. The use of performance bonds on progress payments is recommended only in those exceptional cases where there are extreme risks of loss to the prime contractor.

As an alternative to the performance bond requirement, we believe that the close management of progress payments against the supplier's own cost projections, and the comparison of actual costs to the supplier's physical work performance, will be more than adequate to prevent a loss on a subcontract due to the possible cost risk of exposure, because of the over-funding of progress payments.

Pre-award activity is but one part, albeit a crucial part, of the total effort needed to reduce the risks of loss for prime contractors who provide progress payments. The next chapter will cover other critical half of the process—how best to manage the post-award phase of subcontracts which contain progress payment provisions.

Endnotes

1. FAR 32.503–2 (b).

2. FAR 32.503–3 (b).

3. FAR 32.501–4 (a).

4. DOD-FAR 232.502–1.

5. U.S. Department of Defense, Office of Cost, Pricing and Finance, *Cash Flow Computer Model-User's Guide,* 28 August, 1981, page 9.

6. Flexible Progress Payment Service Contact Points:
   Army: Ms. P. Cake, AMCPP-PC 274-8055.
   Navy: Mr. Michael Righi, ASN(RDA) (PP) 692-3325.
   Air Force: Mr. Terry Shepard SAF/AQCP 695-9043.
   DLA: Mr. William Hill, DLA-AC 274-7726.
   DCAA: Mr. Earl Neuman, HQ DCAA 274-7775.

Chapter 3

Post-Award Management

Once awarded, it is the buyer's responsibility to administer the supplier's progress payments throughout the life of the subcontract. The buyer must determine whether or not there is satisfactory physical work being accomplished by the supplier in order to justify the initial and each subsequent progress payment.

A buyer will normally require technical assistance from other functions in order to make such determinations. For example, routine program status reviews, on site visits by local field representatives, visits by quality assurance and other personnel, and buyer visits themselves, all contribute to the evaluation process. Allowing for the criticality of the procurement, a company or government audit may also be utilized in certain instances.

If it is determined that a supplier is requesting progress payments in advance of their actual physical work achievement, or that the supplier's performance has diminished for whatever reason, or that the supplier's financial condition has deteriorated to the point of endangering completion of the subcontract, it is the buyer who *must* take positive steps to halt further payments. Should the supplier's performance wane, the buyer is both authorized and obligated to delay, suspend, reduce, or request a return of previously paid progress payments to this supplier.

Should a supplier project an overrun on a subcontract, the buyer is obligated by the FAR to impose the "loss ratio adjustment" to the authorized progress payment rate. The loss ratio adjustment reduces the total eligible costs for progress payments by a percentage value representing the subcontract price and the projected total estimated costs at completion, which includes the initial base price plus the overrun being projected by the supplier. The important subject of the loss ratio adjustment, and its impact on both the prime contractor and a subcontractor, will be discussed below in this chapter.

How Do You Manage Progress Payments

Although there will be several individuals in the prime contractor's organization who have an interest in and will monitor the performance of a given subcontractor (such as the program manager, the project engineer, a quality specialist, production control, financial controller, etc.), it is the buyer who is ultimately held responsible for the management of the progress payment provisions of the subcontract. The process of managing progress payments can be divided into three distinct buyer tasks:

1. The **monitoring** of the supplier's performance against the precise language contained in the subcontract document, including all of the terms and conditions, the statement of work, data requirements, and the management of changes to the authorized subcontract baseline.

2. The **review and approval** (or disapproval) of all progress payment invoices requested by the supplier.

3. The taking of appropriate **corrective action**, positive or negative, when warranted.

Each of these tasks will be discussed separately.

Monitoring of Supplier Performance Against the Subcontract Document

A full team approach utilizing all of the functions, organizations and personnel who have a vested interest in the success of a given subcontract is likely the best course for any buyer to take. Depending upon the size and critical nature of the subcontract, a matrixed organization may have been established to collectively manage a particular subcontractor, and this arrangement should be utilized to its fullest potential. Even on a smaller subcontract, there will be functional technical specialists to support the buyer's efforts. No buyer can properly manage a complex subcontract without the benefit of multifunctional support from across the prime contractor's organization.

A given program will often conduct periodic performance status reviews on their various subsystems and components. Such meetings are typically called by the program management office, by engineering, by manufacturing, or sometimes by the procurement organization. The responsible buyer has a vital role to play in such status reviews anytime their subcontract is discussed. At other times there will be visits to the supplier's facility from various functional organizations. Such visits should be coordinated through the buyer by the respective function feeling the need to visit the supplier. In no case should such visits be made without the knowledge of the buyer. Feedback (trip reports) should also be provided to the responsible buyer as soon as possible. True teamwork requires full multilateral communications to be effective. Any organization which bypasses the responsible buyer and makes direct supplier contacts will likely pay a price for such imprudent conduct at a later date.

Many of the larger prime contractors will have a network of geographically located field offices available to coordinate and participate in the periodic visits by its management, procurement, quality, and marketing personnel. It is a wise practice for buyers to utilize these remote offices as an extended team member in the surveillance of the day-to-day activities at a given supplier. In most cases it will be up to the respective buyer to inform these field office personnel of the salient issues at a given supplier. These offices will need to be provided with copies of selected procurement documents, correspondence, change orders, delivery schedules, etc., in order to make their surveillance efforts as meaningful as possible.

Assuming that the proper steps had been taken prior to making the award, the buyer will have in place some type of subcontractor delivery schedule (see the Gantt Chart illustrated in Figure 2-5), and this schedule should be dutifully updated and submitted each month by the supplier as an integral part of their requests for progress payments. The buyer, with assistance from other functions, will want to review the details contained in the monthly schedule submittals to determine whether the supplier is making satisfactory progress in order to justify the disbursement of each additional progress payment.

Review and Approval (or Disapproval) of Progress Payment Invoices

The progress payment invoices (SF1443) received from the supplier each month provide a wealth of cost data to the buyer, which can be used to monitor the supplier's financial performance. This is particularly true if certain cost and progress payment profiles had been established prior to the subcontract's award, as was covered in the previous chapter (Figures 2-2, 2-3, 2-4). An abundance of actual cost performance data is even available on fixed-price procurements whenever progress payments are included in the subcontract.

The actual cost data contained in the monthly invoices may be plotted against the curve reflecting the actual cost performance being experienced by the supplier to determine whether it is consistent with, or somewhere in the range of what the supplier had forecasted prior to the subcontract award. If there are substantial cost deviations from those values originally projected, then some type of query from the buyer to the supplier is probably in order. Reviewing the cost values contained in the Progress Payment Invoices (SF1443) is a full and important subject, which will be discussed in some detail in the next chapter covering the analysis of progress payment data.

In some cases, the buyer may have serious concerns as to the validity of the progress payment requests being made with regards to the overall performance of the supplier. Some examples of situations that should arise a buyer's concerns are where the actual supplier costs incurred are running substantially ahead of the physical performance being reported in the monthly Gantt schedule submittals, the receipt of from negative feedback from the field offices, from information contained in trip reports, or from any other source of supplier information which collectively raises questions which require an immediate answer. In such cases, it may be appropriate for the buyer to take a quick visit to the supplier, or to perhaps request an audit of the supplier's books on the subcontract. Audits should be viewed as a "last resort," to be taken when all else fails and there still are serious questions about conditions at the supplier. Audits can be performed by either the prime contractor or by the United States Government. But audits do take time—a lot of time—and other remedies should be explored prior to requesting such audits.

Taking Appropriate Positive or Negative Corrective Action When Warranted

A prime contractor (through its subcontract buyer) has all the necessary tools and legal authority needed to take decisive action with a subcontractor to either reward them for their outstanding performance, or to admonish them for poor performance. Three types of actions are possible:

1. The progress payment liquidation rate (the loan repayment rate) for subcontract deliveries or line-item completions may be adjusted upward or downward from the initial matching "ordinary" liquidation rate, within a particular range.

2. Progress payments may be "suspended" for certain specific reasons, based on the supplier's performance or on conditions at the supplier which place the prime contractor at risk.

3. The "loss ratio" *must* be imposed when certain conditions are found to exist on the subcontract, namely, whenever the supplier starts to experience an overrun of costs from the subcontract price.

Each of these issues, as well as others, will be covered below.

Adjusting the Progress Payment Liquidation Rate

One of the more viable options available to a subcontract buyer is to adjust the repayment liquidation rate with each line-item delivery, to either *lower* the liquidation rate as a reward for good performance, or to *increase* it for less than acceptable supplier performance. The impact on a subcontractor's cash flow position can be quite dramatic, as the table in Figure 3-1 illustrates. This table will again use Hypothetical Engines as an example, delivering subcontract line items with a value of $1,100,000 each. Remember, the total price of each unit is $1,100,000, which represents a cost of $1,000,000 and a 10 percent profit of $100,000. The cost is critical, because progress payments are based on a percentage of costs incurred. With each unit delivery the supplier may realize variable "net" cash proceeds depending upon the approved liquidation rate in effect.

Under the "ordinary" liquidation rate (which must always match the authorized progress payment rate illustrated here at 80 percent), with each delivery of a unit valued at $1,100,000, the supplier will receive a net cash payment of $220,000. The balance of $880,000 must go to repay or liquidate the progress payment loan.

The cash-flow impact of varying the liquidation rates is illustrated graphically in Figure 3-2, using the four liquidation variables as displayed above in Figure 3-1. This chart displays the progress payment loan reaching a peak value of $4,215,000 when the hardware deliveries begin in month 19, when the loans begin to liquidate. Four liquidation (repayment) rates are displayed: the 80 percent ordinary rate, an adjustment upward to 90 percent, an adjustment upward to a maximum 100 percent, and the more favorable lower alternate liquidation rate (ALR) of 72.7 percent. Admittedly, these values may seem insignificant when displayed graphically, but to any cash conscious supplier, and most are these days, such variations in the repayment of interest-free progress payments can be most important.

Figure 3-1. Cash Flow Impact by Adjusting the Liquidation Rates (000)

With the liquidation rates set at:	"Ordinary" at 80%	Increase to 90%	Increase to 100%	Alt. Liq. Rate at 72.7%
Amount used to liquidate Progress Payments:	$880	$990	$1,100	$800
"Net" cash payment to the supplier:	$220	$110	0	$300
Unit Price of each article:	$1,100	$1,100	$1,100	$1,100

Figure 3-2.   Various Liquidation Rates

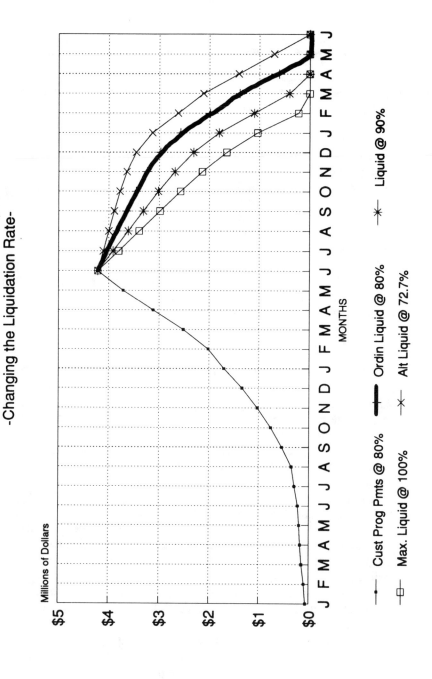

HYPOTHETICAL ENGINES, INC.
-Changing the Liquidation Rate-

Making Adjustments for Poor Supplier Performance

If the buyer and the subcontract management team have determined that the supplier has not performed in an acceptable manner, and based on the supplier's current performance pattern, believe that the supplier is likely to have difficulty fully liquidating all progress payments, a buyer may take steps to either suspend further payments or to simply increase the liquidation rate with each future hardware delivery. The authority for a buyer to take this action is contained in FAR 32.503-6, and is also restated in FAR 52.232-16(c), the subcontract clause covering progress payments.

Two examples are used in Figure 3-1 to illustrate the impact of increasing the liquidation rate from the 80 percent initial ordinary rate, upward to 90 percent, and even upward to a full 100 percent. With a 90 percent liquidation rate the supplier's cash payment with each delivery reduces from $220,000 (ordinary) down to $110,000, and then down to zero cash proceeds with a full 100 percent liquidation. Talk about a "grabber" to get the supplier's management attention. But the buyer must have sound reasons to take such actions, consistent with the language specified in FAR.

Making Adjustments for Good Supplier Performance

By contrast, a supplier who is performing well, and it does happen, may choose to request the "alternate liquidation rate" (ALR), as delineated in FAR 32.503-9. The advantages of moving from the ordinary rate of 80 percent to the alternate liquidation rate are beneficial to both the subcontractor as well as to the prime contractor.

The benefits to the supplier are obvious: they get to keep a larger share of their progress payment loans for a longer period of time. In effect, they perpetuate their "interest free" loans, although the government does not particularly like that description of progress payments. In the table reflected in Figure 3-1, the effect of the alternate liquidation rate is portrayed in the right column. With each delivery, the supplier gets a net cash payment of $300,000 (instead of merely $220,000), and thus only liquidates the loan at $800,000 (instead of $880,000). They get to keep an additional 10 percent of the interest-free funds, and retain some portion of their earned profits with each line-item delivery. Since all legitimate progress payments given to suppliers are reimbursable at 100 percent, there are no additional costs to the prime contractor by going to the alternate liquidation rate (ALR).

One added benefit to the prime contractor is the better visibility it will get over the costs of the work being done by their supplier, and thus receiving additional assurances that supplier's performance is at full expectations.

Suppliers desiring to go to the ALR must meet certain criteria, as will be described below.

To illustrate the cash flow benefits to a supplier of implementing the ALR over the ordinary liquidation rate, a table is provided as Figure 3-3, which compares the "ordinary" liquidation percentage rates on the left with the lower alternate liquidation rates in percentage values in the right columns. This example displays three assumed profit positions: a 5 percent, 10 percent, and 15 percent projected profit for the supplier. Since the ALR formula is profit sensitive, the higher the supplier's profit, the lower will be their ALR, and conversely, the lower the supplier's profit, the higher their resulting ALR. The supplier must demonstrate actual cost experience to the prime contractor, proving that they are achieving their stated profit position. To best understand the concept of alternate liquidation rates, those interested persons should perform their own calculations with actual cost data from a specific subcontract, using the ALR formula displayed in Figure 3-4.[1]

Certain very precise standards must be met before a supplier can qualify for the more attractive terms of the alternate liquidation rate (ALR), somewhat similar to the higher standards which are required for flexible progress payments as covered earlier. Actual cost history must be provided to the prime contractor to support the requested change in liquidation rates. The higher standards to obtain the ALR generally consist of the following ten conditions:

1. The supplier, not the prime contractor, must initiate the request for the lower Alternate Liquidation Rate.

2. The progress payment liquidation rate must not have been changed in the previous twelve months.

3. The time span from the award of the subcontract (and the incurring of costs) until either the first line-item delivery or completion must be at least eighteen months.

4. Actual supplier cost data for the prior twelve months must be available for the prime contractor's review, covering either products actually delivered, or if no deliveries have been made, then cost performance actuals on the subcontract prior to actual deliveries starting.

5. The authorization of the ALR may not impair the prime contractor's ability to obtain a full recoupment of all progress payments already made, and those to be made, to the subcontract.

6. The subcontractor will not be paid for more than the costs of items delivered, together with the earned profits on such items.

Figure 3-3. Profit Impact on the Alternate Liquidation Rate (ALR)

"Ordinary" Liquidation Rate	ALR @ 5% Profit	ALR @ 10% Profit	ALR @ 15% Profit
100.0%	95.2%	90.9%	87.0%
95.0%	90.5%	86.4%	82.6%
90.0%	85.7%	81.8%	78.3%
85.0%	81.0%	77.3%	73.9%
80.0%	76.2%	72.7%	69.6%

Figure 3-4. Alternate Liquidation Rate (ALR) Formula (000)

$$\frac{\text{Costs eligible for PP} \times \text{PP Rate}}{\text{Subcontract Price}} = \text{Alternate Liquidation Rate}$$

$$\frac{\$12,000 \times 80\%}{\$13,200} = 72.7\% \text{ A.L.Rate}$$

7. The unliquidated progress payments may not exceed the limits of either: the progress payments made against incomplete work, including unliquidated next tier subcontractor payments; or, the value of incomplete work, which is defined as supplies and services required by the effort, for which delivery and invoicing are incomplete.

8. The buyer and subcontractor will agree on a new ALR, and the subcontract document will be modified to incorporate the new ALR in lieu of the "ordinary" progress payment liquidation rate.

9. The supplier must agree to: furnish the prime contractor with cost performance actuals at least annually for the remainder of the subcontract; to certify the continued validity of such data; and to be subjected to periodic audits as requested by the prime contractor.[2]

10. Both parties must agree that the ALR will be adjusted upward, monthly if need be, should the supplier's profit rate deteriorate from the agreed to percentage, thereby impacting the supplier's ability to fully liquidate all progress payments by the end of the subcontract period.

While these ten conditions may seem to be overly stringent rules, in the days of severe cash flow challenges, most suppliers are quite happy to comply with such requirements. Thus, if a given supplier can qualify for both flexible progress payments and the alternate liquidation rate, they have in effect the best of all cash flow situations. They have achieved in essence the "Gold Card" of progress payment terms.

Suspending Progress Payments

To interrupt the flow of progress payments to a subcontractor is admittedly a drastic action. Sometimes, however, it is necessary to take such actions to get people's attention and to correct an unsatisfactory performance condition. The prime contractor's buyer has both the authority and the obligation to take this extreme action under certain specific conditions, as defined in FAR 32.503-6.

Any one of six rather broad conditions must exist with the supplier in order for a buyer to take the extreme action of suspending progress payments. They are:

1. Supplier nonconformance with any material requirements of the subcontract.

2. A supplier who is experiencing an unsatisfactory financial condition.

3. A supplier accumulating an inventory of materials for the prime contract which is in excess of reasonable program needs.

4. A supplier becoming delinquent in the payment of costs to its lower-tier suppliers.

5. When the fair market value of the subcontractor's undelivered work exceeds the lesser of "(i) the contract price of the undelivered work, minus the estimated costs required for completing contract performance, or (ii) the incurred costs applicable to the undelivered items."[3]

6. When the subcontract reaches the point of becoming a "loss contract," which occurs when the actual costs to date, plus the estimated costs to complete the effort exceed the subcontract price, or the ceiling price in an incentive type subcontract.

These same six conditions are stipulated in FAR 52.232-16, (c), the progress payment clause, and the DOD-FAR counterpart clause 252.232-7007 (c), which must be incorporated by reference into the subcontract document.

Anyone requiring more information on the requirement for, and the buyer's authority to suspend a subcontractor's progress payments should refer to the unofficial restatement of the FAR as related to progress payments, contained in Appendix B to this book, or better, go directly to the FAR or DOD-FAR itself.

Monitoring the Supplier's Physical Work Performance

Question: *Does the prime contractor have a responsibility or duty to monitor the supplier's "physical work performance" in the management of progress payments?* The FAR provides little guidance in this matter, leaving the issue ambiguous at best, and thus resulting in differing interpretations between the prime contractors and their suppliers.

For example, the pertinent subpart of the FAR is entitled: "Progress Payments Based on Costs." With this title, it is little wonder that many suppliers feel that they are entitled to receive progress payments by simply incurring legitimate costs against a subcontract. However, later in the FAR a prime contractor is required to be in a position to suspend progress payments when there is a "failure to make progress."[4] How does one know if one's supplier is making (or not making) progress if one is obligated to pay invoices based simply on the certification of costs contained in supplier invoices, without the benefit of some type of performance surveillance device? This is the essence of the problem.

The new Defense Logistics Agency's *Contract Administration Manual,* seems to address this question nicely, providing guidance to prime contractors not available in the FAR:

> The progress payments governed by the clause FAR 52.232-16 are based on costs, not on a percentage of physical completion. Nevertheless, the ACO must always compare the actual percent of physical completion to the total costs incurred when paying progress payments in order to avoid overpayment.[5]

Thus with the prime contractor's buyer standing in the place of the Government's ACO in the administration of progress payments, the answer to the question at the beginning of this section is a resounding "YES." It is a wise practice to always monitor the physical performance of any supplier receiving progress payments using United States Government funds. Those who may choose to ignore the supplier's physical performance and its obvious direct relationship to the costs incurred, run the distinct risk of overpayment and loss on any subcontract which contains progress payments.

At present, progress payments based on physical completion are limited by the FAR to only "construction" and "shipbuilding" contracts.[6] A prediction for the future: the FAR will be changed to require proof of physical performance as a precondition to the approval of progress payments. In short, the government will likely require in the future that suppliers, big and small, demonstrate that they are achieving satisfactory physical performance as a prerequisite to receiving progress payment funds. If you were working with your own family's funds, you would do likewise.

Second question: *How does one monitor the physical performance on firm fixed-price subcontracts when suppliers are reluctant (often flatly refuse) to provide such performance information?* Obviously, prime contractors must position themselves to obtain certain performance monitoring tools on their subcontracts to the greatest extent practical. As covered in the last chapter, the use of progress payments can provide a prime contractor with the opportunity to insist on receiving certain basic supplier plans as a precondition to the authorization (flow-down) of progress payments. This is particularly the case with large business suppliers, where the buyer has the authority to withhold the authorization of such progress payment terms. It is important for the prime contractor to periodically conduct onsite reviews as part of the physical performance verification process (i.e., buyers should sometimes see and touch the product being developed for the prime contractor).

The previous chapter discussed the importance of obtaining a solid supplier baseline schedule in the form of a Gantt Chart, which can be used to obtain the supplier's "percentage completion" estimate each month. Remember that the initial Gantt Chart depicted in Figure 2-5 represents the supplier's baseline plan to support the subcontract.

To best illustrate the critical relationship which should exist between the supplier's "physical work completion" and the supplier's "costs spent," let us now review Hypothetical Engine's monthly update to their original baseline schedule. Monthly Gantt Chart updates will be examined through two assumed "time now" periods:

1. After 10 months of performance (through October, 1991), Figure 3-5.

2. After 13 months of performance (through January, 1992), Figure 3-6.

Figure 3-5 shows the supplier's (assumed) schedule status as of month 10. They are indicating a "physical work percentage completion" position of 28 percent, as listed in column five (from the left) on row 25. The important comparison to be made now is the 28 percent physical completion value with the "percentage spent" value as reflected in the progress payment invoice. The percentage spent on the subcontract can be determined by applying the following formula to the data in the progress payment invoice (SF1443):

$$\frac{\text{SF 1443 line item 12a}}{\text{line 12a} + \text{line 12b}} = \text{Percentage Spent}$$

If the percentage spent is at significant variance from the 28 percent as reported in the Gantt Chart, then the buyer should make contact with the supplier to gain insight into the reasons causing the variance. Any supplier should be able to explain the differences between the "money spent" and the physical "work performed," or the buyer may want to consider withholding the authorization of the current invoice until an explanation is received.

However, perhaps of equal importance is the fact that the supplier is now starting to reflect schedule slippages on two of their critical tasks. For example, the receipt of purchased materials (line 5) has slipped by some four months. Also, fabricated parts completion (line 7) has also slipped by two months from the initial baseline schedule. Since the supplier is stating in their

Figure 3-5. **A Gantt Chart to Support a Progress Payment Request**

Hypothetical Engines, Inc.

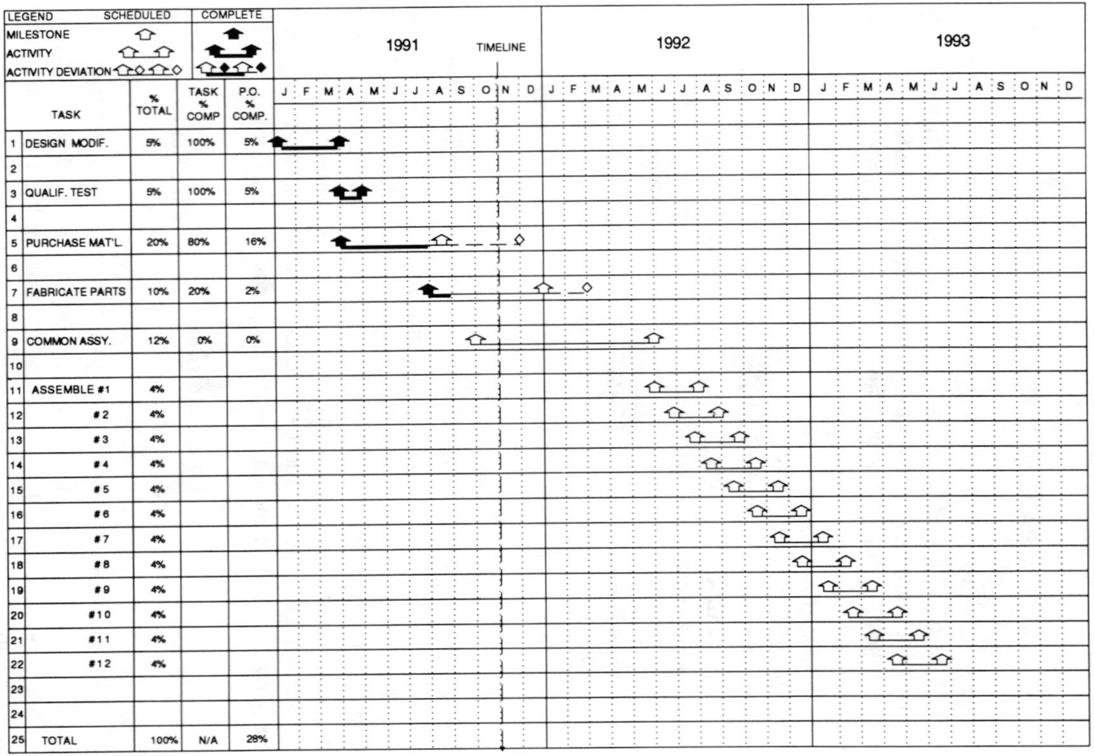
LEGEND
SCHEDULED
COMPLETE
MILESTONE
ACTIVITY
ACTIVITY DEVIATION
1991
TIMELINE
1992
1993
J F M A M J J A S O N D
TASK
% TOTAL
TASK % COMP
P.O. % COMP.
1 DESIGN MODIF. 5% 100% 5%
2
3 QUALIF. TEST 5% 100% 5%
4
5 PURCHASE MAT'L. 20% 80% 16%
6
7 FABRICATE PARTS 10% 20% 2%
8
9 COMMON ASSY. 12% 0% 0%
10
11 ASSEMBLE #1 4%
12 #2 4%
13 #3 4%
14 #4 4%
15 #5 4%
16 #6 4%
17 #7 4%
18 #8 4%
19 #9 4%
20 #10 4%
21 #11 4%
22 #12 4%
23
24
25 TOTAL 100% N/A 28%

update that they feel they can maintain the original delivery schedule dates starting on July 31, 1992, the buyer would likely accept the supplier's request for progress payment—this time. However, it would be wise to watch their performance closely in the future.

Next, Figure 3-6 shows the supplier's (assumed) updated report through month 13. Serious things are starting to emerge, or should we say, not happen as scheduled. The common assemblies (line 9) which should have started October 1, 1991, still have not happened through the reporting period. They are now projected to start next month. However, the supplier still insists that they will maintain their original hardware delivery schedule. Will they? This is a judgement call. Although the supplier has reported continued physical performance up to 34 percent, the buyer and the subcontract management team may want to consider suspending further progress payments to Hypothetical Engines until they start making progress on their critical common assemblies task (line 9), and demonstrate conclusively to the team that the first subcontract hardware delivery (line 11) will happen as promised. Remember, progress payment liquidations do not happen until the hardware articles are delivered.

The fundamental issue here is the prime contractor's ability to gain an insight into their supplier's actual physical performance so as to be in a position to relate physical work accomplishments against the actual funds being spent. This is a cardinal point. Progress payments should be authorized to *only* those suppliers who are willing to comply with a simple minimal requirement—to prepare and submit a monthly Gantt Chart showing a supplier's physical "percentage completion" to support progress payment requests.

Invoking the "Loss Ratio Adjustment"

The government expects to be protected from the overpayment of progress payment loans to a supplier as soon as it becomes known, or can be intelligently forecasted that the supplier will loose money on a given subcontract. And the prime contractor's buyer, who in effect represents the government in the administering progress payments, is required to follow the precise language contained in FAR 32.503-6, (g), covering the subject of "loss contracts." A loss contract/subcontract may be defined simply as a condition whereby the total of the supplier's costs incurred to date (line 12a), plus the estimated costs to complete the job (line 12b), will exceed the subcontract price (line 5) as reported on the progress payment invoice (SF1443).

The theory behind the loss ratio adjustment is quite simple. When progress payment loans are negotiated between a buyer and seller, both parties

Figure 3-6. A Gantt Chart Reflecting a Potential Schedule Slip
Hypothetical Engines, Inc.

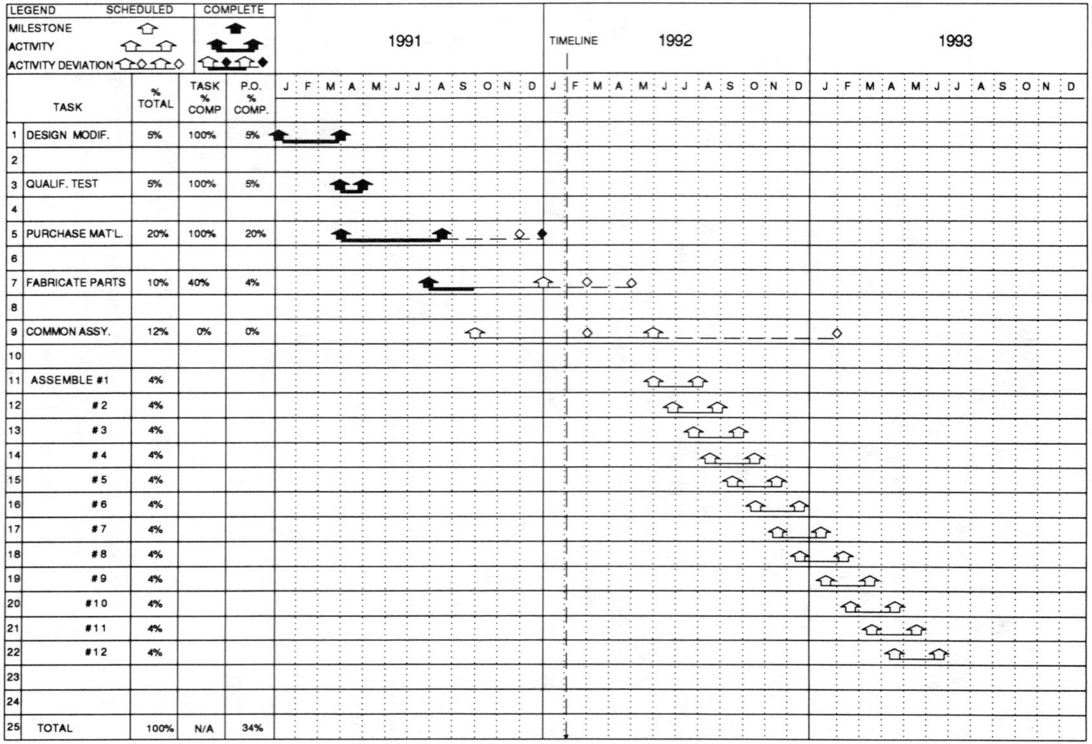

LEGEND SCHEDULED COMPLETE
MILESTONE
ACTIVITY
ACTIVITY DEVIATION

	TASK	% TOTAL	TASK % COMP.	P.O. % COMP.	1991	TIMELINE 1992	1993
1	DESIGN MODIF.	5%	100%	5%			
2							
3	QUALIF. TEST	5%	100%	5%			
4							
5	PURCHASE MATL.	20%	100%	20%			
6							
7	FABRICATE PARTS	10%	40%	4%			
8							
9	COMMON ASSY.	12%	0%	0%			
10							
11	ASSEMBLE #1	4%					
12	#2	4%					
13	#3	4%					
14	#4	4%					
15	#5	4%					
16	#6	4%					
17	#7	4%					
18	#8	4%					
19	#9	4%					
20	#10	4%					
21	#11	4%					
22	#12	4%					
23							
24							
25	TOTAL	100%	N/A	34%			

assume that the seller is going to make a profit on the order. They agree on a progress payment rate as stipulated by the FAR, and a forecasted progress payment expenditure profile based on the assumption that the subcontractor will experience a profit on the order.

When, during the course of performance, it becomes known that those original assumptions are no longer valid, and the supplier will in fact experience a loss, the government insists that the value of progress payments be reduced by the percentage ratio of the supplier's forecasted loss. To do otherwise, which allows the supplier to be overpaid each month during the period of the contract, could invite a potentially greater loss to the government should the supplier be unable to repay the sum of the overpayment at the end of the contract period. The government does not want a "balloon" type payment due from any supplier at the end of the contract or subcontract period. Better to cut such losses early.

An unexpected projected loss on a given contract is an indicator that a supplier is experiencing some unanticipated problems, the extent of which may not be fully known or even quantifiable at the time they are initially revealed. Better to reduce the progress payments early than to allow the unknown risks to grow with each monthly progress payment, thereby increasing the potential losses to the government.

On "incentive" type contracts, the loss ratio adjustment does not automatically start the minute the subcontract price value is forecasted to be exceeded. A buyer does have some latitude over the issue. With incentive type subcontracts, the range between the subcontract target costs and penetration of the subcontract ceiling is a "discretionary" zone for the buyer. In this area, the buyer may or may not invoke a loss ratio adjustment, since technically the supplier is still making a profit, albeit a small one. Once the target ceiling is penetrated on an incentive type contract, however, the loss ratio must be invoked to avoid overpayments.

To establish the loss ratio adjustment, the subcontract price (line 5), including the estimated value of all authorized changes, must be divided by the sum of the supplier's costs incurred to date (line 12a) plus the estimate to complete the job (line 12b). The loss ratio formula is shown in Figure 3-7, again using assumptions and data from Hypothetical Engines.[7] In this example, with a 20 percent projected overrun, the 80 percent progress payment rate will be reduced down to 66.6 percent when the loss ratio factor is applied. The 66.6 percent adjusted rate must be applied to all progress payments, both those paid and to be paid. Obviously, the loss ratio adjustment can be quite dramatic to any supplier!

As painful as the use of the loss ratio adjustment might be for both parties, a buyer has no discretionary latitude in following the strict language

Figure 3-7. Loss Ratio Factor (LRF) Adjustment Formula

(assume a 20% overrun)

$$\frac{\text{Subcontract Price}}{\text{Costs to date + Costs to complete}} = \text{LR Factor}$$
$$= \text{Estimate at Completion}$$

$$\frac{\$13,200}{\$13,200 \times 1.2\% = \$15,840} = 83.3\% \text{ LR Factor}$$

83.3% LRF x 80% PPR = 66.6% new PP Rate

of the FAR requirement any time a loss is forecasted (or reasonably known) for a given subcontract.

Managing Changes to the Subcontract Baseline Price

A full treatment of the subject of managing changes to a subcontract baseline is beyond the intended scope of this book on progress payments. However, in the administration of progress payments, some of the more troublesome issues which will often confront the buyer are related to the subcontract price (line 5 on SF1443), and the incorporation (or exclusion) of authorized changes to the price. Which changes should be included in the subcontract price will often determine whether or not a given invoice may be approved for payment.

The first step is to understand exactly what constitutes the subcontract price for the purposes of administration and approval of progress payments. FAR section 32.501-3 covers the subject of "contract price," and provides specific guidance in this matter.

For the purpose of making progress payments and determining the limitation of such progress payments, the following rules apply in establishing the subcontract price (which will be reflected on line item 5 of the supplier's progress payment invoice, form SF1443):

	The Subcontract Type:	The Subcontract Price:
(1)	Firm-fixed price contracts	is the current contract price, plus unpriced modifications for which funds have been obligated.
(2)	Fixed-price redeterminable or economic price adjustment	is the initial price until modified.
(3)	Fixed-price incentive	is the target price plus unpriced modifications; however, the buyer may provisionally increase the price up to the ceiling or maximum price if the supplier properly incurred such costs.

(4)	Letter subcontracts	is the maximum amount obligated by the contract as modified.
(5)	Unpriced orders under basic ordering agreements	is the maximum amount obligated by the contract as modified.
(6)	Any portion of a contract which allows reimbursement of costs only	is excluded from the subcontract price.

The buyer who is making a determination of what value constitutes the subcontract price is wise to create and maintain a "log" of subcontract changes and the status of each authorized change. Such logs will vary with each given buyer, but will typically consist of the following data fields: the initial subcontract baseline price, award date, nomenclature, date each change was authorized, a not-to-exceed estimated value, date a cost proposal was received, date the price/cost analysis was done, date the fact finding was done, the negotiation date, final negotiated amount, date of the contract modification, modification number, amount of modification, total new subcontract value, etc.

Housekeeping: Staying on Top of Progress Payment Administration

Procurement (subcontract management) organizations are dynamic. Often for a variety of reasons management will move their subcontract buyers around, shifting the responsibility for selected subcontract packages to new buyers. Not infrequently, a buyer who inherits a subcontract package may fail to immediately go back and briefly review the status of the newly acquired procurement file. Rather, they will wait until some future event happens, sometimes an adverse event, to sit down to do their basic homework on the newly acquired procurement file.

When dealing with orders containing progress payment loans, such an approach can be devastating and may ultimately result in a loss to the prime contractor. All subcontracts which contain progress payment terms must be actively monitored in order to avoid possible financial losses to the prime contractor.

What a buyer should do when inheriting a new package containing progress payment provisions is sit down and perform a brief review of certain critical issues. Shown in Figure 3-8 is a basic checklist of ten of the more obvious key issues which a buyer should understand in order to be current on the procurement, and to minimize the risk of (potential) financial losses to the prime contractor.

This same basic checklist may be useful to any procurement organization when preparing themselves to describe their progress payment methodology during any of the formal customer reviews which happen so frequently these days. Examples of these reviews are: the Contractor Purchasing Systems Review (CPSR) as required by FAR 44.3, the Contractor Operations Review (COR), the Contractor Performance Assessment Reviews (CPAR), the System Status Reviews (SSR), or any other customer reviews which may surface in the future.

Cash Management and Progress Payments

Most prime contractors today are feeling a squeeze on their cash flow, and the condition is likely to get even worse moving into the 1990s. It is therefore imperative that those involved with managing progress payments clearly understand that their efforts can have an adverse impact on their prime contractor's cash position, if such activities are not watched closely.

The primary issue is one of subcontract schedule deliveries (including line-item completions), and the delicate balance of making sure that all suppliers deliver their products at the precise scheduled time, not early and most certainly not late. Some people refer to this approach as Just-In-Time scheduling, and perhaps the term applies here. Unfortunately, when it comes to cash flow, many prime contractors are quite sensitive to late supplier deliveries, but rarely exert the same energy or attention on preventing early supplier deliveries. Supplier rating systems often focus on late deliveries, but seldom monitor early deliveries. Moving into the cash-tight 1990s, an equal amount of effort must be spent in preventing early supplier deliveries to remain competitive in this cash tight period.

As way of illustration, Figure 3-9 contrasts a subcontractor's delivery schedule against the actual deliveries made against the subcontract. Here it can be immediately seen that the buyer has permitted the supplier to make early hardware deliveries, completing the total order a full four months in advance of the official subcontract schedule (i.e., thirty-one units were delivered and accepted four months ahead of the official subcontract schedule). This action, as harmless as it may seem, results in the prime contractor having to borrow 20 percent of the unit price of each article accepted early. The full

Figure 3-8.   A Buyer's Checklist of Ten Key Progress Payment Issues

A BUYER'S CHECKLIST OF TEN KEY PROGRESS PAYMENT ISSUES

1. Know the internal procedure which governs the authorization and management of progress payments to fixed-price suppliers.

2. Know which prime contract (or higher tier subcontract) was used to authorize the subcontractor's progress payments, and make sure the standards, terms and conditions are consistent between the prime contract and subcontract.

3. Make sure there was pre-award assessment of the supplier's financial condition, and their cost accounting system which allowed progress payments to be authorized on this supplier, and that such pre-award activity is documented and available in the procurement file.

4. Know if the supplier is a "Big" or a "Small" or a "Small Disadvantaged" business concern.

5. Know the current authorized progress payment rate for the subcontract.

6. Know the current authorized progress payment liquidation rate for the subcontract.

7. Know how many progress payment invoices (SF1443) have been paid to date (line 18 plus line 27), and the unliquidated balance of outstanding progress payments (line 24), and plot these values on the summary of financial projections chart (Figure 2—4) which was prepared based on the supplier's data. Keep copies of all SF1443 progress payment invoices in the procurement file.

8. Know the "dollar" percentage complete on the subcontract, based on the actual funds expended by the supplier as reported in their progress payment (SF1443) invoices, as compared to their "physical" work percentage complete as reported in their monthly Gantt Chart submittal. Compare the SF1443 to the Gantt Chart, to trip reports, to program status reviews, and make sure all these surveillance points are reporting a consistent subcontractor performance pattern.

9. Know how many subcontract deliveries have actually been made, as compared to the official subcontract delivery schedule(s).

10. Know why *you*, the buyer, and your management have authorized the progress payments already paid on this subcontract.

Figure 3-9. **Early Deliveries and Cash Flow**

ONE ACTUAL SUBCONTRACT
-Allowing Early Subcontract Deliveries-

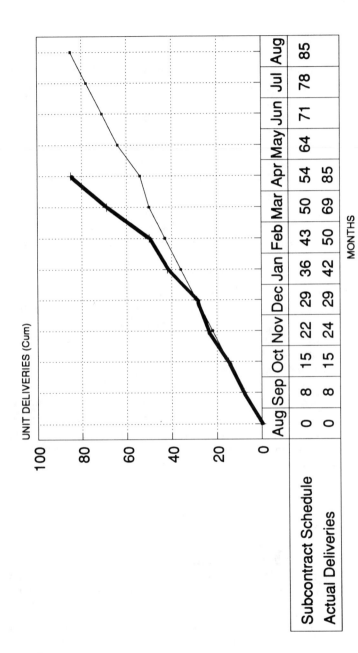

UNIT DELIVERIES (Cum)

	Aug	Sep	Oct	Nov	Dec	Jan	Feb	Mar	Apr	May	Jun	Jul	Aug
Subcontract Schedule	0	8	15	22	29	36	43	50	54	64	71	78	85
Actual Deliveries	0	8	15	24	29	42	50	69	85				

MONTHS

■ Subcontract Schedule   ━━ Actual Deliveries

impact of this action will be illustrated in Figures 3-9 and 3-10, and in the paragraphs that follow.

Historically, most prime contractors and their buyers have been sensitive to late supplier deliveries. A late delivery of even a low-cost part can sometimes hold up a multimillion dollar end-item. So the buyers and management are typically alert to watch for late supplier deliveries. But not infrequently they push too far in this direction, and sometimes (often) allow their suppliers to deliver subcontracted articles earlier than planned or needed by the prime contractor, and as authorized by the subcontract schedule.

People like to get things behind them and move on to the next job, so a buyer may inadvertently allow early supplier deliveries. But such practices can be costly to the prime contractor. This fact is not always understood by those involved in the management of progress payments, or the management of company inventories. Both functions have a vital role to play in cash flow management.

The impact of early deliveries on a prime contractor's cash flow relates to the difference between the approved progress payment rate, illustrated here at 80 percent, and the other unpaid 20 percent balance due on delivery, plus the subcontractor's profit. When a buyer authorizes a progress payment at 80 percent of the subcontractor's costs incurred, the prime contractor folds all such payments into their own progress payment request at 100 percent of the full value of such supplier payments. Remember, supplier progress payments are recoverable by the prime contractor at 100 percent of all legitimate payments made, so there is a zero negative impact on the prime contractor's cash flow. But by contrast, when the supplier makes a delivery of a subcontract line item, they also receive the remaining 20 percent of costs that were not "loaned" as progress payments, plus their fee. Unfortunately, the prime contractor cannot recover these additional cash outlays until the final end unit is delivered to the customer.

To the prime contractor, the category of costs they have now incurred will become one of their own "costs incurred," instead of a "supplier progress payment." Thus, the prime contractor no longer receives full reimbursement from its higher tier customer at 100 percent of such amounts paid. Rather, they can only receive payment at their current authorized progress payment rate, which for illustration purposes is shown at 80 percent. The negative cash flow impact of such actions to the prime contractor is demonstrated in Figure 3-10.

In this illustration, again using Hypothetical Engines with units valued at $1,100,000 each, for each delivery accepted early, the prime contractor must float a value of $220,000 from their own funds, until such time as they can deliver their prime contract end-item to a customer, which may be months

Figure 3-10. Cash Flow Impact from Early Schedule Deliveries

PRIME CONTRACTOR CASH FLOW

(000)

	Cash with 80% Progress Payments	Cash Requirements On Delivery
Subcontractor costs incurred:	$1,000	$1,000
Subcontractor fee paid:	0	$100
Prime contractor's payment:	$800	$1,100
Prime contractor's cash recovery:	$800	$880
Prime contractor's cash outlay:	0	($220)
Category of prime contract cost:	"Suplier progress payment"	"Costs incurred"

into the future. Thus, in this illustration, the prime contractor which accepts early deliveries must float 20 percent ($220,000 divided by $1,100,000) of the unit value of each item they have accepted early from their supplier. And throughout history, as is well known, manufacturing managers have been known to put safety "pads" into their requests for parts. Thus, the "official" subcontract schedule likely contained the manufacturing "pad" when the subcontract was issued.

Obviously the practice of accepting early subcontractor deliveries must be avoided, particularly in times of high interest costs and tight funding. Better to manage all subcontractor deliveries closely, so that they will occur only as contractually scheduled, not early, and not late.

In Summary

Progress payments are something which must be administered properly in order for the prime contractor to avoid sustaining losses in the course of managing their subcontracts. The fact that progress payments can actually result in losses to a prime contractor is not a widely publicized fact. But it happens. The buyers representing their prime contractor organizations must do certain things before the award of the subcontract, and must be alert to supplier performance during the full post-award management phase.

There are at least three important reasons why a buyer must actively manage progress payments during the full term of a subcontract. They are:

1. To provide assurances that physical work is actually being accomplished by the supplier, consistent with the authorization of each progress payment to them, to ensure that the United States Government, and the Buyer's own company, will not sustain a loss on any subcontract by allowing suppliers to receive progress payments in advance of their actual physical work accomplishment.

2. To ensure that a full recovery (an upward flow) of all such subcontractor payments can be made at 100 percent of such payments, by making sure that all supplier payments are both reasonable and proper.

3. Because the FAR requires the monitoring of progress payments by the prime contractor's buyer, who effectively stands in the place of the Government's contracting officers in such matters.[8]

On the more positive side, progress payments provide an "opportunity" for prime contractors to get certain basic performance monitoring information from their fixed-price suppliers, which they could not otherwise get without paying a cost. Such information is vital to the proper post-award management of all fixed-price suppliers, particularly the firm fixed-price (FFP) type orders.

In addition, progress payments can represent possibly one of "the" most important tools any buyer can have, to get the attention and respect they deserve from each of their suppliers.

Endnotes

1. FAR 32.503–10.

2. FAR 32.503–9.

3. FAR 32.503–6, (f), (1).

4. FAR 32.503–6 (c).

5. U.S. Department of Defense, Defense Logistics Agency, Defense Contract Management Command, *Contract Management Manual,* (Cameron Station, Alexandria, Virginia: October, 1990), page 32.590–1.

6. FAR 32.103.

7. Loss ratio formula from FAR 32.503–6 (g).

8. FAR 32.504.

Chapter 4

Analysis of Progress Payment Data

Let us continue our discussion of progress payments by focusing on the subcontractor's request for payment and the data contained therein. Much valuable cost performance information is available on the progress payment invoice, providing actual cost history on firm fixed-price contracts that is roughly comparable to most cost reimbursable type contracts. However, one must know how to read and interpret the data, and discern the subcontractor's performance trends, in order for this data to be useful as a subcontract management tool.

The Progress Payment Request (SF 1443)

The official form which a subcontractor will use to request progress payments from a prime contractor is entitled the "CONTRACTOR'S REQUEST FOR PROGRESS PAYMENT," FAR Standard Form 1443. Figure 4-1A and 4-1B contain the frontside and backside facsimiles of the SF 1443.

In the 1980s, the SF 1443 replaced an earlier Department of Defense form DD 1195, which was identical in format and content. When requesting payment, a supplier may use either a photocopy of the SF 1443 or a computer generated imitation, as long as the format and content remain identical to the SF 1443, and the certification box at the bottom contains an original signature from the appropriate official representing the supplier. However, before using a computer generated SF 1443, it might be wise protocol to first discuss the

Figure 4-1A.   Progress Payment Request SF 1443—Frontside

CONTRACTOR'S REQUEST FOR PROGRESS PAYMENT

Form Approved
OMB No. 3090-0105

IMPORTANT: This form is to be completed in accordance with instructions on reverse.

SECTION I – IDENTIFICATION INFORMATION

1. TO: NAME AND ADDRESS OF CONTRACTING OFFICE (Include ZIP Code)

PAYING OFFICE

2. FROM: NAME AND ADDRESS OF CONTRACTOR (Include ZIP Code)

3. SMALL BUSINESS ☐ YES ☐ NO
4. CONTRACT NO.
5. CONTRACT PRICE $

6. RATES
A. PROG. PYMTS. ___ %
B. LIQUIDATION ___ %

7. DATE OF INITIAL AWARD
A. YEAR
B. MONTH

8A. PROGRESS PAYMENT REQUEST NO.
8B. DATE OF THIS REQUEST

SECTION II – STATEMENT OF COSTS UNDER THIS CONTRACT THROUGH _____ (Date)

9. PAID COSTS ELIGIBLE UNDER PROGRESS PAYMENT CLAUSE	$
10. INCURRED COSTS ELIGIBLE UNDER PROGRESS PAYMENT CLAUSE	
11. TOTAL COSTS ELIGIBLE FOR PROGRESS PAYMENTS (Item 9 plus 10)	
12. a. TOTAL COSTS INCURRED TO DATE	$
b. ESTIMATED ADDITIONAL COST TO COMPLETE	
13. ITEM 11 MULTIPLIED BY ITEM 6a	
14. a. PROGRESS PAYMENTS PAID TO SUBCONTRACTORS	
b. LIQUIDATED PROGRESS PAYMENTS TO SUBCONTRACTORS	
c. UNLIQUIDATED PROGRESS PAYMENTS TO SUBCONTRACTORS (Item 14a less 14b)	
d. SUBCONTRACT PROGRESS BILLINGS APPROVED FOR CURRENT PAYMENT	
e. ELIGIBLE SUBCONTRACTOR PROGRESS PAYMENTS (Item 14c plus 14d)	
15. TOTAL DOLLAR AMOUNT (Item 13 plus 14e)	
16. ITEM 5 MULTIPLIED BY ITEM 6b	
17. LESSER OF ITEM 15 OR ITEM 16	
18. TOTAL AMOUNT OF PREVIOUS PROGRESS PAYMENTS REQUESTED	
19. MAXIMUM BALANCE ELIGIBLE FOR PROGRESS PAYMENTS (Item 17 less 18)	

SECTION III – COMPUTATION OF LIMITS FOR OUTSTANDING PROGRESS PAYMENTS
*SEE SPECIAL INSTRUCTIONS ON BACK FOR USE UNDER THE FEDERAL ACQUISITION REGULATION.

20. COMPUTATION OF PROGRESS PAYMENT CLAUSE (a(3)(i) or a(4)(i)) LIMITATION*	$
a. COSTS INCLUDED IN ITEM 11, APPLICABLE TO ITEMS DELIVERED, INVOICED, AND ACCEPTED TO THE DATE IN HEADING OF SECTION II.	
b. COSTS ELIGIBLE FOR PROGRESS PAYMENTS, APPLICABLE TO UNDELIVERED ITEMS AND TO DELIVERED ITEMS NOT INVOICED AND ACCEPTED (Item 11 less 20a)	
c. ITEM 20b MULTIPLIED BY ITEM 6a	$
d. ELIGIBLE SUBCONTRACTOR PROGRESS PAYMENTS (Item 14e)	
e. LIMITATION a(3)(i) or a(4)(i) (Item 20c plus 20d) *	
21. COMPUTATION OF PROGRESS PAYMENT CLAUSE (a(3)(ii) or a(4)(ii)) LIMITATION *	
a. CONTRACT PRICE OF ITEMS DELIVERED, ACCEPTED AND INVOICED TO DATE IN HEADING OF SECTION II	
b. CONTRACT PRICE OF ITEMS NOT DELIVERED, ACCEPTED AND INVOICED (Item 5 less 21a)	
c. ITEM 21b MULTIPLIED BY ITEM 6b	
d. UNLIQUIDATED ADVANCE PAYMENTS PLUS ACCRUED INTEREST	
e. LIMITATION (a(3)(ii) or a(4)(ii)) (Item 21c less 21d) *	
22. MAXIMUM UNLIQUIDATED PROGRESS PAYMENTS (Lesser of Item 20e or 21e)	
23. TOTAL AMOUNT APPLIED AND TO BE APPLIED TO REDUCE PROGRESS PAYMENT	
24. UNLIQUIDATED PROGRESS PAYMENTS (Item 18 less 23)	
25. MAXIMUM PERMISSIBLE PROGRESS PAYMENTS (Item 22 less 24)	
26. AMOUNT OF CURRENT INVOICE FOR PROGRESS PAYMENT (Lesser of Item 25 or 19)	

27. AMOUNT APPROVED BY CONTRACTING OFFICER

CERTIFICATION

I certify that the above statement (with attachments) has been prepared from the books and records of the above-named contractor in accordance with the contract and the instructions hereon, and to the best of my knowledge and belief, that it is correct, that all the costs of contract performance (except as herewith reported in writing) have been paid to the extent shown herein, or where not shown as paid have been paid or will be paid currently, by the contractor, when due, in the ordinary course of business, that the work reflected above has been performed, that the quantities and amounts involved are consistent with the requirements of the contract. That there are no encumbrances (except as reported in writing herewith, or on previous progress payment request No. _____) against the property acquired or produced for, and allocated or properly chargeable to the contract which would affect or impair the Government's title, that there has been no materially adverse change in the financial condition of the contractor since the submission of the most recent written information dated _____ by the contractor to the Government in connection with the contract, that to the extent of any contract provision limiting progress payments pending first article approval, such provision has been complied with, and that after the making of the requested progress payment the unliquidated progress payments will not exceed the maximum unliquidated progress payments permitted by the contract.

NAME AND TITLE OF CONTRACTOR REPRESENTATIVE SIGNING THIS FORM

SIGNATURE

NAME AND TITLE OF CONTRACTING OFFICER

SIGNATURE

NSN 7540-01-140-5523   1443-101

STANDARD FORM 1443 (10-82)
Prescribed by GSA (FPR 1-16.808)
FAR (48 CFR 53.232)

Figure 4-1B.   Progress Payment Request SF 1443—Backside

INSTRUCTIONS

GENERAL - All entries on this form must be typewritten - all dollar amounts must be shown in whole dollars, rounded up to the next whole dollar. All line item numbers not included in the instructions below are self-explanatory.

SECTION I — IDENTIFICATION INFORMATION. Complete Items 1 through 8c in accordance with the following instructions:

Item 1. TO — Enter the name and address of the cognizant Contract Administration Office. PAYING OFFICE — Enter the designation of the paying office, as indicated in the contract.

Item 2. FROM · CONTRACTOR'S NAME AND ADDRESS/ZIP CODE — Enter the name and mailing address of the contractor. If applicable, the division of the company performing the contract should be entered immediately following the contractor's name.

Item 3. Enter an "X" in the appropriate block to indicate whether or not the contractor is a small business concern.

Item 5. Enter the total contract price, as amended. If the contract provides for escalation or price redetermination, enter the initial price until changed and not the ceiling price; if the contract is of the incentive type, enter the target or billing price, as amended until final pricing. For letter contracts, enter the maximum expenditure authorized by the contract, as amended.

Item 6A. PROGRESS PAYMENT RATES — Enter the 2-digit progress payment percentage rate shown in paragraph (a)(1) of the progress payment clause.

Item 6B. LIQUIDATION RATE — Enter the progress payment liquidation rate shown in paragraph (b) of the progress payment clause, using three digits - Example: show 80% as 800 - show 72.3% as 723.

Item 7. DATE OF INITIAL AWARD — Enter the last two digits of the calendar year. Use two digits to indicate the month. Example: show January 1982 as 82/01.

Item 8A. PROGRESS PAYMENT REQUEST NO. — Enter the number assigned to this request. All requests under a single contract must be numbered consecutively, beginning with 1. Each subsequent request under the same contract must continue in sequence, using the same series of numbers without omission.

Item 8B. Enter the date of the request.

SECTION II — GENERAL INSTRUCTIONS. DATE. In the space provided in the heading enter the date through which costs have been accumulated from inception for inclusion in this request. This date is applicable to item entries in Sections II and III.

Cost Basis. For all contracts with Small Business concerns, the base for progress payments is total costs incurred. For contracts with concerns other than Small Business, the progress payment base will be the total recorded paid costs, together with the incurred costs per the Computation of Amounts paragraph of the progress payment clause in FPR 1-30.510-1(a) or FAR 52.232-16, as appropriate. Total costs include all expenses paid and incurred, including applicable manufacturing and production expense, general and administrative expense for performance of contract, which are reasonable, allocable to the contract, consistent with sound and generally accepted accounting principles and practices, and which are not otherwise excluded by the contract.

Manufacturing and Production Expense, General and Administrative Expense. In connection with the first progress payment request on a contract, attach an explanation of the method, bases and period used in determining the amount of each of these two types of expenses. If the method, bases or periods used for computing these expenses differ in subsequent requests for progress payments under this contract, attach an explanation of such changes to the progress payment request involved.

Incurred Costs Involving Subcontractors for Contracts with Small Business Concerns. If the incurred costs eligible for progress payments under the contract include costs shown in invoices of subcontractors, suppliers and others, that portion of the costs computed on such invoices can only include costs for: (1) completed work to which the prime contractor has acquired title; (2) materials delivered to which the prime contractor has acquired title; (3) services rendered; and (4) costs billed under cost reimbursement or time and material subcontracts for work to which the prime contractor has acquired title.

SECTION II — SPECIFIC INSTRUCTIONS

Item 9. PAID COSTS ELIGIBLE UNDER PROGRESS PAYMENT CLAUSE — Line 9 will not be used for Small Business Contracts.

For large business contracts, costs to be shown in Item 9 shall include only those recorded costs which have resulted at time of request in payment made by cash, check, or other form of actual payment for items or services purchased directly for the contract. This includes items delivered, accepted and paid for, resulting in liquidation of subcontractor progress payments.

Costs to be shown in Item 9 are not to include advance payments, downpayments, or deposits, all of which are not eligible for reimbursement; or progress payments made to subcontractors, suppliers or others, which are to be included in Item 14. See "Cost Basis" above.

Item 10. INCURRED COSTS ELIGIBLE UNDER PROGRESS PAYMENT CLAUSE — For all Small Business Contracts, Item 10 will show total costs incurred for the contract.

Costs to be shown in Item 10 are not to include advance payments, downpayments, deposits, or progress payments made to subcontractors, suppliers or others.

For large business contracts, costs to be shown in Item 10 shall include all costs incurred (see "Cost Basis" above) for: materials which have been issued from the stores inventory and placed into production process for use on the contract; for direct labor; for other direct in-house costs; and for properly allocated and allowable indirect costs as set forth under "Cost Basis" above.

Item 12a. Enter the total contract costs incurred to date; if the actual amount is not known, enter the best possible estimate. If an estimate is used, enter (E) after the amount.

Item 12b. Enter the estimated cost to complete the contract. The estimate may be the last estimate made, adjusted for costs incurred since the last estimate; however, estimates shall be made not less frequently than every six months.

Items 14a through 14e. Include only progress payments on subcontracts which conform to progress payment provisions of the prime contract.

Item 14a. Enter only progress payments actually paid.

Item 14b. Enter total progress payments recouped from subcontractors.

Item 14d. For Small Business prime contracts, include the amount of unpaid subcontract progress payment billings which have been approved by the contractor for the current payment in the ordinary course of business. For other contracts, enter "0" amount.

SECTION III — SPECIFIC INSTRUCTIONS. This Section must be completed only if the contractor has received advance payments against this contract, or if items have been delivered, invoiced and accepted as of the date indicated in the heading of Section II above. EXCEPTION: Item 27 must be filled in by the Contracting Officer.

Item 20a. Of the costs reported in Item 11, compute and enter only costs which are properly allocable to items delivered, invoiced and accepted to the applicable date. In order of preference, these costs are to be computed on the basis of one of the following: (a) The actual unit cost of items delivered, giving proper consideration to the deferment of the starting load costs or, (b) projected unit costs (based on experienced costs plus the estimated cost to complete the contract), where the contractor maintains cost data which will clearly establish the reliability of such estimates.

Item 20d. Enter amount from 14e.

Item 21a. Enter the total billing price, as adjusted, of items delivered, accepted and invoiced to the applicable date.

Item 23. Enter total progress payments liquidated and those to be liquidated from billings submitted but not yet paid.

Item 25. Self-explanatory. (NOTE: If the entry in this item is a negative amount, there has been an overpayment which requires adjustment.)

Item 26. Self-explanatory, but if a lesser amount is requested, enter the lesser amount.

SPECIAL INSTRUCTIONS FOR USE UNDER FEDERAL ACQUISITION REGULATION (FAR).

Items 20 and 20e. Delete the references to a(3)(i) of the progress payment clause.

Items 21 and 21e. Delete the references to a(3)(ii) of the progress payment clause.

STANDARD FORM 1443 BACK (10-82)

issue with the recipient, your customer. Most customers are typically recep-
tive to the use of computers for any activity which improves contractor
efficiency.

The reverse side of the FAR Standard Form 1443 contains the "official"
detailed instructions on the proper interpretation and ways to complete the
SF 1443. But, like so many examples of administrative and/or bureaucratic
instructions, there are gaps, questions and ambiguities associated with these
guidelines.

Therefore, what follows below is an "unofficial" and pragmatic interpretation of what each line item on the SF 1443 is presumed to contain.
However, please keep in mind that any definitive interpretation of this form
must be whatever your customer and/or the government requires of you in
order to receive prompt payment.

As a starting point the FAR provides us with guidance as to what the
government expects to receive with each SF 1443:

Each contractor request for payment shall—

(a) Be submitted on Standard Form 1443, Contractor's Request for
Progress Payment;

(b) Comply with the instructions on the reverse of the applicable form,
and the contract terms, and

(c) Include any additional information reasonably requested by the contracting officer.[1]

Since the contract is between prime and subcontractor, the term buyer
may be substituted for the contracting officer when used on the SF 1443.

Let us now trace through the SF 1443 line item by line item. The
language displayed in *italics* represents direct quotations from the SF 1443.

"SECTION I—IDENTIFICATION INFORMATION"

Section I of the SF 1443 is used to indicate the prime contractor, the name
of the subcontractor, and details of the subcontract under which the progress
payments are being requested.

"1. TO: NAME AND ADDRESS OF CONTRACTING OFFICE:"

In the case of a subcontract, this item must reflect the name and address of
the prime contractor.

"2. FROM: NAME AND ADDRESS OF CONTRACTOR:"

This line item will contain the name and address of the subcontractor.

"3. SMALL BUSINESS: YES OR NO:"

The subcontractor must indicate its legal status as either a large or small supplier, as defined in FAR 19.001, and as specified in the subcontract document.

"4. CONTRACT NO. _____"

The supplier must specify the document number under which the payment is being requested, i.e., the prime contractor's subcontract or purchase order number.

"5. CONTRACT PRICE $_____"

This is one of the more critical and difficult line items on the form. Everything in item 5 is straightforward *until* there are changes in the subcontract statement of work, either authorized or constructive, in which case the monthly entries on line item 5 can get most interesting and debatable.

Normally, item 5 will always equal the value of the subcontract price. One exception would be if only selected contract line items in a subcontract were subject to progress payments, and other line items were not. In this case, the value to be shown in item 5 would be the sum price of only those contract line items which were subject to progress payments, which would be a lesser value than the total subcontract price.

The subcontract price is that value which has been authorized in the subcontract document, plus any supplemental agreements. However, it can also reflect authorized but unnegotiated work, provisionally increased at some value by the buyer to allow for an increase in the amounts available for progress payments. If the buyer has received a legitimate cost proposal from a supplier, supported by adequate cost detail, up to 75 percent of this proposed new increment may be provisionally authorized as increased subcontract price, for purposes of billing progress payments.

In letter contracts, the price is that value which has been obligated (budgeted) for the subcontract. Some prime contractors find it an advisable practice to "self-impose" a limitation on their buyers as to what they may authorize on letter contracts or undefinitized changes, at say 40 to 50 percent of any proposed values. They take this step to cap their liability, and to encourage early definitization.

In an incentive type contract, the subcontract value is always the target price, unless and until the buyer elects to increase it up to the full ceiling price.

"6. RATES: A. PROGRESS PAYMENTS__%; B. LIQUIDATION__%"

Both these specified rates must conform to the current rates as delineated in the subcontract document, as may be modified over time. Item 6A, the progress payment rate, will be used to express a percentage value (in two digits, e.g., 80) of supplier costs incurred, whereas item 6B, the liquidation rate will be used to reflect a percentage value (in three digits, e.g., 727) of the subcontract price for line items.

"7. DATE OF INITIAL AWARD: A. YEAR __; B. MONTH__"

This reflects the award date as contained in the subcontract.

"8A. PROGRESS PAYMENT REQUEST NO.____"

In order to keep positive control of all requests for progress payments, the subcontractor will add a consecutive invoice number to each request, starting with number 1. A separate sequence is used for each discrete subcontract. These numbers must be controlled by the supplier and an assigned number can be used only once. There are exceptions: (1) invoices may be revised, (2) invoices may be returned to be rebilled later. There cannot be any gaps in invoice numbers, and all subsequent invoices should be assigned a new number even if a prior invoice has not been paid.

"8B. DATE OF THIS REQUEST____"

This is the date of the invoice request, which will most likely reflect a date later than the (costs through) date as listed in the Section II below, to allow time for administrative processing.

"SECTION II—STATEMENT OF COSTS UNDER THIS CONTRACT THROUGH (date)"

Section II of the SF 1443 is used to specify the costs incurred and/or paid in precise detail through the costs through date. This section also requests the subcontractor's forecasted estimate to complete the job—the sum total of items 12a plus 12b, a very important issue in subcontract management.

The date shown in Section II is distinct from the date of invoice submittal contained in line item 8B above, in that the Section II date must reflect the accounting cutoff period for all cost data contained in both Sections II and III.

"9. PAID COSTS UNDER PROGRESS PAYMENT CLAUSE $____"

This item will contain costs which have been paid to other suppliers, for work which has been completed. Note these two important characteristics which must be met: *paid* costs, for *completed* work.

Typically, this item is used only by a large business firm. Small business firms do not generally fill out this item, but they could if they so elected, and it would not be improper. However, item 9 is normally for use by large business firms only.

"10. INCURRED COSTS ELIGIBLE UNDER PROGRESS PAYMENT CLAUSE $____"

This is typically the item used by a small business firm to reflect their costs, both those paid and those simply incurred.

A large business may use this item to reflect their incurred costs for some types of labor, those materials which are owned by the supplier and withdrawn from a company stockroom, indirect burdens, inter-divisional work, etc. Backup data is sometimes required to support the amounts claimed on this item.

"11. TOTAL COSTS ELIGIBLE FOR PROGRESS PAYMENTS (Item 9 plus 10) $____"

Item 11 contains the sum of items 9 and 10, and represents the costs which are *eligible* for progress payments. Item 11 must always equal the total of items 9 plus 10, or the request will be rejected.

Item 11 is also significant in that this is the item where the "loss ratio" is applied, whenever the estimate at completion exceeds the value in item 5, and the subcontract is, therefore, in an overrun condition.

"12a. TOTAL COSTS INCURRED TO DATE $____"

Item 12a costs must always be equal to or greater than item 11 costs, or the request must be rejected. Item 12a may include costs which are paid by the subcontractor, but which are not eligible for progress payments for some reason.

A large business will sometimes include their accrued costs on this item, which are not eligible for progress payments until they are actually paid.

Sometimes estimated costs are also included in this item, which are signified by an "(E)" designation.

Some firms will include their paid costs for supplier progress payments, costs from item 14e, which have been paid to their next tier suppliers.

"12b. ESTIMATED ADDITIONAL COSTS TO COMPLETE $____"

This is an item which has caused much discussion over the years between the government and prime contractors, and between prime contractors and their subcontractors. This item is intended to reflect a periodic and legitimate estimate to complete the total job by a supplier.

Too often (it is suspected), the value displayed in item 12b is simply a value derived by subtracting item 12a from the total of the work to be done, and not by a conscientious supplier estimate to complete the effort. A supplier *must* prepare a bona fide estimate to complete a subcontract at least every six months, in order to strictly comply with the precise instructions contained on the backside of the SF 1443.

If the value of item 12b, when added to item 12a, exceeds the contract price as reflected in item 5, and there are no authorized changes to account for the difference, then the contract is determined to be in a "loss" condition. In such cases the "loss ratio" must be applied against line item 11, to reduce the value of eligible progress payments by a percentage value of the projected overrun.

In those cases where a contract has not yet been definitized, the supplier will sometimes leave item 12b blank, or they might list a value which could possibly exceed item 5, when items 12a and 12b are combined, reflecting simply their negotiating plan or strategy. This situation would not necessarily call for a loss ratio adjustment to be applied to a subcontract prior to definitization.

Much common sense and intelligence must be used to assess the values shown in item 12b, when there are authorized but still unnegotiated changes in the pipeline.

"13. ITEM 11 MULTIPLIED BY ITEM 6a. $____"

This item sets the upper limitation of a supplier's costs which are eligible for progress payments. It is a straight mathematical calculation of the subcontractor's eligible costs (item 11) multiplied by the approved progress payment rate as specified in item 6a. It signifies the ceiling amount available for progress payment billings, without any costs of next tier subcontractor payments which are additive to the invoice at 100 percent of all such payments made.

"14a. PROGRESS PAYMENTS PAID TO SUBCONTRACTORS $____"

The sum of all progress payments actually paid to the next tier suppliers, as of the Section II date above, the cutoff date of costs paid through.

"14b. LIQUIDATED PROGRESS PAYMENTS TO SUBCONTRACTORS $____"

The sum of all liquidations of progress payments actually recouped from the next tier suppliers, as of the Section II date above.

"14c. UNLIQUIDATED PROGRESS PAYMENTS TO SUBCONTRACTORS (Item 14a less 14b) $____"

This item is a straight subtraction of item 14a less 14b, representing the sum of all next tier progress payments eligible for inclusion in this current invoice.

"14d. SUBCONTRACTOR PROGRESS BILLINGS APPROVED FOR CURRENT PAYMENT $____"

This item is for a "small business" supplier only. It represents any next tier supplier progress payments which have been approved for payment, but not yet paid. This line item is not for use by any supplier designated as a "large business" firm.

"14e. ELIGIBLE SUBCONTRACTOR PROGRESS PAYMENTS (Item 14c plus 14d) $____"

The sum of 14c plus 14d. For a large business, items 14c and 14e will always be the same. A small business with costs listed in item 14d could have a different amount in this item.

"15. TOTAL DOLLAR AMOUNT (Item 13 plus 14e) $____"

This item is a straight calculation of item 13 (the maximum eligible progress payments), plus the value of item 14e (100 percent of next tier supplier payments). It signifies the maximum amount of costs eligible for payment to the subcontractor.

"16. ITEM 5 MULTIPLIED BY ITEM 6b. $____"

This is a straight calculation of item 5 (representing the contract price), multiplied by item 6b (the authorized liquidation rate). It is used in conjunction with item 15 to indicate the maximum allowable ceiling, based on the subcontract price, that is available for progress payments on this contract, which will be shown on item 17 below.

"17. LESSER OF ITEM 15 OR 16 $____"

This item sets the maximum cumulative amount permissible for progress payments under this contract.

"18. TOTAL AMOUNT OF PREVIOUS PROGRESS PAYMENTS REQUESTED $____"

This item is used to signify the cumulative amount of all progress payments previously *requested* by the supplier, but not necessarily paid as of the date of this request. The value in item 18 will not include the costs contained this current invoice.

"19. MAXIMUM BALANCE ELIGIBLE FOR PROGRESS PAYMENTS (Item 17 less 18) $____"

A simple calculation of item 17, less item 18.

"SECTION III—COMPUTATION OF LIMITS FOR OUTSTANDING PROGRESS PAYMENTS"

Section III of the SF 1443 is to be used only if the supplier has received an advance payment, or after the supplier has begun the delivery of hardware, software, or services, as specified on subcontract line items, and the liquidation process for progress payments has started. Section III is also used to calculate limitations of progress payments, designed to prevent the overpayment for inventory or work-in-progress values.

"20. COMPUTATION OF PROGRESS PAYMENT CLAUSE LIMITATION"

The item 20 series relates to the *costs* associated with subcontract line items delivered, and to be delivered.

"20a. COSTS INCLUDED IN ITEM 11, APPLICABLE TO ITEMS DELIVERED, INVOICED, AND ACCEPTED TO THE DATE IN HEADING OF SECTION II $____"

The cost value contained in item 11 above for all subcontract articles delivered, invoiced, and accepted, as of the date listed in Section II above.

"20b. COSTS ELIGIBLE FOR PROGRESS PAYMENTS, APPLICABLE TO UNDELIVERED ITEMS AND TO DELIVERED ITEMS NOT IN-VOICED AND ACCEPTED (Item 11 less 20a) $____ "

The remaining cost value of items listed in item 11 above, which are not delivered as of the Section II date. Note: the values of items 20a plus 20b must equal item 11 above, or the invoice will be rejected.

"20c. ITEM 20b MULTIPLIED BY ITEM 6a $____ "

A straight calculation of the costs experienced for undelivered work multiplied by the approved progress payment rate.

"20d. ELIGIBLE SUBCONTRACTOR PROGRESS PAYMENTS (Item 14e) $____ "

This is the same value as listed above under item 14e.

"20e. LIMITATION (Item 20c plus 20d)"

A summation of eligible progress payments on undelivered work plus eligible supplier progress payments paid.

"21. COMPUTATION OF PROGRESS PAYMENTS CLAUSE LIMITATION"

The item 21 series relates to the *price* of subcontract items already delivered, and to be delivered in the future.

"21a. CONTRACT PRICE OF ITEMS DELIVERED, ACCEPTED AND INVOICED TO DATE IN HEADING OF SECTION II, $____ "

The billing "price" of items delivered, accepted, and invoiced, but not necessarily paid, as of the Section II date listed above. This is the same value as listed in item 20a, plus the supplier's estimated profit for the articles delivered.

In a loss contract, where the sum of item 12a plus item 12b exceeds the contract price of item 5, the cost values listed in item 20a will always equal the price values of item 21a.

"21b. CONTRACT PRICE OF ITEMS NOT DELIVERED (Item 5 less 21a) $____ "

This item is the difference between the subcontract price as listed on item 5, and the price value of items delivered, item 21a. Again, this is the same value as listed in 20b, plus the supplier's estimated profit on the articles not yet delivered.

"21c. ITEM 21b MULTIPLIED BY ITEM 6b $____"

The price value of items yet to be delivered, multiplied by the approved liquidation rate. This is another limitation check to ensure that outstanding progress payments can be liquidated.

"21d. UNLIQUIDATED ADVANCE PAYMENTS PLUS ACCRUED INTEREST $____"

Applies only if there were advance payments given to the subcontractor.

"21e. LIMITATION (Item 21c less 21d) $____"

This sets the ceiling at the price level of work to be delivered.

"22. MAXIMUM UNLIQUIDATED PROGRESS PAYMENTS (Lesser of item 20e or 21e) $____"

This sets the permissible ceiling for all progress payments, representing the lesser of either costs for undelivered work plus eligible supplier progress payments, or, the price value for undelivered work.

"23. TOTAL AMOUNT APPLIED AND TO BE APPLIED TO REDUCE PROGRESS PAYMENT $____"

This is the cumulative value of all progress payment liquidations, those already paid from prior invoices, plus those requested but not yet paid. This item would normally be the result of the price value of delivered items (item 21a) multiplied by the liquidation rate (item 6b), but there can be exceptions which should be recognized.

One exception could be where the subcontract had selected line items which were either not subject to progress payments, or perhaps subject to a different progress payment rate, which is possible but rare. Another exception could occur when the supplier is in the transition over to flexible progress payments at a lower progress payment rate with a new corresponding higher liquidation rate. As a safe rule of thumb, always look for a value of item 21a times item 6b.

"24. UNLIQUIDATED PROGRESS PAYMENTS (Item 18 less 23) $__"

This is the cumulative outstanding unliquidated progress payment balance, and is derived by taking the prior cumulative progress payments (item 18), and subtracting the calculated amount (item 23) to be used to liquidate such payments.

"25. MAXIMUM PERMISSIBLE PROGRESS PAYMENTS (Item 22 less 24) $____"

This item sets the ceiling for progress payments by subtracting cumulative unliquidated outstanding progress payments (item 24) from the maximum permissible progress payments (item 22).

"26. AMOUNT OF CURRENT INVOICE FOR PROGRESS PAYMENT (Lesser of Item 25 or 19) $____"

Allows for a payment of the lesser value of either the net due from item 19, or the net from item 25. Sometimes a supplier will request a lesser value, which should be the amount authorized for payment.

"27. AMOUNT APPROVED BY CONTRACTING OFFICER $____"

This space should not be filled in by the supplier requesting payment. It is reserved for the exclusive use of the Government's Contracting Officer, or in the case of a subcontractor, for the prime contractor's buyer to add an approved amount for payment to the subcontractor. This amount may be different than the amount requested in item 26.

"CERTIFICATION"

"I certify that the above statement (with attachments) has been prepared from the books and records of the above-named contractor in accordance with the contract and the instructions hereon, and to the best of my knowledge and belief, that it is correct, that all the costs of contract performance (except as herewith reported in writing) have been paid to the extent shown herein, or where not shown as paid have been paid or will be paid currently, by the contractor, when due, in the ordinary course of business, that the work reflected above has been performed, that the quantities and amounts involved are consistent with the requirements of the contract. That there are no encumbrances (except as reported in writing herewith, or on previous progress payment request No.____) against the property acquired or produced for, and allocated or properly chargeable to the contract which would affect or impair the government's title, that there has been no materially adverse change in the financial condition of the contractor since the submission of the most written information dated____by the contractor to the government in connection with the contract, that to the extent of any contract provision

limiting progress payments pending first article approval, such provision has been compiled with, and that after the making of the requested progress payment the unliquidated progress payments will not exceed the maximum unliquidated progress payments permitted by the contract."

This is "heavy" stuff which should not be taken lightly by anyone signing and certifying both to the truthfulness and accuracy of the data contained on the invoice. As one expert on progress payments puts it:

> If, through audit or investigation, it is found that any of the information on the form is substantially or significantly inaccurate (i.e., costs overstated), then the person who signs the certification could be sued, fined, or even jailed, as a violation of civil and/or criminal law.[2]

"Name and Title of Contractor Representative Signing this Form"

This line is to be signed by the subcontractor's representative who has the authority to sign and certify the authenticity of the costs contained in the invoice.

"Name and Title of Contracting Officer"

This line should be signed by the prime contractor's representative who has authority to approve the payment of the amount on item 27. Typically this will be the buyer; or the buyer plus the buyer's immediate manager; or sometimes a specific person in the accounts payable department. These individuals will vary by contractor.

A Progress Payment Analysis Log

Let us now address the administration of progress payments in an efficient and painless manner. Face it, progress payments require paper, much paper. Each month there will be an invoice (SF 1443) with the cover page, and often detailed supporting documentation, for each invoice. There will be routing slips and sign-off sheets, Gantt Charts, etc. Procurement files will bulge just to maintain the documentation on progress payments.

One of the best ways for a buyer to stay on top of this mound of paper is to utilize a one-page log to summarize some of the more important data points which should be monitored during the course of subcontractor performance. Shown in Figure 4-2 is an example of one sample log. This log will

Figure 4-2. Progress Payment Analysis Log

PROGRESS PAYMENT ANALYSIS LOG QWF

1. Buyer: _____   Manager: _____
2. Subcontractor: _____   5. Subcontract Price: _____
4. Subcontract Number: _____   6A. Progress Payment Rate: _____ %   6B. Liquidation Rate: _____ %
7. Date of Award: _____

Invoice Number (8A)	Section II Costs Thru Date	Eligible P.P. Costs (11)	Costs Incurred (ACWP) (12a)	Est to Comp (ETC) (12b)	Est At Comp (EAC) (12a + 12b)	% Spent SF1443 (12a / EAC)	% Complete Gantt Chart (BCWP)	Cum Amount Prev. P.P. (18)	Cum. Price Units Devd (21a)	Uniliquid. Balance (24)	Amount Payment Approved (27)	Cumulative "Gross" P.P. (18 + 27)	Cumulative "Net" P.P. (24+27)
(a)	(b)	(c)	(d)	(e)	(f)	(g)	(h)	(i)	(j)	(k)	(l)	(m)	(n)

allow the buyer to summarize those data points dealing with progress payments which should be monitored each month. Of the 42 items of data which are available on the SF 1443 each month, roughly half are displayed on this sample log.

Starting with the initial invoice requesting payment, each subsequent progress payment invoice submitted by a supplier must build on what was previously requested and approved by the prime contractor in all earlier invoices. Each invoice must have a sequential controlling number, which may only be used once. Therefore, it is both efficient and prudent to keep track of progress payment history by the use of a simple log which summarizes the chronology of what has occurred with earlier requests.

True, the maintenance of the log will take some of the buyer's time to update each month. But it will save much time later when compared to the alternative of having to wade through pages of past invoices and supporting data just to understand what had been requested and approved for payment in earlier periods.

One word of caution on the use of a log. Certain of the line items of data which are contained on the SF 1443 have been dropped from display on this log. That is not to infer that each line is not important. Many of the line items will relate to limitation formula, which must also be monitored, but not necessarily summarized each month. Also, mathematical accuracy of the data displayed on the SF 1443 must be checked by someone, and if the figures do not add, then the invoice must be returned to the supplier. The log in Figure 4-2 is no substitute for common sense administration.

Shown across the top of the log are straight duplicate titles of items listed from the SF 1443. The numbers correspond to those contained on the SF 1443, but need be listed only once.

The 14 columns of monthly performance data are designated as (a) through (n), and a few words on each is in order:

(a) Displays the sequential number assigned by the subcontractor to identify and control each SF 1443, as listed on item 8A.

(b) Displays the "costs through date" straight from Section II of the supplier's SF 1443.

(c) Total costs "eligible" for progress payments, from item 11.

(d) Total costs incurred to date, from item 12a, which must be equal to or greater than item 11. This line item is important because it represents the total costs incurred and actually spent by the supplier. As such it represents the total dollars already consumed by the supplier.

In a performance measurement environment, represented by C/SCSC (Cost/Schedule Control Systems Criteria) which will be covered in the next chapter, item 12a corresponds to what is called the "Actual Cost of Work Performed," or "ACWP," or simply the "actual costs."

(e) The supplier's periodic (every six months) estimate to complete the job, directly from item 12b.

(f) The sum of items 12a and 12b, which represents the supplier's total "estimate at completion" (EAC) for the effort, corresponding to the term EAC in C/SCSC.

(g) The "% dollars spent" by the supplier, which is a simple calculation of item 12a, column (d), divided by the supplier's estimate at completion (EAC), column (f), expressed as a percentage.

(h) The "% of physical work completed," as taken directly from the supplier's monthly Gantt Chart, from the bottom of column 5 (see Figure 3-5), submitted to support each progress payment request.

In a C/SCSC performance measurement environment, the term "% of physical work completed" corresponds to what is called the "Budgeted Costs for Work Performed" (BCWP), divided by the "Budget at Completion" (BAC).

By comparing the "% dollars spent" in column (g) with the "% physical work completed" in column (h), the buyer can quickly discern whether or not there is some relationship between the money going out and the work being done.

(i) The cumulative total amount of all prior progress payments directly from item 18.

(j) The price value of work completed and delivered, from item 21a.

(k) The cumulative unliquidated balance, from item 24.

(l) The amount approved for payment this time, from item 27. This item may sometimes differ from item 26 (the supplier requested amount) on the SF 1443.

(m) The cumulative "Gross" progress payments, which is the sum of columns (i) plus (l) (or items 18 plus 27 on the SF 1443). This value should be plotted against the supplier's own cost plan, as was discussed with Figure 2-4.

(n) The cumulative "Net" progress payments, which is the sum of columns (k) plus (m) (or items 24 plus 27 on the SF 1443). This value should also be plotted against the supplier's own cost projection as displayed in Figure 2-4. The "Net" progress payments are critical to monitor to prevent a potential financial loss by the prime contractor. Column (n) is sensitive and dependent on a supplier meeting its subcontract schedule commitments.

The Progress Payment Analysis Log (Figure 4-2) should be maintained and updated each month by the buyer who will screen each invoice prior to approval by the buyer, and the buyer's immediate management for payment. The log should be kept available as an integral part of the procurement file for all subcontracts which contain progress payment provisions.

The progress payment log is not a utopia for any buyer. Perhaps a given buyer will want to tailor their own log, incorporating those items which are felt to be more meaningful than those listed in Figure 4-2. Fine. The key issue is that the buyer must stay on top of progress payments, and actively manage them until all loan values are properly returned. The log should facilitate this important process.

Using the Log to Analyze Progress Payments

Let us now address a specific subcontract and what one buyer was able to display utilizing the log. Shown in Figure 4-3 is the same sample format, but with recorded invoice history on a specific subcontract in which some fifteen progress payment invoices have been received and paid. Deliveries and liquidations have not yet begun, so no data was recorded from item 21a.

Also, no Gantt Chart was required from the supplier at the time of subcontract award, so the buyer on this subcontract has missed an opportunity to be able to compare physical work progress with the dollars being spent. Unfortunate.

However, this subcontract does have some rather interesting chronology. Some of the circumstances surrounding these data are worth our discussion.

Going directly to the log, items 1 through 7 displayed in the header across the top follow the line-item numbering of the SF 1443, modified only to incorporate subcontracting nomenclature. The 14 columns from left to right are the same as were designated as items (a) through (n) in Figure 4-2 earlier.

The subcontract was awarded on 12-5-87 in the amount of $119,490. Invoices 1 through 7 were submitted and paid and everything looked proper. The order had new statement of work added and was increased on 8-10-88 to a revised value of $280,784. Invoices 8 through 11 were submitted and paid, also in a routine manner.

Figure 4-3. A "Completed" Progress Payment Analysis Log

PROGRESS PAYMENT ANALYSIS LOG

1. Buyer: A. JONES   Manager: B. SMITH
2. Subcontractor: HYPOTHETICAL ENGINES
3. Subcontract Number: 150-990080

5. Subcontract Price: ~~$449,400~~ 280,784
6A. Progress Payment Rate: 75 %   6B. Liquidation Rate: 75 %
7. Date of Award: ~~12-5-87~~ 8-10-88

PAGE 1 OF 2

Invoice Number (8A)	Section II Costs Thru Date	Eligible P.P. Costs (11)	Costs Incurred (ACWP) (12A)	Est to Comp (ETC) (12B)	Est At Comp (EAC) (12A + 12B)	% Spent SF1443 (12A / EAC)	% Complete Gantt Chart (BCWP)	Cum Amount Prev. P.P. (18)	Cum. Price Units Devd (21A)	Unliquid. Balance (24)	Amount Payment Approved (27)	Cumulative "Gross" P.P. (18 + 27)	Cumulative "Net" P.P. (24+27)
1	1-17-88	3,007	5,608	103,020	108,628	5%	—	-0-	-0-	-0-	2,255	2,255	2,255
2	2-14-88	6,029	9,313	99,315	108,628	9%	—	2,255	-0-	2,255	4,517	6,772	6,772
3	3-20-88	10,961	11,337	97,291	108,628	10%	—	6,772	-0-	6,772	1,449	8,221	8,221
4	4-17-88	13,028	13,474	95,154	108,628	12%	—	8,221	-0-	8,221	1,550	9,771	9,771
5	5-15-88	16,291	17,229	91,399	108,628	16%	—	9,771	-0-	9,771	2,699	12,470	12,470
6	6-12-88	20,518	23,006	85,622	108,628	21%	—	12,470	-0-	12,470	2,919	15,389	15,389
7	7-18-88	32,111	33,044	75,587	108,628	30%	—	15,389	-0-	15,389	8,694	24,083	24,083
8	8-14-88	38,415	39,993	215,268	255,261	16%	—	24,083	-0-	24,083	4,736	28,819	28,819
9	9-11-88	40,852	42,430	212,831	255,261	17%	—	28,819	-0-	28,819	1,820	30,639	30,639
10	10-16-88	53,568	64,549	190,712	255,261	25%	—	30,639	-0-	30,639	9,537	40,176	40,176
11	11-13-88	64,199	69,345	185,881	255,261	27%	—	40,176	-0-	40,176	6,348	46,524	46,524
12	12-18-88	94,873	109,030	172,089	279,099	38%	—	46,524	-0-	46,524	22,631	71,155	71,155
13	1-15-89	118,587	129,159	144,940	279,099	46%	—	71,155	-0-	71,155	17,785	88,940	88,940
14	2-19-89	136,928	148,413	130,126	279,099	53%	—	88,940	-0-	88,940	13,753	102,693	102,696
15	3-19-89	116,474	123,644	157,140	280,784	44%	—	102,696	-0-	102,696	(51,340)	87,352	87,352

However, starting with the submittal of invoice 12, which was submitted after a very intense review of the supplier's performance by all members of the subcontract management team, performance problems began to surface. Note: starting with invoice number 12, the supplier's estimate at completion (EAC) had risen to over 99 percent of the subcontract price, as listed in item 5. The supplier in now admitting that they will earn less than 1 percent profit on this order!

Also, it must be of a concern that the supplier may well be in a "loss position," but not yet ready to admit this fact out of concern that the loss ratio will be applied, and therefore, progress payments already paid will be reduced. Admitting to be in a loss position is a big psychological pill for any subcontractor to swallow. Suppliers will admit to a loss of their profit, but a loss contract is something else!

In this example the prime contractor had another legitimate reason to question the validity of the invoice costs being submitted to it for payment. The prime contractor's quality control inspector, working closely with the buyer, had reported back to the buyer that he did not see evidence that this supplier had physically completed over 50 percent of their order, as had been reported in progress payment invoice 14 (reflecting 53 percent spent). The buyer therefore had sent out an auditor to examine the supplier's progress payment bookings, and the costs allocated to this order. The results of the audit was a revised (downward) request with the fifteenth invoice submittal. Their eligible progress payment costs from line item 11 actually went down from $136,928 in invoice 14, to $116,474 with their fifteenth invoice. A supplier credit in the amount of ($15,340) was processed by the supplier.

Much of what should happen in the analysis of a supplier's requests for progress payments can be placed into the category of simply using common sense on the part of the buyer. When dealing with progress payments, a buyer has 27 line items of actual supplier cost performance data with which to work. When these 27 line items break out into individual detailed line categories, they equate to 42 line items of valuable and "certified cost" data.

A fixed-price subcontract with progress payments can thus provide almost as much information to the buyer as a cost reimbursable subcontract, if the buyer and the supporting subcontract management team only knows what to look for when reviewing these data.

Profit: The First Thing to Go

The other area which the buyer must monitor closely is that of a supplier's profit—the initial negotiated rate versus the forecasted rate based on the supplier's own performance.

Going back to the actual data displayed in Figure 4-3, one can see that this supplier had two profit positions: one as was reflected in invoice 1, and later in invoice 8 when the price was increased. Both were consistent with the supplier's original negotiated profit position of 10 percent.

These positions were:

	Invoice No. 1	Invoice No. 8
Price item 5:	$119,490	$280,784
Estimate at Completion:	-$108,628	-$255,261
Profit dollars:	$ 10,862	$ 25,523

	Invoice No. 1	Invoice No. 8
Profit dollars:	$ 10,862	$ 25,523
Divided by EAC:	$108,628	$255,261
Equals a profit rate of:	=.10%	=.10%

Initially they had been forecasting a profit achievement of 10 percent on this order. However, conditions changed dramatically as was reflected in their invoices #12 and #15:

	Invoice No. 12	Invoice No. 15
Price item 5:	$280,784	$280,784
Estimate at Completion:	-$279,099	-$280,784
Profit dollars:	$ 1,685	0

	Invoice No. 12	Invoice No. 15
Profit dollars:	$ 1,685	0
Divided by EAC:	$279,099	$280,099
Equals a profit rate of:	=.006%	=.000%

What this supplier stated when submitting invoice 15 is that they will make no profit on this order. But they are not yet admitting to an overrun of price. A highly questionable position for the supplier to take, and one which the subcontract management team should monitor closely.

In this case the buyer should press the subcontractor for an examination of the supplier's estimate to complete the subcontract, and the supporting detail behind line item 12b of the SF 1443. It would appear from the data as submitted, that the subcontractor is merely "backing" into their estimate to complete by simply subtracting their actual costs from the subcontract price. An improper practice.

This examination of the estimate to complete-ETC (item 12b) becomes a critical one in the administration of progress payments because the government expects the employment of a loss ratio adjustment at the proper time (i.e., any time there is a forecast whereby costs 12a + 12b exceed the subcontract price, item 5).

There is an additional "profit" monitoring method available with progress payments, which has not yet appeared on this subcontract as displayed in Figure 4-3. Once a supplier starts to make hardware deliveries or complete line items, they must disclose their profit position of the work completed, versus the work to be done. This information is available in the SF 1443 line items 20a, b, c, d, e (the costs of work), and may be compared to line items 21a, b, c, d, e (the price of work). The difference between the price (item 21) less costs (item 20) represents the supplier's profit. This is illustrated as below.

Profit of work already completed and already delivered:

Price of work delivered (item 21a)	$
Less costs of work delivered (item 20a)	-$ __
Profit dollars on work delivered:	$

Profit dollars on work delivered:	$ __
Divided by EAC (12a + 12b):	$

Equals the profit rate on work delivered:	= __%

Profit of work to be completed and to be delivered:

Price of undelivered work (item 21b	$
Less costs of undelivered work (item 20b)	-$ __
Profit dollars on undelivered work:	$

Profit dollars on undelivered work:	$ __
Divided by EAC (12a + 12b):	$

Equals the profit rate on work to be delivered:	= __%

The significance of monitoring a supplier's profit on the articles delivered, versus those to be delivered, is that the supplier may be losing money on the order but is not ready to admit it because of the loss ratio adjustment. This fact could be hidden for a while by reporting different forecasted profit values on the items delivered (21a/20a), versus the items to be delivered (21b/20b).

Supplier profit should be monitored closely, because profit is the first thing to go.

Things Can (And Sometimes Do) Go Wrong

A wise American once said: "A picture is worth a thousand number crunchers."[3] There is nothing profound in this statement, except that it seems to fit nicely with what is about to follow. Many people in industry now rely heavily (almost exclusively) on statistical data, prepared by financial spreadsheets or electronic data bases. These are fine. But nothing quite takes the place of a physical display chart to articulate the intended message in the very clearest form.

In earlier chapters the importance of obtaining the supplier's cost and schedule performance plans was discussed, along with relating their actual performance against their own plans. The supplier's physical work performance was covered in the discussion in Figures 3-5 and 3-6. Now let us focus on the supplier's cost and financial performance against their own forecasts or plans.

Sometimes conditions with a given supplier will deteriorate for a multitude of reasons. It is up to the buyer and the subcontract management team to monitor the supplier's performance and to correctly access all signals being transmitted from the supplier. This is particularly true when progress payment terms and conditions are included in the procurement.

Perhaps a few specific examples will best illustrate what can go wrong in such relationships. Five specific examples will be described from the "chronicles" of actual case histories, graphically displayed with a series of financial charts. Again, our old friend Hypothetical Engines will be used to illustrate these conditions in an anonymous format.

Example 1: "Whose Subcontract Are You Working?"

It is January, the thirteenth month of subcontract performance (see Figure 4-4). In their financial plan submitted prior to award, the supplier had forecasted a requirement for about $1.824 million in progress payment funding by the thirteenth month.

Figure 4-4.   SF 1443 Behind the Plan

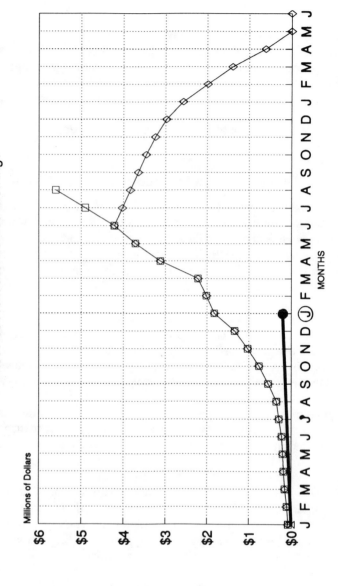

HYPOTHETICAL ENGINES, INC.
"Whose Subcontract Are You Working?"

In their very first progress payment invoice they request only $200,000, or about 10 percent of what they had forecasted. Should a buyer be concerned when a supplier underspends, significantly, from its own cost projections? Answer: absolutely.

In this case the supplier was suspected of working on someone else's order, allocating their resources to another job. At the very least a phone call or visit was in order to determine why the supplier's own projections were so far off target.

Also important, there were serious doubts as to whether the first subcontract delivery would be made on time, just five months away. There could be legitimate reasons for the lower costs incurred, but the buyer must find out why in very specific terms, in order to protect against a possible schedule slip.

In this case the subcontractor was, in fact, working another order.

Example 2: "Excessive Inventory"

It is the fifteenth month of subcontract performance, March, and the supplier's own projections called for progress payment requirements of about $2.218 million (see Figure 4-5). In their performance to date they had been spending ahead of their own forecasts.

Now, they submit an invoice in the amount of $9.600 million, representing the full value of all of their projected progress payment requirements (at 80 percent of the target costs). Should this invoice be approved for payment? Answer: absolutely not, and for a variety of reasons.

In the first place, this supplier has incurred an inventory which can only be described as "in excess" of the requirements of the subcontract. The United States Government is concerned about suppliers creating actual inventories in excess of their requirements, and approving this request would only add credence to their position.

However, from the buyer's own perspective, it would be unwise to fund such inventory for the simple reason of potential future changes in the purchased (design) configuration. Changes in procurement specifications are more often the rule than the exception. One minor engineering change could obsolete all parts made in advance under this order. If inventory was authorized in advance of current requirements, it would make it more difficult for the buyer to recover such funds in subsequent negotiations with the supplier.

But perhaps of greater concern should be the distinct possibility that this supplier may be experiencing a lesser profit (or even a loss) on this particular order, but is not yet ready to acknowledge the loss condition. The buyer under these conditions has all the authority needed to halt additional progress

Figure 4-5.   **Supplier Excessive Inventory**

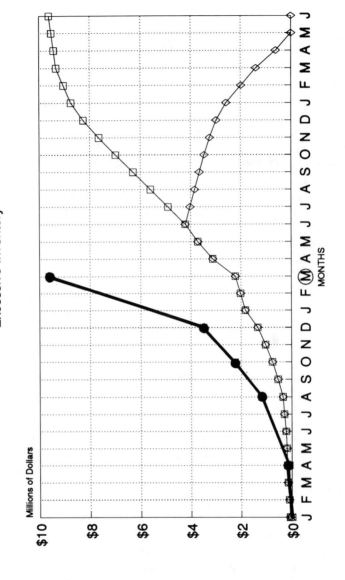

HYPOTHETICAL ENGINES, INC.
"Excessive Inventory"

payments based on the supplier producing inventory in excess of reasonable subcontract requirements, as was covered in an earlier chapter. In this case, the buyer would be wise to exercise such options and halt further progress payments until an assessment of the circumstances can be made.

In this case the subcontractor was in an overrun condition, but was not about to admit it.

Example 3: "We Must Invoke the Loss Ratio"

It is the eighteenth month of performance, June, and the supplier is right on target with its projection of progress payment funding requirements of $4.215 million (see Figure 4-6). However, the supplier in their invoice has indicated that they anticipate incurring an overrun in subcontract price by some 20 percent. What do you do? Answer: The buyer is obligated to invoke a "loss ratio adjustment," in which case only $3.5 million can be paid in progress payments to this supplier.

And, if prior progress payments made to the supplier actually exceed this lower (loss ratio) value, then the buyer is further obligated to request a return of prior funds paid to the subcontractor. As unfortunate as it may be, the FAR requirements are very specific about what is required from a prime contractor whenever an overrun of subcontract value is projected. The loss ratio adjustment is an absolute requirement of a buyer, unless specifically waived by a Government Contracting Officer, which is unlikely.

Example 4: "Missing the First Subcontract Delivery"

It is the twentieth month of performance, August, and the supplier has submitted an invoice for $5.597 million, which is exactly 80 percent of their costs incurred as authorized by the terms of the subcontract (see Figure 4-7). However, of greater consequence, their first subcontract hardware delivery should have been made in the prior month, and it was missed. What do we do?

Under the concept of "net" progress payments, the supplier is not entitled to full progress payments of $5.597 million (representing 80 percent of their costs incurred). Rather, the first subcontract delivery, if it had been made as scheduled, would have reduced the "gross" value of outstanding progress payments down to a "net" value of $3.837 million. Thus, because of the supplier's own schedule performance, if prior progress payments have exceeded a "net" value of $3.837 million, then the supplier should be notified that they are to return all funding in excess of this "net" progress payment value. Suppliers are expected to meet the authorized subcontract schedule

Figure 4-6.   Invoking the Loss Ratio

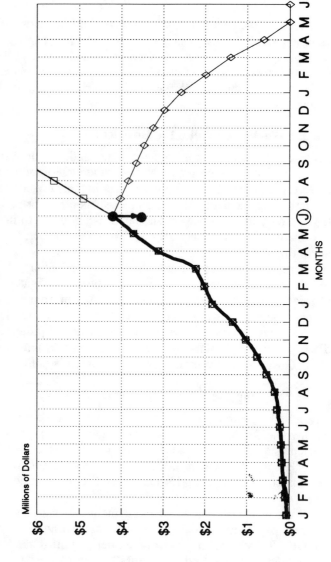

HYPOTHETICAL ENGINES, INC.
"We Must Invoke the Loss Ratio"

Millions of Dollars

$6

$5

$4

$3

$2

$1

$0

J F M A M J J A S O N D J F M A M J J A S O N D J F M A M J

MONTHS

—□— (F) "Gross" Prog Pmt   —◇— (J) "Net" Prog Pmt.   —●— SF 1443 Request

Figure 4-7. **Missing a Delivery**

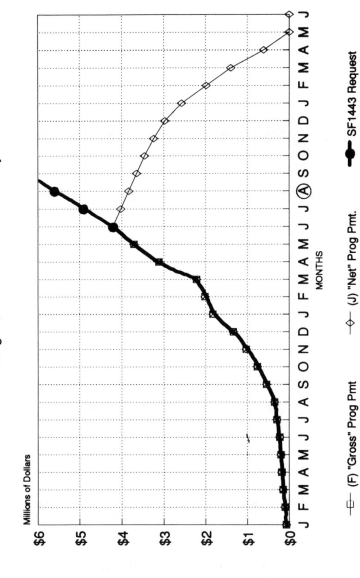

HYPOTHETICAL ENGINES, INC.
"Missing the First Subcontract Delivery"

and liquidate their outstanding balances down to the "net" progress payment levels.

The precise monitoring of subcontractor performance against the official subcontract schedule, and its relationship to progress payment liquidations based on the supplier's deliveries, sends a clear message to all subcontractors that they are expected to perform to the subcontract document. Halting further funds, and perhaps requesting a return of prior progress payments, sends an unambiguous message to the supplier.

Allowing suppliers to be paid along a "gross" progress payment curve, and failing to take corrective action whenever performance or deliveries are missed, is perhaps the greatest cost risk which can be experienced by a prime contractor in the management of progress payments to fixed price suppliers.

Example 5: "A High Risk (Schedule) Arrangement"

It is the twenty-ninth month of performance in a thirty month subcontract (see Figure 4-8). This particular subcontract calls for a *single* item delivery at the end of the subcontract period. The supplier has been paid a full 80 percent of all of their costs incurred in the form of progress payment loans.

In month twenty-nine the buyer contacts the supplier for delivery arrangements and the supplier admits for the first time that the single unit is months away from completion. Unfortunately, this information comes as a complete surprise to the buyer and the subcontract management team. The subcontract management team was, shall we say, "asleep at the switch!"

The problem was clear: The team was not monitoring the supplier's physical work performance. Rather, they were relying entirely on the supplier's past reputation, and the certification of costs on the SF 1443.

The moral to this story: Always monitor the supplier's physical work performance. And if there is only *one* contract delivery at the end of the subcontract period: Always monitor the supplier's physical work performance "very closely." Late supplier deliveries may happen, but they should not come as a surprise to the buyer and the subcontract management team, who should be monitoring the performance of the supplier.

Supplier Performance and Progress Payments

Often we meet the enemy and it is us.

It should be mentioned that sometimes the fault for a missed subcontract delivery, or other impaired supplier performance, will lie directly with the buyer's own organization. The buyer must be sensitive to that distinct possibility. Not infrequently some type of management redirection may have

Figure 4-8.   A "High Risk" Arrangement

HYPOTHETICAL ENGINES, INC.
-A Single Subcontract Delivery-

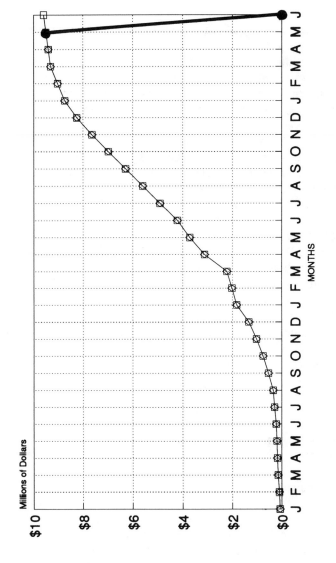

Millions of Dollars

$10

$8

$6

$4

$2

$0

J F M A M J J A S O N D J F M A M J J A S O N D J F M A M J

MONTHS

—□— (F) "Gross" Prog Pmt   —●— (J) "Net" Prog Pmt.

occurred for a variety of legitimate (or nonlegitimate) reasons, and the buyer may not have gotten the (official) word. Buyers are often the last to find out. An engineering change may have been processed and "unofficially" released to the supplier which interfered with a supplier's ability to meet a schedule commitment. These are practical issues which do happen, and good suppliers should not be penalized for being responsive to your company's needs.

However, if after review of the circumstances, the supplier still has no reasonable excuse for missing a subcontract delivery, a safe course of action would be to notify the subcontractor that further progress payments on this order are held pending a recovery to their schedule commitments. There is probably no stronger inducement to get a supplier back on the delivery track than to cut off the flow of progress payment funding.

In such cases, the buyer should prepare a memorandum to the accounts payable organization directing a specific course of action, and hand carry it (do not mail) to the appropriate accounting people. Because of the significance of such actions, it is likely a good practice for a buyer to get at least one level of procurement management to concur in the action to stop payments. Likely, the supplier will take drastic actions to retaliate (e.g., call a vice president, call their Congressman, call the press) whenever their progress payment funding gets cut-off. It is not uncommon for a supplier to threaten to stop work when progress payments are halted, and that possibility must be recognized by the prime contractor's most senior management and their legal staff.

In Summary

The subject of progress payments to fixed-price suppliers is one of critical importance to any buyer or subcontract manager. Progress payments can provide them with an important and unique tool in the management of fixed-price subcontracts.

Interestingly, more often than not, progress payment administration and the "data" available from the invoices is not used decisively in the management of subcontracts. Rather, progress payments and the data they provide are too often administered as a "proforma" exercise, something which must be done, rather than viewed as an opportunity to assist the prime contractor in the management of these most challenging fixed-price orders. Progress payments offer the prime contractor a management "tool" of considerable importance.

Endnotes

1. FAR 32.503-1.

2. Alan I. Fleischmann, *Progress Payment Handbook,* (Naugatuck, Connecticut: Progress Payments Ltd., 1989), page 8–7.

3. Gary E. Christle, Office of the Assistant Secretary of Defense (Comptroller), at a conference sponsored by the Institute of Cost Analysis on *Cost/Schedule Control Systems and Performance Measurement Systems,* in a talk in Atlanta, Georgia, October 26, 1987.

Chapter 5

Progress Payments and the Earned Value (C/SCSC) Concept

On January 7, 1991, Secretary of Defense Richard B. Cheney canceled the A-12 Avenger Program. This has been reported to be the largest contract ever terminated by the DOD. Upwards of 9,000 employees immediately lost their jobs because of this single action.

Without debating the rightness or wrongness of the Cheney decision, to those of us who are interested in management control systems for government programs, particularly major programs, the A-12 Avenger cancellation provides a case study which will likely be discussed for years. To those who are specifically interested in the subset elements of "progress payments" and "earned value" performance management, the A-12 incident provides a "lessons learned" opportunity of major importance.

The exact circumstances surrounding the A-12 will not be available to the general public for several years. It was what is called a secret SAR (special access required) program, which kept it out of the main monitoring processes of the DOD and certainly the general public. Nevertheless, enough public information has surfaced for us to draw certain conclusions.

The prime contracts were awarded on January 13, 1988, under a fixed-price incentive contractual arrangement, which contained a target price of $4.379 billion, a target cost of $3.981 billion, and a ceiling price of $4.777 billion.[1] Full compliance with the Cost/Schedule Control Systems Criteria

(C/SCSC) and periodic Cost Performance Reports (CPR) were required from the two prime contractors: McDonnell Douglas, St Louis, and General Dynamics, Fort Worth.[2] Progress payments were included in the fixed price contractual arrangement.

It has been acknowledged by reliable DOD sources that the C/SCSC management control systems were implemented properly and were functioning well at both the principle contractors.[3] But as early as April 10,1991, (some 90 days after cancellation), it was reported that the government was demanding a return of $1.35 billion in "over payments" made to the two principle contractors.[4] And by June 8, 1991 (five months after cancellation), the two prime contractors have filed a 78 page lawsuit against the government arguing they are entitled to keep the questioned overpayment of funds.[5] Stay tuned—this saga will be continued.

Final settlement of this "major difference of opinion" between the United States Government and two of its largest contractors will likely take years to settle in the courts. However, if it is generally acknowledged that: the C/SCSC management control systems were working well with both of the prime contractors; and there was an over payment of one-third of the total program's target costs only part way through the contractual period; then one can only conclude that the C/SCSC administrators appear not to have been communicating well with the progress payment administrators! Thus, contractor progress payments would appear not to have been linked with earned value (C/SCSC) performance measurement. Time will tell.

This final chapter will not focus on the A-12 program cancellation. The A-12 merely provides us with a case study, a role model, of what can go wrong, and perhaps some examples of practices to avoid.

Rather, this chapter will want to address four basic subjects in a generic sense, attempting to "link" the activities of progress payments with the earned value performance measurement concept.

1. A brief overview of the "earned value" (C/SCSC) performance measurement concept;

2. Relating progress payment data to earned value performance measurement data when full C/SCSC *is* formally imposed on the subcontractor;

3. Relating progress payment data to performance on firm fixed-price (FFP) type subcontracts when there is *no* formal C/SCSC imposed on the supplier;

4. Methods (the formula) used by earned value (C/SCSC) practitioners to forecast an independent estimate of costs at completion (EAC),

based on the actual cost and schedule performance of the subcontractor.

The Earned Value (C/SCSC) Concept in a Nutshell

The earned value performance measurement concept is a complex subject which is difficult to present in a "nutshell." One of the best introductions to the theory of the earned value concept comes from one of its founders, in a recent article he wrote after retirement from the government:

> Since 1967, the DOD has employed the Cost/Schedule Control Systems Criteria (C/SCSC) as a means to ensure that major contractor's internal management systems are sound and can provide government program managers with reliable, objective cost performance information for use in management decision making. The "criteria approach" allows contractors to adopt the systems and controls of their own choosing, provided those systems can satisfy the criteria. Compliance is determined by government teams which review the systems in operation after contract award.
>
> The C/SCSC require that a contractor establish an integrated cost and schedule baseline plan against which actual performance on the contract can be compared. Performance must be measured as objectively as possible based on positive indicators of physical accomplishment rather than on subjective estimates or amounts of money spent. Budget values are assigned to scheduled increments of work to form the performance measurement baseline (PMB).
>
> In order to measure contract performance, budgets for all work on the contract must sum to the contract target cost (CTC) so that each increment of work is assigned a value (budget) that is relational to the contract value. When an increment of work is done, its value is earned; hence the term earned value. By maintaining the budgetary relationship to contract target cost, variances from the budget baseline reflect ongoing contract cost performance.[6]

To properly put the earned value performance measurement concept into historical perspective, we must go back in time some three decades and trace the evolution of Cost/Schedule Control Systems Criteria (C/SCSC) from its two ancestors: PERT/Time and PERT/Cost.

The Program Evaluation and Review Technique (PERT) was introduced by the United States Navy in 1957 to support the development of its Polaris missile program. PERT was a technique which attempted to simulate the necessary work to develop the Polaris missile by creating a logic network of dependent sequential events. Its purpose was threefold: to plan the required effort, to schedule the work, and to predict the likelihood of accomplishing the objectives of the program within a given time frame. The initial focus of PERT was on the management of time, and predicting the probability of program success.

There was great excitement surrounding the new PERT program management concept. Unfortunately, the technique's successes fell far short of the proponent's expectations. Part (perhaps most) of the difficulty with PERT was not with the concept itself, but rather with the computers at the time. Both computer hardware and software were not up to the required challenges in 1957. Computers were scarce, and PERT network processing had to compete with the processing of the company's payroll—and somehow the company payroll always won. Also, the software programs, evolving initially out of simple linear network concepts, just could not provide the needed flexibility to support the program management requirements at the time.

While the PERT planning, scheduling, and probability forecasting concepts have survived to this day, the technique for use as a program management tool initially "suffocated" a few short years after its introduction. The technique was too rigid for practical applications with the computer hardware and software available at the time. And there was also the problem of the overzealous government mandate to use PERT. Industry management rightfully resented being told what tools they must use in the management of their contracts.

Then, before PERT was accepted by program management in industry, the United States Air Force came up with an extension of PERT by adding resource estimates to the logic networks. "PERT/Cost" was thus born in 1962, and just plain "PERT" was thereafter known as "PERT/Time." Needless to say that if PERT/Time as a management technique was too rigid for practical applications at the time, PERT/Cost with the added dimension of resources only exacerbated the problem. PERT/Cost as a management control tool had a lifetime of perhaps two years.

What was significant about PERT/Cost, however, was not the technique itself, but rather what evolved from it. The "earned value" measurement concept was first introduced to industry when the government issued their *Supplement No. 1 to DOD and NASA Guide, PERT/Cost Output Reports*, in March, 1963, in which they provided industry with a simple definition of the earned value concept:

VALUE (Work Performed to Date): The total planned cost for work completed within the summary item.[7]

Thus, instead of relating cost plans to cost actuals, which historically had been the custom, PERT/Cost related the "VALUE" of work performed against the cost actuals, to determine the utility/benefits from the funds spent. What was *physically accomplished* for what was *actually spent* was a simple but fundamentally important new concept in program management. Hence, the earned value concept was first introduced in 1963, but it had to wait until the issuance of the formal C/SCS Criteria to have its full and lasting impact on American industry.

For various reasons the United States Air Force gave up on the PERT/Cost technique in the mid-1960s, but correctly held on to the "earned value" concept. When the Department of Defense formally issued their Cost/Schedule Control Systems Criteria (C/SCSC) in 1967, the earned value concept was solidly contained therein. With the subsequent adoption of these same identical criteria by the Department of Energy in 1975, and the reaffirmation of the criteria by the Department of Defense in their major 1991 defense acquisition policy statement, the earned value concept of cost and schedule management is firmly established in the United States Government acquisition process.[8]

A detailed discussion of the 35 specific criteria contained in the C/SCSC is beyond the limited scope of this book. There are full textbooks, and week-long seminars, and practitioners/consultants available to cover these matters should one have the requirement or even the inclination. Rather, this book merely attempts to summarize some of the more significant features of the concept so as to be able to relate the earned value concept to the primary subject: progress payments to fixed price subcontractors. The thirty-five actual C/SCS Criteria contained in the new government regulation (DODI 5000.2, part 11, section B, attachment 1) are provided in Attachment D.

The C/SCSC are divided into five logical groupings, which contain the thirty-five criteria:

1. *ORGANIZATION (5 criteria):* To define the required contractual effort with use of a work breakdown structure (WBS), to assign the responsibilities for performance of the work to specific organizational components (i.e, the organizational breakdown structure (OBS)), and to manage the work with use of a single "integrated" contractor management control system.

2. *PLANNING AND BUDGETING (11 criteria):* To establish and maintain a performance measurement baseline (PMB) for the planning and control of the authorized contractual work.

3. *ACCOUNTING (7 criteria):* To accumulate the actual costs of work performed (ACWP) and materials consumed in a manner which allows for its comparison with the actual performance measurement (BCWP).

4. *ANALYSIS (6 criteria):* To determine the earned value, to analyze both cost variances (CV) and schedule variances (SV), and to develop reliable estimates of the total costs at completion (EAC).

5. *REVISIONS AND ACCESS TO DATA (6 criteria):* To incorporate changes to the controlled performance measurement baseline (PMB) as required, and to allow appropriate government representatives to have access to contract data for determining C/SCS Criteria compliance.

Some of the critical elements of these five criteria groupings will be briefly discussed to provide a quick overview of the earned value concept. Each of the acronyms used above will be defined in the discussion which follows.

Criteria Group 1

The five criteria required by the first group covering *organization* can best be illustrated by a review of the diagram in Figure 5-1. Criterion one (1a) requires the use of a work breakdown structure (WBS) to define the required effort, whether it be a contract, subcontract, a company funded internal project, etc. The WBS approach allows program management to comprehensively define and then to perform a given contract within the maze of a company's functional organization. The use of a WBS to define the program is illustrated in Figure 5-1, at the extreme left side.

The second criterion (1b) requires assignment of the defined WBS work tasks to the organizational breakdown structure (OBS) for performance. This concept is illustrated in Figure 5-1, the upper portion. Internal functional organizations (OBS) will perform the contract tasks as were defined by the WBS.

The third criterion (1c) requires the integration of the contractor's management control functions with each other, and with the defined WBS and OBS elements. This requirement is achieved by the creation of "management control cells," which are referred to in C/SCSC as Cost Accounts and are displayed in Figure 5-1. Tasks which are "make items" (work to be performed internally by the contractor) must be identifiable to both the WBS and OBS. Likewise, "subcontracts" must also be identifiable to both the WBS and OBS.

Figure 5-1. Work Breakdown and Organizational Breakdown Structures

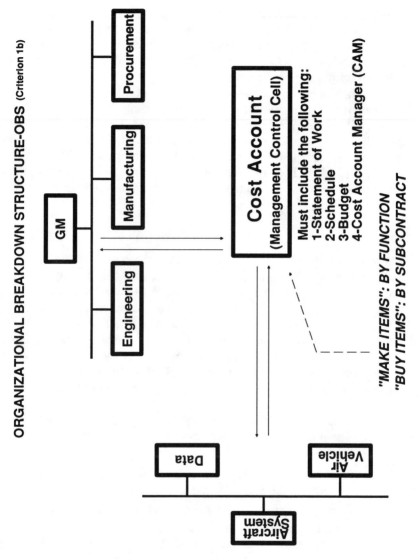

ORGANIZATIONAL BREAKDOWN STRUCTURE-OBS (Criterion 1b)

GM

Engineering

Manufacturing

Procurement

Cost Account
(Management Control Cell)

Must include the following:
1-Statement of Work
2-Schedule
3-Budget
4-Cost Account Manager (CAM)

"MAKE ITEMS": BY FUNCTION
"BUY ITEMS": BY SUBCONTRACT

Data

Air Vehicle

Aircraft System

WORK BREAKDOWN STRUCTURE-WBS (Criterion 1a)

Thus, all of the hundreds (or more) of these self-contained management control cells (Cost Accounts) in C/SCSC must be relatable to either the WBS to comply with the precise language of the prime contract's statement of work, or by the OBS to satisfy the requirements of internal functional management within a given company.

Each management control cell (cost account) must have four elements to maintain the integrity of the management control unit, and for the performance measurement of data contained therein: (1) a statement of work for the cell; (2) a time frame or schedule for the cell; (3) a budget of financial resources; (4) a responsible manager, typically referred to as the Cost Account Manager (CAM). The cost account concept or management control cell is fundamental to C/SCSC and is displayed in Figure 5-1, in the lower right corner.

Criteria Group 2

The eleven criteria contained in the second group covering *planning and budgeting* require the formation of a measurement baseline against which the supplier's performance may be measured. This requirement can be illustrated by our reviewing Figure 5-2, the Performance Measurement Baseline (PMB). There are twelve specific components to what is called the C/SCSC Performance Measurement Baseline, and to follow the discussion, one must have some understanding of what is meant by each of the elements contained in the baseline. Therefore, these twelve PMB elements must be defined for us, relatable by number to the elements displayed in Figure 5-2:

1. **CONTRACT (or SUBCONTRACT) TARGET PRICE (CTP):** The negotiated estimated cost plus profit or fee for the contract or subcontract.

2. **FEE/MARGIN/PROFIT**: The excess in the amount realized from the sale of goods, minus the cost of goods.

3. **CONTRACT (or SUBCONTRACT) BUDGET BASE (CBB):** The negotiated contract cost plus the contractor's (or subcontractor's) estimated cost of authorized but unpriced work.

4. **CONTRACT (or SUBCONTRACT) TARGET COST (CTC):** The negotiated cost for the original definitized contract and all contractual changes which have been definitized, but excluding the estimated cost of any authorized, unpriced changes.

Figure 5-2.   The Performance Measurement Baseline (PMB)

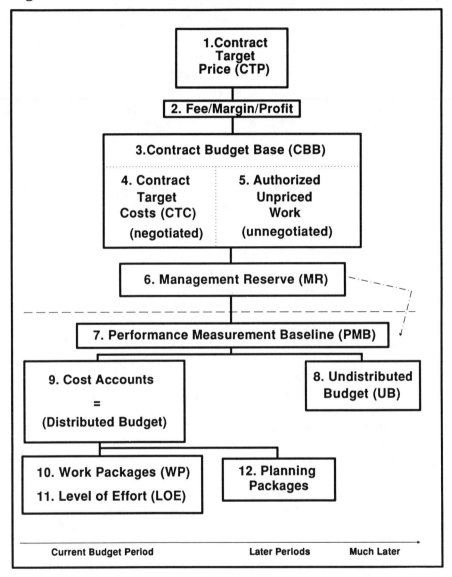

5. **AUTHORIZED UNPRICED WORK**: The effort for which definitized contract costs have not been agreed to, but for which written authorization has been received by the contractor/subcontractor.

6. **MANAGEMENT RESERVE (MR)**: A portion of the Contract Budget Base that is held for management control purposes by a contractor to cover the expense of "unanticipated" program requirements. MR is not initially a part of the Performance Measurement Baseline (PMB), but is expected to be consumed as PMB prior to completing a contract. Any MR not consumed at program completion becomes pure profit, (2) above, or profit and some portion returned to the buying customer under an incentive type arrangement.

7. **PERFORMANCE MEASUREMENT BASELINE (PMB)**: The time-phased budget plan against which project performance is measured. It is formed by the summation of budgets assigned to scheduled cost accounts and their applicable indirect budgets. For future effort that is not currently planned to the cost account level, the Performance Measurement Baseline also includes those budgets assigned to higher level WBS elements. The PMB normally equals the contract budget base, less management reserve.

8. **UNDISTRIBUTED BUDGET (UB)**: Budget applicable to contract effort which has not yet been identified to WBS elements at or below the lowest level of reporting to the government or prime contractor.

9. **COST ACCOUNT (CA)**: A natural intersection point between the work breakdown structure (WBS) and the organizational breakdown structure (OBS), at which functional management responsibility for the work is assigned, and where actual direct labor, material, and other direct costs are compared with earned value for management control purposes. Cost accounts are the focal point of cost/schedule control.

10. **WORK PACKAGES (WP)**: Detailed short-span jobs or material items, identified by the contractor for accomplishing work required to complete a contract. Work packages are discrete tasks that have specific end products or end results.

11. **LEVEL OF EFFORT (LOE)**: Work that does not result in a final product (e.g., liaison, coordination, follow-up, or other support activities) and which cannot be effectively associated with a definable

end product process result. It is measured only in terms of resources actually consumed within a given time period.

12. **PLANNING PACKAGE**: A logical aggregation of far term work within a cost account that can be identified and budgeted but not yet defined into work packages. Planning packages are identified during the initial baseline planning to establish the time phasing of the major activities within a cost account and the quantity of the resources required for their performance. Planning packages are placed into work packages consistent with the "rolling wave" scheduling concept prior to the performance of the work.

It sometimes comes as a surprise to some that the C/SCSC Performance Measurement Baseline (PMB) represents a value less than the total contract or subcontract amount. However, this fact is true only for the initial PMB. Profit or fee is not intended to be used in the performance of the contract, or else the result will be zero profit to the contractor or subcontractor. By contrast, management reserve (MR) is expected to be consumed during contractual performance, and when it is needed, MR is shifted into the PMB. Any management reserve remaining at the end of the contract is used to offset unfavorable variances, or may represent contract underrun, and/or profit.

Criteria Group 3

The seven criteria in the *accounting* group require that both cost actuals and schedule performance be relatable in the same time period with the "earned value" achievement, or what PERT/Cost called simply "value." Important point: by definition in C/SCSC, a cost variance (CV) is the difference between the earned value achieved and the cost actuals for the same period. A schedule variance (SV) is the difference between the value of the scheduled work for the period and the earned value achieved in the same period. Let us discuss this simple but fundamental concept with a review of the data displayed in Figures 5-3 and 5-4.

Figure 5-3 presents an imaginary four year, $100 million contract, using the "conventional" cost control method. The plan calls for the expenditure of exactly $25 million each year for the four years. At the end of exactly two years of performance, $40 million was spent compared to the planned expenditure of $50 million. How is the plan doing? Truthful answer: it is not really possible to know using the "conventional" planned costs versus actual costs method.

Figure 5-3. Conventional Cost Control

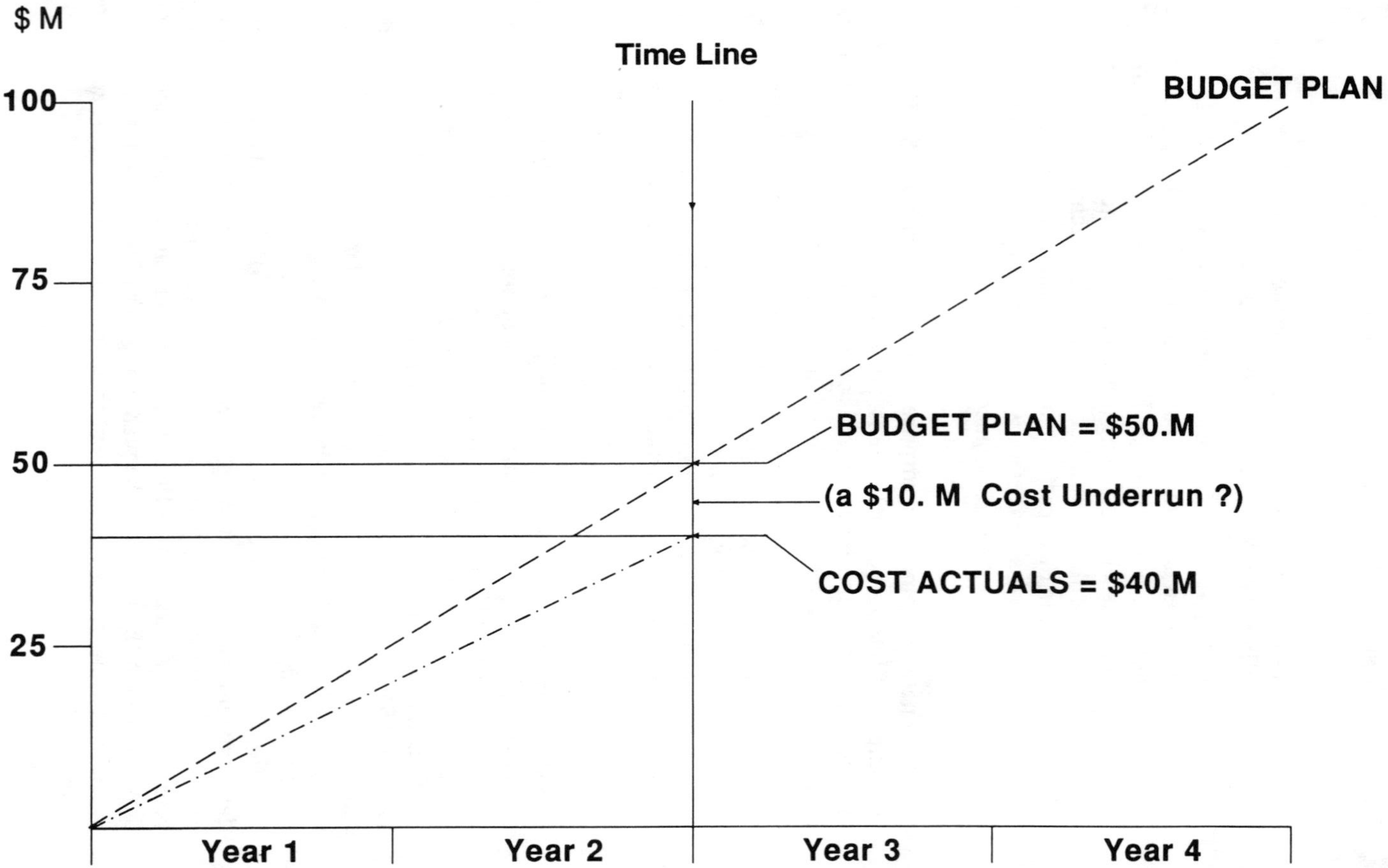

$M

Time Line

BUDGET PLAN

BUDGET PLAN = $50.M

(a $10. M Cost Underrun ?)

COST ACTUALS = $40.M

100

75

50

25

Year 1   Year 2   Year 3   Year 4

Figure 5-4. "Earned Value" Performance Measurement

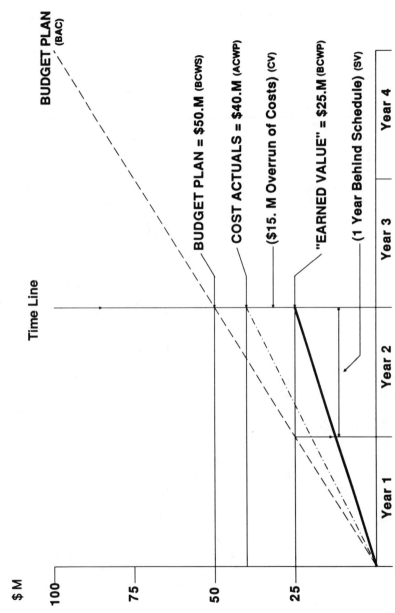

An optimist might look at the data in Figure 5-3 and say $50 million dollars of work was accomplished and only $40 million in actual costs was spent, so therefore the costs were underrun to date by some $10 million. And remember, most program managers and senior executives and CEOs are optimists by their very nature!

Or, a pessimist might look at this same chart and conclude that some $40 million dollars of the planned work was completed and exactly $40 million in actual costs was spent, so therefore the equivalent of $10 million dollars of work is behind schedule. But on the other hand, the cost performance is just fine!

In reality, it is not possible to tell how well or poorly the plan is doing by simply using the "conventional" cost control method of comparing planned cost expenditures with actual cost expenditures. The conclusions can and will likely be most deceiving. And, it is not possible to tell if the plan has overrun or underrun the costs, or is ahead or behind the schedule using the traditional methods of cost management. And being an optimist or a pessimist or a realist will not improve the process. To determine the actual dollars spent in a given time frame, the amount of work performed against the physical work plan is needed. To be able to make an objective assessment of the program accomplishments, "earned value" performance measurement is needed.

Going on to Figure 5-4, the critical third dimension of "earned value" performance measurement has been added, and the results are shocking. Only $25 million in physical work has been accomplished. Therefore, since $40 million was spent, there are in fact $15 million in overrun costs. And more distressing, of the $50 million of work scheduled to be completed in the initial two years, only $25 million has been accomplished. Thus, the plan is $25 million in equivalent work behind schedule, or stated another way, it is one year behind schedule!

By equating the cost dollars spent to the earned value, it is possible to exactly how well or poorly the plan is doing in the cost performance. By equating the planned schedule with earned value, it is possible to know how much of the authorized contract work has been accomplished against the schedule. Earned value performance measurement is "objective" measurement. It takes the guesswork out of the management of cost and schedule management of contracts or subcontracts. And perhaps of greatest importance, the supplier's actual cost and schedule performance can be used to intelligently forecast the final estimate of costs and the necessary time to complete the effort.

In order to follow the discussion which will be covered in the final section in this chapter on using C/SCSC performance data to predict the final outcome, it will be necessary to master some of the C/SCSC jargon. To help master these terms, let us look at the following definitions and relate them to the data contained in Figure 5-4.

BUDGETED COST FOR WORK SCHEDULED (BCWS): The sum of the budgets for all work packages scheduled to be accomplished (including in-process work packages) plus the amount of level of effort scheduled to be accomplished within a given time period.

(The BCWS is nothing more than the "plan," against which contractor performance will be measured. In Figure 5-4 the plan or BCWS through year two was $50 million).

BUDGETED COST FOR WORK PERFORMED (BCWP): The sum of the budgets for completed work packages and completed portions of open work packages, plus the appropriate portion of the budgets for level of effort. Also known as "Earned Value."

(The BCWP is the "earned value," the physical value of the work done at a given point in time. In Figure 5-4 the BCWP or earned value at year two was $25 million.)

ACTUAL COST OF WORK PERFORMED (ACWP): The costs actually incurred and recorded in accomplishing the work performed within a given time period.

(The ACWP is the "actual costs" for a given period. The ACWP through year two was $40 million.)

COST VARIANCE (CV): The numerical difference between earned value (BCWP) and actual costs (ACWP).

(The CV is the difference between the earned value BCWP, less the actual cost, ACWP. In Figure 5-4 the earned value BCWP is $25 million, less actual costs ACWP of $40 million, for a CV of "$15 million.)

Note the important difference in C/SCSC performance measurement: there is no comparison of the plan (BCWS) with the actual costs (ACWP), as with the "conventional cost" method.

SCHEDULE VARIANCE (SV): The numerical difference between Earned Value (BCWP) and the Budget Plan (BCWS).

(The SV is the difference between what was scheduled to be done, BCWS, and what was accomplished, or the earned value,

BCWP. In Figure 5-4 the BCWP is $25 million, less the BCWS of $50 million, for a SV of "$25 million.)

BUDGET AT COMPLETION (BAC): The sum of all budgets (BCWS) allocated to the contract. It is synonymous with the term Performance Measurement Baseline (PMB).

(The BAC is important as a comparison with the estimate at completion, which will take place during the period of performance. In Figure 5-4 the BAC is $100 million at the end of four years, synonymous with the BCWS in this case).

ESTIMATE AT COMPLETION (EAC): A value periodically developed to represent a realistic appraisal of the final cost to complete an effort. It is the sum of direct and indirect costs to date, plus the estimate of costs for all authorized work remaining. EAC = ACWP + the Estimate to Complete.

(Thus, whenever sound business practices are applied—to ourselves, or with progress payment administration or with C/SCSC performance measurement—periodically there will be a need to estimate what it will take to complete a given job. In Figure 5-4 there is no EAC forecasted by the supplier. However, with a CV of "$15 million and a SV of "$25 million only half way through the contract period, a realistic EAC is definitely in order.)

COST PERFORMANCE INDEX (CPI): The cost efficiency factor achieved by relating earned value (BCWP) performance to the actual dollars spent (ACWP).

(The CPI is the critical indicator of program performance using the earned value technique. The CPI is derived by dividing the earned value BCWP ($25 million) performance by the dollars actually spent ACWP ($40 million), which provides the cost efficiency factor for work accomplished after two years. The result of $25 million divided by the $40 million provides an efficiency factor of .625 percent. Stated another way, for every dollar spent to date, this program achieved a benefit of only .625 cents on the dollar!).

SCHEDULE PERFORMANCE INDEX (SPI): The schedule efficiency factor achieved by relating earned value (BCWP) against the scheduled work (BCWS).

(The SPI is a critical corollary index to the CPI, and is often used in conjunction with the CPI to forecast the final outcome. The SPI is derived by dividing the earned value BCWP ($25 million) performance by the scheduled work BCWS ($50 million), which provides the schedule efficiency factor for work after two years. The result of $25 million divided by $50 million equates to a factor of only 50 percent. Stated another way, for every dollar of equivalent work planned, this contract only accomplished one-half of it).

(Thus, one must conclude that the work initially scheduled to be done in years one and two, will now be performed in an extended contract period into years five or even six. And everyone knows the simple truth that work done in later periods likely will cost more to accomplish, caused by inflation).

With these nine definitions, related back to the data contained in Figure 5-4, will be easier to understand the forecasting techniques in the final EAC section below.

Criteria Group 4

The *analysis* section contains six criteria which require the contractor or subcontractor to make an assessment of what has occurred with its cost and schedule performance to date. Most important, however, this criteria group requires the supplier to analyze the cost and schedule performance to date, and then to estimate the cost and schedule requirements necessary to complete the effort, to forecast the EAC. Estimates at Completion will be covered thoroughly later in this chapter.

Criteria Group 5

The *revisions and access to data* section contains six criteria which require that the supplier maintain the performance measurement baseline (PMB) throughout the life of the contract by incorporating all new work into the PMB in a timely manner. Obviously, the maintenance of the baseline is vital to the integrity of any performance measurement system. Also, this group requires the contractor to provide access of performance data to the customer's representatives in order to verify strict compliance with the criteria.

Since the issuance of the C/SCS Criteria by the DOD in 1967, the application of the concept has been intentionally limited to only those contracts in which the customer (the buyer) has retained the risks of cost growth (i.e., on cost or incentive type contracts/subcontracts). The dollar thresholds for formal C/SCSC implementation will vary from period to period and will be set by the buying customer, but are currently generally imposed at $50 million dollars on prime contracts ($25 million for subcontracts) for developmental type work, and $160 million ($60 million for subcontracts) for production type efforts. Any full application of C/SCSC will require a periodic report (typically monthly) called the Cost Performance Report (CPR).

The lesser Cost/Schedule Status Reports (C/SSR) or the Cost Performance Reports/No Criteria (CPR/NC) are now generally set on smaller contracts at $5 million in contract value and a minimum of twelve months in program duration. However, program and subcontract management should weigh the risk factors involved in a given effort and decide the earned value applications on a case by case basis.

This overview was out of necessity a very limited discussion of a very large subject. One last question needs to be addressed: does the earned value (C/SCSC) performance measurement concept really work, or is it just another government requirement? To best answer this question, let us should review the results of an impressive Department of Defense study.

Covering the period from 1977 to 1990, over 400 DOD contracts in which formal C/SCSC was implemented were studied. The results of the analysis are most impressive, and without exception their findings were consistent for all of the 400 plus contracts monitored.

Once the C/SCSC performance measurement baseline (PMB) is in place and at least 15 percent of the planned work has been performed, the following conclusions can be made on the future performance of a given program:

- The overrun at completion will not be less than the overrun to date.

- The percent overrun at completion will be greater than the percent overrun to date.

- The conclusion: You can't recover.

- Who says: More than 400 major DOD contracts since 1977.

- Why: If you underestimated the near, there is no hope that you will do better on the far term planning.[9]

In closing on this section covering the basics of the earned value concept, let us cover the objectives sought to be gained through the use of the performance measurement concept to monitor and manage contractors/subcontractors. Once again, going to one of the originators of the concept who did so much to implement the technique during his tenure with the DOD and later at the DOE, Robert R. Kemps summarized the four objectives which can obtained from employing the earned value (C/SCSC) performance measurement concept:

- Sound Contractor Systems.
- Reliable, Auditable Data.
- Objective Performance Measurement.
- No Surprises.[10]

Four simple programmatic objectives, not always easy to obtain.

Comparing Progress Payments Data with C/SCSC Cost Performance Report (CPR) Data

When comparing the cost data contained on progress payment invoices with the cost data contained in the formal C/SCSC Cost Performance Report (CPR), or the lesser C/SSR or CPR/NC, there are two issues which require a reconciliation when there are differences reported from a contractor or subcontractor, and the reporting of differences will likely be the norm, not the exception:

1. The comparison of the *cost actuals* (ACWP) reported to date—between those contained in the progress payment invoice versus the cost actuals reflected on the CPR;

2. The comparison of the *estimates* to complete (EAC) the effort—between those forecasted on the progress payment invoice versus those forecasted on the CPR.

For purposes of this discussion, three distinct C/SCSC cost and schedule performance reports (CPR, C/SSR, CPR/NC) will be considered as being identical for the purpose of reviewing the data contained therein. Any generic differences in these three reports deal with other matters, not the actual costs (ACWP) or the estimate at completion (EAC) contained in these reports.

One would expect that there is, or that there should be, some direct relationship between what a contractor/subcontractor reports as their cost actuals position when they submit progress payment invoices versus what they may reflect on other cost reports (e.g., a CPR). After all, the cost data does come from the same supplier, reporting their cost status from a single accounting system.

However, in practice, it is not unusual to receive multiple cost reports from a supplier reflecting different financial actuals for the same reporting period. Anytime this happens, it is incumbent on the buyer to request a reconciliation from the subcontractor, requiring an explanation of any differences in the cost reports.

The culprit in such discrepancies can be attributed to several factors which can make the data contained in any of these cost reports unique. These factors are:

1. Different cut-off dates for the reports, or the data contained or reported therein. In some cases the reports are to reflect a specific accounting closure date, but at other times the date will reflect the date of report submittal. Not infrequently, progress payment closure dates will have a different cut-off date from the general ledger closure date.

2. Cost data only (which excludes fee or profit) versus "price" data (which will include some estimate of earned fee or profit on lower tier subcontracts). Often there are distinct professional differences of opinion between a buyer and seller as to how much profit or fee a given supplier will likely have earned on the effort at a given point in time.

3. Progress payments to lower tier suppliers being included or excluded in the cost actuals being reported.

4. Negotiated statement of work versus unnegotiated statement of work—that is, changes. Unnegotiated work will often be placed into categories such as: (1) authorized, priced and proposed; (2) authorized but unpriced, and unproposed effort; and (3) unauthorized and still under discussion. Not infrequently, there are legitimate differences of opinion between buyer and seller as to the correct value of the "yet to be negotiated" work.

5. The projected estimated supplier costs at completion, in absolute overrun or underrun terms—with the cost sharing impact it may have on a supplier's earned profits under an incentive type contractual arrangement.

6. Termination liability projections at any given point in time, which will include either a supplier's open commitments, or their expenditures only. Remember, small businesses may include accounting accruals as cost actuals for purposes of requesting progress pay-

ments. Large businesses must actually pay the bills in order for them to quality as actual expenditures.

7. Materials purchased (e.g., raw stock, nuts, bolts, chemicals, etc.), received, and placed directly into inventory but not yet charged to work in process—the costs of which may or may not be incorporated into the cost actuals reported.

There are doubtless additional factors, all legitimate reasons, which may cause differences in the reported data between the progress payment requests (SF1443) and the C/SCSC cost performance reports (CPR). These seven items are not intended to be all inclusive.

What all this means to the buyer and the seller is that they should insist that those who prepare such cost reports invest in a few choice narrative words in order to better describe the cost reports they send out—or in other words what assumptions they may have made when the data was submitted. This is particularly true when there are similar financial terms being used in multiple cost reports, which can have different meanings to the practitioners.

However, in every case when there are different values reported, the buyer has a programmatic responsibility to understand the reasons causing these discrepancies prior to authorizing funds for the progress payment invoice.

Comparing Progress Payment Data without the Benefit of Formal C/SCSC on Firm Fixed-Price (FFP) Subcontracts

How do you get earned value performance measurement on subcontracts which do not have formal C/SCSC requirements imposed? One approach would be to universally impose full C/SCSC requirements on all contracts and subcontracts which are funded by the U.S. Government. One individual from the government has suggested exactly that in his timely article on the subject of managing contractor progress payments. Note, in this quote he uses the term "flexible" to mean cost or incentive type contracts, and "inflexible" to refer to firm fixed-price (FFP) type contracts:

The DOD would be well advised to insist validated cost/schedule procedures be implemented on all large dollar contracts—flexible and inflexible, prime and subcontracts—that require payments reviews by the government. Validated cost/schedule reporting will ensure proper program controls and provide the government with a more effective and efficient method of conducting government payment reviews.[11]

The point made above is that since there are hundreds of contractors which have fully validated C/SCSC systems, and since it is important to connect the approval of progress payments with the physical performance of a contractor, why not extend C/SCSC to all programs which are funded by the government. Certainly valid points, but not recommended for a number of reasons.

In the first place, although there are currently over two hundred actively validated C/SCSC management control systems in the United States, that number represents only a small fraction of the total contracts and subcontracts which are covered by government progress payments. Most of the firm fixed-price FFP type contracts and subcontracts would not be impacted by such an edict, because most suppliers do *not* possess a validated C/SCSC management control system. Two hundred approved management systems out of several thousand suppliers is but a small percentage of the total.

But of greater significance, extending full C/SCSC to all programs which have progress payments would simply increase the costs of the government's procurement of major systems. The full application of formal C/SCSC with their thirty-five specific criteria have too much "nonvalue" added requirements to be universally and indiscriminately applied to all programs which have progress payments. Full C/SCSC applications should be limited to cost or incentive type contracts, with their inherent cost risks, which can benefit from having an early warning monitoring system.

In 1967, when C/SCSC was first introduced, there was some confusion as to whether or not the criteria should be imposed on other than cost or incentive type contracts/subcontracts. It was decided at that time to limit the formal application of C/SCSC to only those efforts where the risk of cost growth was on the buyer (i.e., on cost or incentive type contracts). That principle is still valid today. There are better, less costly ways to achieve the same goals, that of linking progress payment approvals to the physical performance of the supplier requesting payment.

When a supplier requests progress payments and the buyer is prudent enough to require the creation and monthly submittal of a Gantt Chart, the prime contractor (buyer) has all that is needed to employ at least a modified version of the earned value concept. Even a modified earned value approach can be significant when monitoring fixed-price suppliers, who traditionally have refused to allow any performance monitoring by prime contractors.

Remember our earlier discussion in Chapter 2 which covered the importance of imposing a requirement for Gantt Charts, which was displayed in Figure 2-5. The Gantt Chart was in all cases to be prepared by the subcontractor, who was required to list all of the planned tasks necessary to perform the order. Each of the listed tasks was to receive a weighted value, the sum of which must add up to 100 percent of the purchase order price. What the Gantt Chart with weighted values provides is in effect a simple form of an "earned value" plan, which in the C/SCSC vernacular is referred to as the Budgeted Costs for Work Scheduled (BCWS). With the supplier's own plan, each task can be qualified with its value into a time frame to form a cumulative percentage curve. In Figure 5-5, the data presented by the subcontractor in Figure 2-5 was used to quantify Hypothetical Engine's performance plan, their own BCWS, monthly and cumulative.

Each month, as the supplier reports the actual performance against their Gantt schedule, they must report a percentage completion against the plan. In Figures 3-5 and 3-6 the supplier was reporting 28 percent complete as of October, 1991, and later, 34 percent as of January, 1992. This compares unfavorably with assessment of their own data in Figure 5-5. To best illustrate what this supplier is reporting in their schedule performance, the data should be laid out as follows:

	Oct. 1991	Jan. 1992
BCWS Plan (from Figure 5-5)	37%	46%
BCWP Performance (Figures 3-5 and 3-6)	28%	34%
Schedule Variance Position	–9%	–12%
SPI (BCWP divided by BCWS)	76%	74%

One can immediately see that with the passage of time, this supplier is getting progressively further behind in accomplishing the work they set out to do in their own plan from Figure 2-5. And by measuring their schedule position with earned value performance indices, one can quantify precisely how well or poorly they are doing. Their schedule performance index (SPI) went down from 76 percent of accomplishing planned work in October, 1991, then to 74 percent ninety days later.

What this percent complete estimate provides is a sort of modified earned value, or BCWP (Budgeted Costs for Work Performed) in the C/SCSC terminology. The difference between their planned BCWS versus what they accomplished in their BCWP, provides the schedule performance (SV) position for a subcontractor. It tells the prime contractor whether the supplier is accomplishing the work they had set out to do, and in a timely fashion. The performance of Hypothetical Engines is not going well, twelve months into a thirty month effort.

Figure 5-5. Establishing the BCWS

Hypothetical Engines, Inc.

Item#	Task	%	J	F	M	A	M	J	J	A	S	O	N	D	J	F	M	A	M	J	J	A	S	O	N	D	J	F	M	A	M	J
1	Des.Mod.	5	1	2	2																											
3	Qual.Test	5				5																										
5	Pur.Mat.	20				4	4	4	4	4																						
7	Fab.Parts	10								2	2	2	2	2																		
9	Comm.Assy	12										1	2	1	2	1	2	1	2													
11	#1	4																		2	2											
12	#2	4																			2	2										
13	#3	4																				2	2									
14	#4	4																					2	2								
15	#5	4																						2	2							
16	#6	4																							2	2						
17	#7	4																								2	2					
18	#8	4																									2	2				
19	#9	4																										2	2			
20	#10	4																											2	2		
21	#11	4																												2	2	
22	#12	4																													2	2
BCWS	Month%	100	1	2	2	9	4	4	4	6	2	3	4	3	2	1	2	1	2	2	4	4	4	4	4	4	4	4	4	4	4	2
BCWS	Cum.%		1	3	5	14	18	22	26	32	34	37	41	44	46	47	49	50	52	54	58	62	66	70	74	78	82	86	90	94	98	100

Now to relate the earned value (percent complete) to the costs this supplier is experiencing. Each month as the supplier submits their request for progress payments they must complete a SF1443 invoice form. Line 12a of the SF1443 contains their total actual costs incurred, cumulative to date. The amount listed on line 12a is equivalent to the actual cost values in C/SCSC, or what is called the ACWP, Actual Costs for Work Performed. When you relate the ACWP to the earned value (BCWP), you have the cost variance (CV) for performance by a supplier. With this information one can deduce the cost performance efficiency factor for the supplier (BCWP divided by the ACWP) to determine how much a supplier has earned for every dollar it has spent. If the supplier spends $1.00, but only accomplishes $.85 in earned value, one should watch the supplier closely. They could be heading for a loss which will require the application of the loss ratio to all progress payments made once their total "projected" costs penetrates the subcontract price value.

Thus, by requiring that a subcontractor put in place a few elementary cost and schedule plans prior to a subcontract award, a buyer can employ a simple but effective earned value performance measurement concept. With this, the performance of even firm-fixed price suppliers may be monitored during the life of their subcontracts, and provide a linkage between progress payment approvals and earned value measurement.

Using C/SCSC Performance Indices to Predict the EAC

The best Estimate at Completion (EAC) forecast for a given program is typically referred to as a "bottoms-up" or "grass-roots" EAC. Here, each of the remaining tasks to be worked is examined by the very functions who will perform the tasks, and a detailed estimate to complete all of the work is prepared. However, to do a legitimate bottoms-up EAC takes a lot of program resources to accomplish—the very same resources who are trying to complete the job in a timely manner. Therefore, grass roots EACs can only be accommodated once or twice each year per program in order for such exercises to not interfere with the primary mission of completing the contractual effort. At the upper extreme, a grass roots EAC may be done quarterly, but that frequency may well over-tax the limited resources of any program and have an adverse impact on successful contractual performance.

However, and this is the good news, the cost and schedule performance data generated by the earned value C/SCSC activities provides an effective way of complimenting the periodic (annual, semi-annual, or quarterly) "grass roots" EACs done by the functional organizations. Without disrupting personnel in the performing organizations, and with the help of computer software programs in place today, a monthly (or even weekly) full range of EAC forecasts may be efficiently provided, based upon the actual C/SCSC performance data.

In addition, work being performed by all subcontractors is also subject to monthly EAC analysis, independent of what the supplier may be "officially" forecasting. Periodic subcontractor EACs should be verified independently by the responsible cost account manager (CAM), and one of the best ways to accomplish this is by examination of the supplier's earned value performance. And should the CAM also be the same individual who approves all progress payment invoices, a critical linkage will have been established between the two management processes. The preparation of an independent EAC forecast for subcontractors also provides better assurance to the government that a "loss ratio adjustment" will be invoked at the appropriate time to preclude any overpayment of government funds.

In 1991, when the Department of Defense made their long awaited changes to the C/SCSC requirements documentation and incorporated them directly into their new acquisition policy statement in DODD 5000.1 and DODI 5000.2, there were no changes to the C/SCS Criteria. There were, however, two important changes with respect to the analysis of the C/SCSC data, particularly as related to providing the estimates of costs at completion (EAC) on a given program.

The first change requires a "range of EAC estimates" to be provided by the military service program manager who is responsible for the management of a given acquisition system. The service program manager must, from the cost/schedule performance data:

(1) Enter the range of estimates at completion, reflecting best and worst cases.[12]

The second DOD change to C/SCSC requires a justification, again from the military service program manager, whenever an estimate of costs at completion is forecasting a final value that is *less* than an amount using the cumulative Cost Performance Index (CPI) to forecast the EAC:

(2) Provide the estimate at completion reflecting the best professional judgement of the servicing cost analysis organization. If the contract is at least 15 percent complete and the estimate is lower than that calculated using the cumulative cost performance index, provide an explanation.[13]

The "15 percent" thresholds referred to in the second quote relates to the DOD (Christle) empirical study of over 400 contractors who performed using C/SCSC, which was covered earlier. After performing 15 percent of a contract, what the contractor has achieved thus far is likely to be the *lower* end value of what they will do by the end of the contract.

With the added emphasis on using earned value performance data to forecast the final cost/schedule outcomes of contracts, it would be wise to make sure that some of the formulas available to forecast a "range of estimates" are fully understood. While there are a multitude of EAC formulas in use by the C/SCSC practitioners, only the basic three are presented here since these three constitute the more accepted methods in use. The three EAC methods are:

1. The *low-end* Estimate at Completion (the Mathematical EAC).

2A. The *middle-range* Estimate at Completion (the CPI EAC).

2B. What CPI Performance factor it will take "to complete" an effort, called the To Complete Performance Index (TCPI), in order to achieve the "CPI EAC" forecast.

3. The *high-range* Estimate at Completion (the CPI x SPI EAC).

Each of these mathematical forecasting methods will be addressed individually, building on the definitions of C/SCSC terms covered earlier in this chapter.

Note: in order to follow this discussion it is necessary to understand the C/SCSC jargon covered around the display of data in Figure 5-4, particularly the Cost Performance Index (CPI) and the Schedule Performance Index (SPI). A perfect CPI is 1.0, which means that for each dollar actually spent, one dollar of physical work was performed. A perfect SPI is also 1.0, which means that for each dollar of work planned to be accomplished, one dollar of physical work was accomplished.

If a contractor achieves what it sets out to achieve in its cost and schedule baseline plans (PMB), that is considered acceptable or even "perfect" efficiency in a performance measurement environment. This concept is illustrated in the diagram in Figure 5-6.

If after establishing the performance measurement baseline (PMB) the contractor achieves a cost performance factor of 1.0, this is considered excellent results. For every dollar they spend, they have achieved one dollar in physical earned value accomplishments. Anything less than 1.0 is considered

Figure 5-6.   Monitoring Earned Value (C/SCSC) Performance

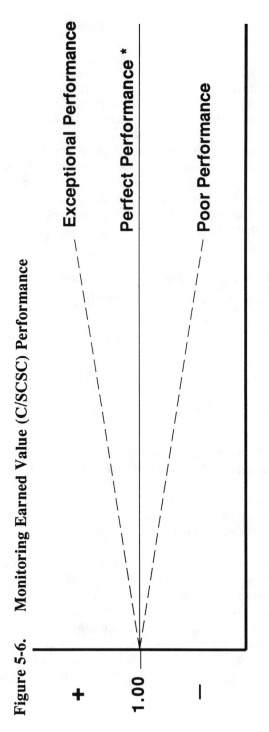

* Perfect Cost Performance: Cost Performance Index (CPI) = 1.0
    $1.00 Cost Actuals = $1.00 Earned Value

* Perfect Schedule Performance: Schedule Performance Index (SPI) = 1.0
    $1.00 Work Planned = $1.00 Earned Value

negative performance. Anything greater than 1.0 is considered positive or even exceptional efficiency.

On occasion, a contractor may actually achieve a greater than 1.0 performance. It is sometimes possible for a contractor to perform slightly under 1.0 in the first part of a contractual period, then exceed 1.0 in the final stage. This may be the result of conservative planning of the performance baseline, where the final 100 percent achievement of various tasks are restrained in order to stimulate exemplary performance by program personnel.

However, if a contractor claims achievement "significantly" greater than 1.0, perhaps 1.5, then someone might want to pay the supplier a visit and find out how such "miracles" have occurred. Often, but not always, a performance attainment much greater than 1.0 is the result of an improper original performance measurement plan. And sometimes, exceptional performance is just plain "gamesmanship" by those who are preparing and/ or approving the cost/schedule reports.

Likewise, schedule performance of 1.0 is considered as good as it can get, under normal circumstances. For every one dollar of work planned to be accomplished, one dollar of performance was achieved.

Now to address the range of EAC possibilities. The low-end EAC forecast is called the "Mathematical EAC," which is displayed in Figure 5-7. Some people refer to the Mathematical EAC formula as being "useless," or "unrealistic," and even "optimistic." And yet, many firms in the industry have been using this EAC method since the C/SCSC were issued in 1967. The formula for the mathematical EAC is Budget at Completion (BAC), less the cumulative earned value (BCWP), plus the cumulative actual costs to date (ACWP). What this EAC does in effect is to "buy-out" any poor performance to date, but assumes that starting tomorrow, all remaining work will be performed at perfect or 1.0 efficiency (on the average).

While the mathematical EAC forecasting method is not a useful device for accurately forecasting what a program will likely cost at the end, it does provide a "floor" EAC, that value which represents the absolute minimum cost for the program. Such revelations sometimes come as a shock to management and does provide the lower-end range of EAC possibilities.

The middle-range EAC forecast is called the "Cumulative CPI EAC," which is displayed in Figure 5-8. The formula is the Budget at Completion (BAC), divided by the cumulative Cost Performance Index (CPI). There are a number of variations for this mid-range EAC, which will serve no value to us in this limited discussion of the subject. Some people will use only the last three or six months of the CPI, to reflect a recent trend or change the direction of the CPI. For our purposes we need only to understand that the total budget available is divided by the cumulative performance efficiency

Figure 5-7. The "Mathematical" Estimate at Completion (EAC)
"optimistic" / "unrealistic" / "useless"

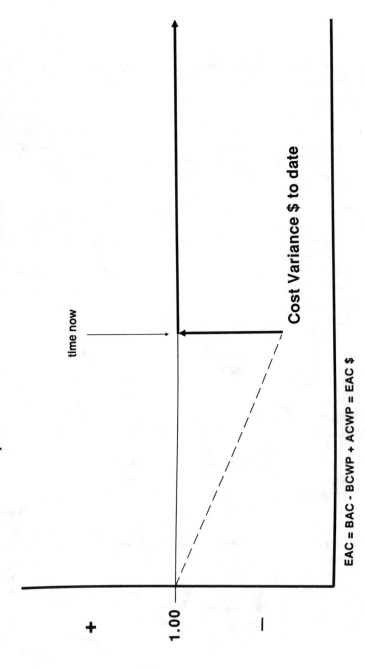

EAC = BAC - BCWP + ACWP = EAC $

Figure 5-8.   The "Cumulative CPI" Estimate at Completion (EAC)
"most likely" / "minimum"

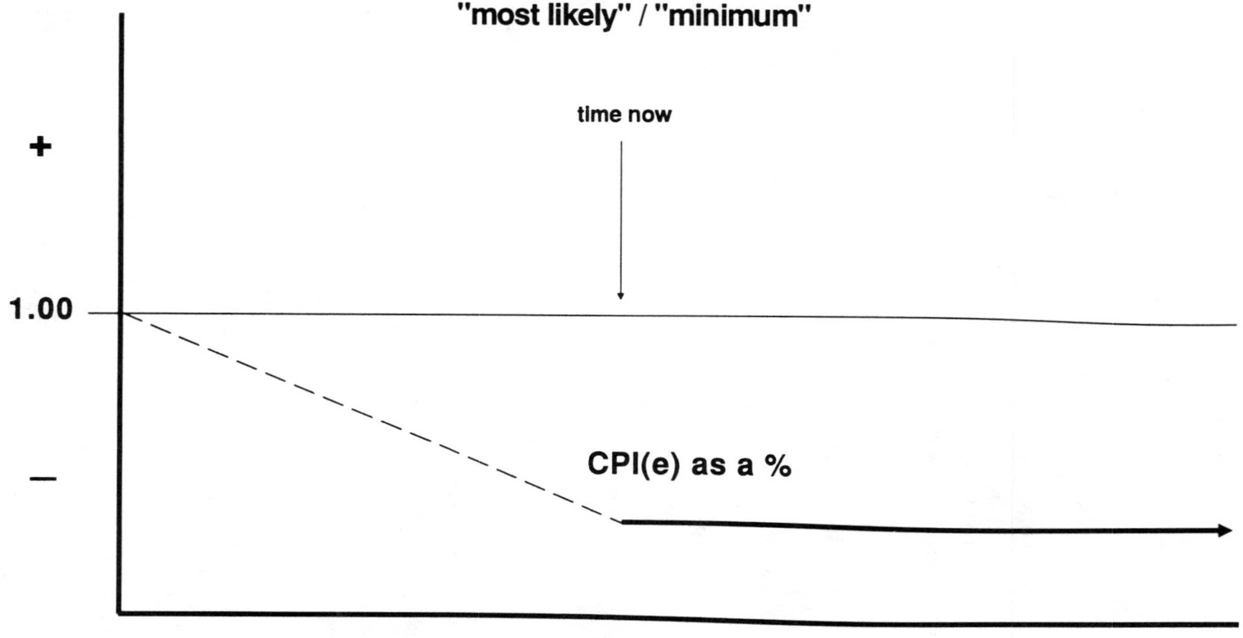

time now

+

1.00

–

CPI(e) as a %

$$EAC = \frac{BAC}{CPI(e)} = EAC\ \$$$

factor. If that efficiency factor is less that 1.0, then the estimate to complete the job will grow from the original allocated budget.

The CPI EAC is the most common and accepted EAC method. Some people consider this method to reflect the "most likely" EAC forecast, while other more conservative individuals feel it only reflects the "minimum" EAC. Whatever. In the recent DODD 5000.2-M, as quoted earlier, the military service program manager must now "provide an explanation" for any EAC forecasts that predict a final performance value that is less than that using the cumulative CPI EAC method.

One of the most important tools in C/SCSC forecasting does not deal with how much it will cost, or how long it will take to complete the job. Rather, the "To Complete Performance Index (TCPI)" has its utility in determining what performance efficiency factor it will take to do what you say you will do. Simply put, if you complete one half of a job with a CPI of .95 percent, then one must assume that in order to complete the job within the approved budget for the remaining work, one must achieve a CPI of 1.05 percent for the balance of the effort. This concept is illustrated in Figure 5-9, as well as the formula to calculate the TCPI.

The value of the TCPI formula is that it can be used to answer a number of questions, all related to achieving some future objective. For example, what efficiency factor it will take: (1) to stay within the Budget at Completion (BAC); (2) to stay within the latest Estimate at Completion (EAC); (3) to stay within the latest Over the Target Budget (OTB); (4) to stay within the Fixed Price Incentive (FPI) ceiling, etc. The TCPI is used to "puncture" blind optimism, which sometimes inflicts our management, particularly our more senior management.

The high-end EAC forecast is called the CPI x SPI EAC forecast. It adds the dimension of scheduled but unfinished work, which was in the original plan, but has not been completed. This concept is illustrated in Figure 5-10, and the formula is the work remaining to be performed (BAC less BCWP), divided by the product of the Cost Performance Index (CPI) times the Schedule Performance Index (SPI), plus the ACWP. Obviously, if one performed under 1.0 in both the CPI and SPI, the resulting estimate at completion will be substantial.

This EAC method can get to be quite emotional to those involved in managing programs. Some consider this technique to represent the "most likely" EAC, while others call it the "worst case" scenario. Some program managers, attempting to keep their costs under control refer to this technique irreverently as a "self-fulfilling prophecy."

This method is generally considered to be the high-end EAC method, and was used by the DOD cost analysts on the A-12 program to forecast its

Figure 5-9. To Complete (the work) Performance Index (TCPI)
"what will it take to stay within the BAC / EAC / OTB / FPI ceiling"

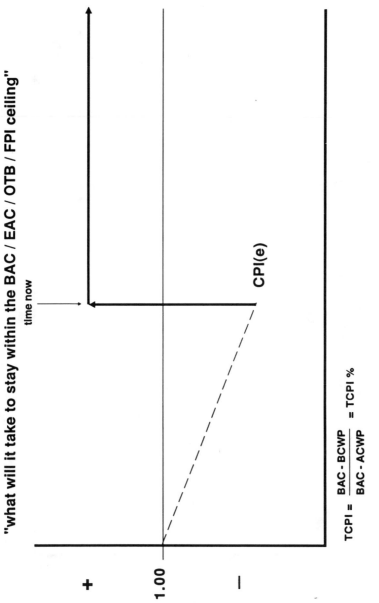

$$TCPI = \frac{BAC - BCWP}{BAC - ACWP} = TCPI\ \%$$

Figure 5-10. The "Cumulative CPI × SPI" Estimate at Completion (EAC) "worst-case" / "most likely" / "a self-fulfilling prophecy"

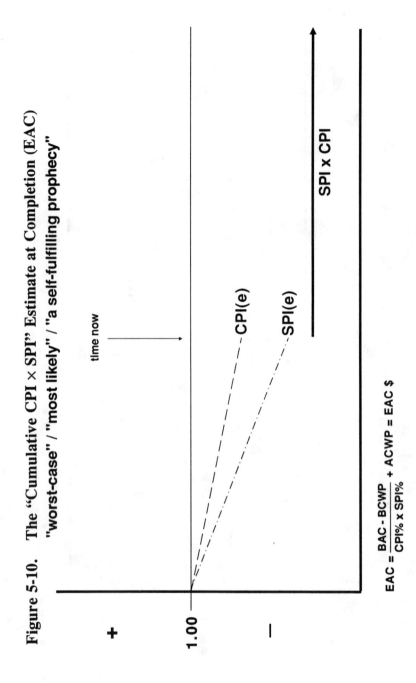

$$EAC = \frac{BAC - BCWP}{CPI\% \times SPI\%} + ACWP = EAC\ \$$$

total estimate at completion. It is a most valuable high-end EAC forecasting technique.

Now, what benefit do all of these EAC methods actually provide when attempting to forecast the final costs of a given program? To discern the value in employing these EAC techniques, let us take each of the formulas as displayed in Figures 5-7 to 5-10 and relate them to the data provided from the performance in Figure 5-4.

Starting from the low-end EAC method, the following is a range of EAC forecasts.

(1) The "Mathematical EAC":

BAC − BCWP + ACWP = EAC$

$100M − $25M + $40M = EAC **$115M.**

(2A) The "CPI EAC":

BAC / CPI = EAC$

$100M /.625% = EAC **$160M.**

(2B) The "TCPI":

BAC − BCWP / BAC − ACWP = TCPI

$100M − $25M / $100M − $40M = $75M / $60M = TCPI **1.25%**

(3) The "CPI x SPI EAC":

(BAC − BCWP) / (CPI x SPI) + ACWP

($100M − $25M) / (.625% x .500%) + $40M = EAC **$280M.**

The low-end EAC method (mathematical EAC) tells us that $115 million will be spent, the minimum floor. The mid-range EAC (CPI EAC) forecasts a total cost requirement of $160 million, and if anyone predicts a lesser amount, a military program manager will have to justify the lesser amount in order to comply with the new DOD 5000.2-M. The high-end EAC (CPI x SPI EAC) tells us $280 million is needed to complete the job, quite an increase over the budget of $100 million! A full range of EAC estimates are possible with these formulas.

What is also significant is the fact that in order to stay within the original approved budget of $100 million, the contractor must achieve a CPI performance efficiency factor of 1.25 percent for all of the remaining effort. A very ambitious goal for any mortal person or group to achieve.

The various EAC forecasting methods available to us when earned value methods are employed can be most beneficial in the management of contracts or subcontracts, and provide a complimentary adjunct in the effective administration of contractor progress payments.

In Summary

While there is not universal acceptance for the concept that there should be, or must be, a linkage between the progress payments being made to suppliers and the physical performance they are achieving on such work, the A-12 program experience will likely require such relationships in the future. This important linkage will likely improve both management processes: progress payments and cost/schedule performance measurement.

By linking physical performance measurement to the approval of progress payments, the prime contractor should avoid the potential cost risks of making overpayments to the supplier. Also, the FAR covering progress payments specifically require that there be some monitoring of the supplier's performance, in order to know when it might be necessary to adjust the repayment rate, or to suspend further progress payments, or to invoke the loss ratio, among other things.

By linking progress payments with C/SCSC performance measurement the buyer will have a better understanding of what the suppliers are actually achieving in satisfying their statement of work. To exclude progress payment data from the actuals being reported in the Cost Performance Report (CPR) does nothing but distort the desired earned value measurements. And with the subcontracted portions (the buy content) becoming such a major part of most prime contractor dollars (upwards of 80 percent in some cases), the exclusion of progress payment data in performance measurement can reflect major distortions in the data being reported. A better approach, it is felt, would be to measure the physical performance of all suppliers which have progress payments, including firm fixed-price suppliers, and to incorporate these actual dollars into all cost performance reports (CPR).

Having touched on a couple of issues rather hurriedly in the discussion above, it might be beneficial to reemphasize these points. It is important that the buyer—the individual who has delegated procurement authority to issue the subcontract—be given the responsibility for the review and approval of each and every progress payment invoice before any such payments are made. This is a fundamental issue. Also important, it is believed, is the concept that this same buyer be held responsible for the total management of his/her subcontract, including that of functioning in the role of Cost Account Manager (CAM) for the performance measurement of the supplier.

If a prime contractor thus places the responsibility for: (1) the full administration of progress payments, including the approval or disapproval of all payment invoices, and (2) the management of a subcontract earned value cost account in a single individual, then the prime contractor will have achieved a "linkage" of both activities. This critical coupling should prevent any future overpayment of suppliers, in advance of their actual physical work accomplishments, and improve the overall subcontract management processes.

We hope we have made the case for employing this approach.

Endnotes

1. Chester Paul Beach, Jr., Inquiry Officer, in a memorandum for the Secretary of the Navy, "A-12 Administrative Inquiry," November 28, 1990, page 2.

2. Ibid, pages 3 and 4.

3. Mr. Wayne Abba, office of Acquisition Policy and Program Integration, Office of the Secretary of Defense, in public remarks made on the A-12 program, to the management systems subcommittee of the National Security Industrial Association, Costa Mesa, California, January 16, 1991.

4. Mrs. Eleanor Spector, Director of Defense Procurement, Office of the Secretary of Defense, in Congressional testimony April 9, 1991.

5. *Los Angeles Times,* from Reuters, June 8, 1991.

6. Robert R. Kemps, Humphreys & Associates, Inc., formerly with the Department of Defense and later the Department of Energy, in an article he wrote entitled "Solving the Baseline Dilemma," for the Performance Management Association's newsletter, Autumn, 1990.

7. Russell D. Archibald and Richard L. Villoria, *Network-Based Management Systems (PERT/CPM),* (New York: John Wiley & Sons, Inc., 1967), page 475.

8. Department of Defense Directive 5000.1, dated February 23, 1991, *"Defense Acquisition" ;* Department of Defense Instruction 5000.2, same date, *"Defense Acquisition Management Policies and Procedures."*

9. Gary E. Christle, Deputy Director for Cost Management, Office of the Under Secretary of Defense for Acquisitions, in a paper entitled "Con-

tractor Performance Measurement–Projecting Estimates at Completion," Atlanta, Georgia, October 26, 1987. Data updated from 200 to
400 contracts from the Beach report, November 28, 1990, page 6.

10. Robert R. Kemps, Director of the Office of Project and Facilities Man-
    agement for the Department of Energy (DOE), in his paper entitled
    "Cost/Schedule Control Systems Criteria (C/SCSC) for Contract Perfor-
    mance Measurement," at the Performance Management Association
    conference in San Diego, California, April, 1989.

11. William J. Hill, "Toward More Effective Management and Control of
    Contractor Payments," appearing in Defense Systems Management
    College's *Program Manager* magazine, January–February, 1991, page
    21.

12. DOD 5000.2-M, page 16-H-6.

13. DOD 5000.2-M, page 16-H-6.

Appendix A

Glossary of
Progress Payment Terms

AACE—*See* American Association of Cost Engineers.

ABNORMAL PAYMENTS—Any payment which is not consistent with the norm, in conflict with the FAR, or laws which govern such payments. Often synonymous with the term unusual payments.

ACO—*See* Administrative Contracting Officer.

ACTIVITY—Something that occurs over time, and generally consumes resources. Also referred to as a Task.

ACTUAL COST—A cost sustained in fact, on the basis of costs incurred, as distinguished from forecasted or estimated costs.

ACTUAL COST OF WORK PERFORMED (ACWP)—The costs actually incurred and recorded in accomplishing the work performed within a given time period.

ACTUAL DIRECT COSTS—Those costs specifically identified with a contract, based upon the contractor's cost identification and accumulation system as accepted by cognizant auditing representatives (*see also* Direct Costs).

ACWP—*See* Actual Costs of Work Performed.

ADMINISTRATIVE CONTRACTING OFFICER (ACO)—The official primarily responsible for monitoring contract performance and negotiating certain contract modifications.

ADVANCE ORDER AUTHORIZATION—The means by which long-lead material may be ordered to preclude schedule delays.

ADVANCE PAYMENTS—Cash advances to contractors, suppliers, or subcontractors, prior to shipment of materials or performance of services.

ADVANCED MATERIAL RELEASE (AMR)—A document typically used by engineering organizations to release long-lead time or time critical material requirements prior to the formal release of a design. AMRs are used to start the procurement process without waiting for the design of something to be completed.

AFIT—Air Force Institute of Technology.

ALTERNATE LIQUIDATION RATE—A more attractive method of providing for the repayment or liquidation of progress payment loans by contractors which is allowed by the FAR, and which permits the contractor to retain some portion of their earned profit element of the contract price with the delivery of each item. Specific performance rules must be met by the contractor in order to go from the ordinary to the alternate liquidation rate.

AMERICAN ASSOCIATION OF COST ENGINEERS (AACE)—A professional organization which exists for the advancement of the science and art of cost engineering.

AMERICAN PRODUCTION & INVENTORY CONTROL SOCIETY (APICS)—A professional organization which focuses on manufacturing and inventory control issues.

AMR—*See* Advanced Material Release.

APICS—*See* American Production & Inventory Control Society.

APPLIED DIRECT COSTS—The actual direct costs recognized in the time period associated with the consumption of labor, material, and other direct resources, without regard to their date of commitment or their date of payment. These amounts are to be charged to the appropriate work-in-progress when any of the following takes place: (1) When labor, material, and other direct resources are actually consumed; (2) Material resources are withdrawn from inventory for use; (3) Material resources are received that are uniquely identified to the contract and scheduled for use within sixty days; (4) Major components or assemblies that are specifically and uniquely identified to a single serially numbered end-item are received on a line flow basis.

APPORTIONED EFFORT—Effort that by itself is not readily divisible into short span work packages, but which is related in direct proportion to some other measured effort.

ARBITRATION—The process of two parties presenting their grievances to a third party for resolution of any differences.

AT COMPLETION VARIANCE (ACV)—The difference between the Budget at Completion (BAC) and Estimate at Completion (EAC). At any point in time, it represents a forecast of budget overrun or underrun.

AUTHORIZED UNPRICED WORK (AUW)—The effort for which definitized contract costs have not been agreed to, but for which written authorization has been received by the contractor.

AUTHORIZED WORK—That effort which has been definitized and is on contract, plus that for which definitized contract costs have not been agreed to but for which written authorization has been received.

AVERAGE UNIT (FLYAWAY/ROLLAWAY/SAILAWAY) COSTS—The average unit costs related to the production of a useable end-item of military hardware. Such values include the costs of procuring the basic unit, a percentage of the basic unit cost to cover changes, other installed Government-furnished equipment, and nonrecurring production costs.

BAC—*See* Budget at Completion.

BASED-ON PRICE—A price may be considered to be based on established catalog or market prices of commercial items sold in substantial quantities to the general public if the item being purchased is sufficiently similar to the commercial item to permit the differences between the prices of the items to be identified and justified without resort to cost analysis.

BASELINE—*See* Performance Measurement Baseline. *See also* Contract Budget Base.

BASELINE REVIEW (BR)—A customer review conducted to determine with a limited sampling that a contractor is continuing to use the previously accepted performance system and is properly implementing a baseline on the contract or option under review. A baseline review is particularly applicable to follow-on contracts, where key C/SCSC knowledgeable contractor personnel are retained from previous efforts.

BCWP—*See* Budgeted Costs for Work Performed.

BCWS—*See* Budgeted Costs for Work Schedules.

BEST AND FINAL OFFER (BAFO)—A final proposal submission by all offerors in the competitive range submitted at a common cut-off date at the request of a Contracting Officer or buyer, after conclusion of negotiations.

BID—An offer submitted in response to a formally advertised invitation for bids.

BID & PROPOSAL (B&P)—The effort associated with the preparation and submittal of cost bids and technical proposals.

BIDDERS CONFERENCE—In sealed procurements, a meeting of prospective bidders arranged by the contracting officer during the solicitation period to help prospective bidders to fully understand the buyer's requirements and to give them an opportunity to ask questions.

BILL OF MATERIAL (BOM)—A listing of all the sub-assemblies, parts and raw materials that go into a parent assembly showing the quantity of each required to make an assembly. There are a variety of formats of Bill of Material, including single level, indented, modular (planning), transient, matrix, costed, etc.

BOOKING RATES—Rates used during the course of a year to record estimated actual indirect costs to a project. The overhead booking rates are applied to direct labor, materials and other direct costs.

BOTTOM UP COST ESTIMATE—*See* Engineering Cost Estimate.

BR—*See* Baseline Review.

BUDGET—A plan of operations for a fiscal period in terms of: (a) estimated costs, obligations, and expenditures; (b) source of funds for financing including anticipated reimbursements and other resources; and (c) history and workload data for the projected programs and activities.

BUDGET AT COMPLETION (BAC)—The sum of all budgets (BCWS) allocated to the contract. It is synonymous with the term Performance Measurement Baseline (PMB).

BUDGETED COST FOR WORK PERFORMED (BCWP)—The sum of the budgets for completed work packages and completed portions of open work packages, plus the appropriate portion of the budgets for level of effort and apportioned effort. Also known as "Earned Value."

BUDGETED COST FOR WORK SCHEDULED (BCWS)—The sum of the budgets for all work packages, planning packages, etc., scheduled to be accomplished (including in-process work packages) plus the amount of level of effort and apportioned effort scheduled to be accomplished within a given time period.

BUDGETING—The process of translating approved resource requirements into time-phased financial requirements.

BURDEN—*See* Indirect Cost.

BURDEN—Overhead expenses not conveniently chargeable directly to a specific job order, and therefore distributed over the appropriate direct labor and/or material base.

CA—*See* Cost Account.

CAIG—*See* Cost Analysis Improvement Group.

CAM—*See* Cost Account Manager.

CAO—*See* Contract Administration Office.

CAP—Cost Account Plan, a term typically used by firms to describe a "Cost Account." *See* Cost Account.

CBB—*See* Contract Budget Base.

CCDR—*See* Contractor Cost Data Reports.

CDRL—*See* Contractor Data Requirements List.

CFSR—*See* Contract Funds Status Report.

CHANGE ORDER—Unilateral direction to a contractor to modify a contractual requirement within the scope of the contract, pursuant to the changes clause contained in the contract.

CHANGES CLAUSE—A provision in a contract which allows for unilateral redirection by the buyer, subject to a subsequent agreement by both parties as to the affect of such re-direction, commonly called an equitable adjustment to the contract.

CHART OF ACCOUNTS—A formally established and controlled identification of accounting cost elements.

CO—*See* Contracting Officer.

COMMONALITY—One of two conditions that must be met if an item is to qualify for the established catalog or market price exemption from the requirement for submission of cost or pricing data.

COMMITMENT—A binding financial obligation in the form of a purchase order, or as used in the military, the amount administratively reserved for future obligation against available funds based upon firm requisitions.

COMPARABILITY—A condition that exists between an offered price and some other price against which it is compared. This condition is necessary for effective price comparison and exists when all price related differences have been identified and accounted for so that the prices being compared are based on relatively equal assumptions.

COMPETITION—Part of an acquisition strategy whereby more than one contractor is sought to bid on performing a service or function, with the winner being selected on the basis of criteria established by the party for whom the work is to be performed.

CONSTRUCTIVE CHANGE—Happens during contract performance, when an oral or written act or omission by the contracting officer or other authorized official, which is of such a nature that it is construed to have the same effect as a written change order.

CONTRACT—An agreement, enforceable by law, between two or more competent parties, to do or not to do something not prohibited by law, for a legal consideration.

CONTRACT ADMINISTRATION OFFICE (CAO)—The activity assigned by the DOD to perform contract administration responsibilities for the government, which is now delegated to the DPRO.

CONTRACT BUDGET BASE (CBB)—The negotiated contract cost plus the estimated cost of authorized but unpriced work.

CONTRACT DATA REQUIREMENTS LIST (CDRL)—A listing of data requirements specified for a contract.

CONTRACT FUNDS STATUS REPORT (CFSR)—A DOD report which provides information to forecast contract funding requirements.

CONTRACT LINE ITEM NUMBER (CLIN)—The number used to identify a specific contract deliverable item.

CONTRACT TARGET COST (CTC)—The negotiated cost for the original definitized contract and all contractual changes which have been definitized, but excluding the estimated cost of any authorized, unpriced changes. The CTC equals the value of the BAC plus management reserve, when there is no authorized, unpriced work.

CONTRACT TARGET PRICE (CTP)—The negotiated estimated cost (CTC) plus profit or fee.

CONTRACT WORK BREAKDOWN STRUCTURE (CWBS)—The CWBS is a customer prepared family tree sub division of a program which: (1) subdivides an entire program into all its major hardware, software, and service elements, (2) integrates a customer and contractor effort, and (3) provides a framework for planning, control and reporting from the lowest levels to the total contract level.

CONTRACTING OFFICER (CO)—Any person who by virtue of a position or appointment in accordance with prescribed Government regulations, is vested with the authority to enter into and administer Government contracts, and make determinations and findings with respect such activities. Three types of contracting officers are typically identified: the procurement contracting officer (PCO); the administrative contracting officer (ACO); and the termination contracting officer (TCO).

CONTRACTOR—An entity in private industry which enters into contracts with the Government. The term also applies to Government-owned, Government-operated activities which perform work on major defense programs.

CONTRACTOR COST DATA REPORT (CCDR)—A report developed to provide the DOD components with a means by which contract cost and related data can be collected to aid in acquisition management. It is designed to collect data on defense material items in a standard format in carrying out cost estimating, programming, budgeting and procurement responsibilities.

CONTRACTOR PURCHASING SYSTEM REVIEW (CPSR)—A periodic formal Government review of a contractor's purchasing system and the processes. Such CPSR's are required by the FAR, and result in the approval (or disapproval) of the contractor's procurement system.

COST ACCOUNT (CA)—An identified level at the natural intersection point of the work breakdown structure (WBS) and organizational breakdown structure (OBS) at which functional responsibility for work is assigned, and actual direct labor, material, and other direct costs are compared with earned value budget for management control purposes. Cost accounts are the focal point of cost/schedule control.

COST ACCOUNT MANAGER (CAM)—A member of a functional organization responsible for task performance detailed in a cost account and for managing the resources authorized to accomplish such tasks.

COST ACCOUNTING STANDARDS (CAS)—Standards established under public law intended to achieve uniformity and consistency in cost accounting practices of government contractors.

COST ANALYSIS—The review and evaluation of a contractor's cost or pricing data and of the judgmental factors applied in projecting from the data to the estimated costs. The purpose is to form an opinion leading to a position on the degree to which a contractor's proposed costs represent what contract performance should cost, assuming reasonable economy and efficiency. It includes appropriate verification of cost data, evaluation of specific elements of cost, and projection of these data to determine the effect on price factors like cost necessity, allowances for contingencies, and the basis used for allocation of overhead costs.

COST ANALYSIS IMPROVEMENT GROUP (CAIG)—An OSD/DOD advisory body established to perform cost analysis of current and future weapon systems. The CAIG also develops common cost estimating procedures for the DOD.

COST BREAKDOWN STRUCTURE—A system for subdividing a program into (a) hardware elements and sub-elements; (b) functions and subfunctions; and (c) cost categories to provide for more effective management and control of the program.

COST CENTER—A subdivision of an activity or a responsibility center, for which identification of costs is desired and which is amenable to cost control through one responsible supervisor.

COST CONTROL—Any system of keeping costs within the bounds of budgets or standards based upon work actually performed; applicable at any level of management.

COST ELEMENT—Typical elements of cost are: direct labor; direct material; other direct costs (ODC), and indirect costs.

COST ESTIMATE—A result or product of an estimating procedure which specifies the expected dollar cost required to perform a stipulated task or to acquire an item. A cost estimate may constitute a single value or a range of values.

COST INCURRED—A cost identified through the use of the accrued method of accounting and reporting or otherwise actually paid. Cost of direct labor, direct materials, and direct services identified with and necessary for the performance of a contract, and all properly allocated and allowable indirect costs as shown by the books of the contractor.

COST OF MONEY—A form of indirect cost incurred by investing capital in facilities employed on government contracts.

COST OVERRUN—The amount by which a contractor exceeds the estimated cost and/or the final limitation (ceiling) of a contract.

COST PERFORMANCE INDEX (CPI)—The value earned for every measurable unit of actual cost expended.

COST PERFORMANCE REPORT (CPR)—A monthly DOD report generated by the contractor to obtain cost and schedule status information for program management. The CPR is intended to provide early identification of problems having significant cost impact, effects of management actions and program status information for use in making and validating management decisions.

COST PLUS AWARD FEE (CPAF) CONTRACT—A cost reimbursable subcontract that provides for a smaller than normal base fee, plus an agreed to additional fee value which may be earned or lost by the supplier based on its performance during the life of the subcontract. The amount of award fee paid to the seller is determined solely by a subjective assessment of the supplier's performance by the buyer, according to guidelines, but no formula.

COST PLUS FIXED FEE (CPFF) CONTRACT—A cost reimbursable type contract which provides for reimbursement of all legitimate subcontractor costs, but with a fixed fee which does not change as costs go up or down from the initial negotiated values. Changes in subcontract scope may alter the original fixed fee. This type of contract places the risk of cost growth on the buyer, and the seller is under no obligation to complete the work without reimbursement for all legitimate costs.

COST PLUS INCENTIVE FEE (CPIF) CONTRACT—A cost reimbursable subcontracts which provides for an initially negotiated target cost and target fee; the fee may go up or down based on the agreed to relationship of total allowable costs to negotiated costs. Factors in addition to costs may be used as incentives, for example, technical performance, deliveries, etc.

COST REIMBURSEMENT CONTRACTS—A category of contracts whose use is based on payment by the government to a contractor of allowable costs as prescribed by the contract. Normally only best efforts of the subcontractor are involved, and includes (1) cost, (2) cost sharing, (3) cost-plus-fixed fee, and (4) cost-plus-incentive fee contracts.

COST/SCHEDULE CONTROL SYSTEMS CRITERIA (C/SCSC)—Government established standards which a contractor's internal management system must meet in order to insure the government of effective planning and control of contract work.

COST/SCHEDULE STATUS REPORT (C/SSR)—The scaled down C/SCSC requirement generally imposed on contracts smaller than would warrant a full DODI 7000.2 or DODI 5000.2 application.

COST TO COMPLETE FORECAST—A forecast spread by time periods for indicated remaining costs for the completion of contractual tasks. This term refers to the contractor's estimate of the cost-to-complete remaining tasks. Synonymous with Estimate to Complete.

COST VARIANCE (CV)—The numerical difference between earned value (BCWP) and actual costs (ACWP).

COULD COST—A new concept in the DOD acquisition process which provides a method of introducing competition into sole-source, follow-on, and/or special access procurements. It is an estimating process whereby the contractor and government work together to eliminate nonvalue added work, or waste. It focuses on what the procurement could cost if the plant were operating at full efficiency.

CPAF—*See* Cost plus award fee (CPAF) contracts.

CPFF—*See* Cost plus fixed fee (CPFF) contracts.

CPI—*See* Cost Performance Index.

CPIF—*See* Cost plus incentive fee (CPIF) contracts.

CPSR—*See* Contractor Purchasing System Review.

CRITICAL PATH—A sequential path of activities in a network schedule which represents the longest duration of a contract. Any slippage of the tasks in the critical path will increase the duration of a contract.

CRITICAL SUBCONTRACTOR—A contractor performing a complex portion of a contract which requires a flow down of C/SCSC or C/SSR requirements and integration, reviews, acceptance and control of subcontractor system and reporting. Critical subcontractors are designated as a result of customer negotiation or by management direction.

CTC—*See* Contract Target Cost.

CTP—*See* Contract Target Price.

CURE NOTICE—A notice by the contracting officer indicating that the contractor will be subject to a default termination unless it corrects a specific noncompliance issue, or makes satisfactory progress to eliminate the condition.

CUSTOMARY PROGRESS PAYMENT RATE—The specific rate authorized by the FAR for progress payments to contractors. Such rates may vary from period to period as defined by the FAR, may vary from large to small businesses, and between the FAR and the DOD-FAR.

CV—*See* Cost Variance.

CWBS—*See* Contractor Work Breakdown Structure.

DCAA—*See* Defense Contract Audit Agency.

DCAS—*See* Defense Contract Administration Services.

DEBARMENT—Actions taken by the Government to exclude a contractor from Government contracting and Government approved subcontracting for a specific period of time. A contractor so designated is termed "debarred."

DEFAULT—The actual or anticipated failure of a contractor to fulfill the terms and conditions of a contract, giving the right of a buyer to terminate the contract.

DEFECTIVE COST OR PRICING DATA—Certified cost or pricing data subsequently found to have been inaccurate, incomplete, or noncurrent as of the effective date of the certificate. In this case, the Government is entitled to an adjustment of the negotiated price, including profit or fee, to exclude any significant sum by which price was increased because of the defective data, provided the data were relied upon by the Government.

DEFENSE CONTRACT ADMINISTRATION SERVICES (DCAS)— Government offices located at numerous contractor facilities throughout the United States. These units are roughly equivalent to Army, Navy and Air Force Plant Representative Offices and their primary function is that of contract administration.

DEFENSE CONTRACT AUDIT AGENCY (DCAA)—A government agency that provides accounting and financial services on DOD contracts.

DEFENSE PLANT REPRESENTATIVE OFFICE (DPRO)—The DOD office which combined all of the individual service AFPRO, ARPRO, and NAVPRO offices into one consolidated organization to provide contract administration and other oversight functions at contractor facilities. The DPRO receives their specific authority from the FAR, and a delegated oversight authority from the Procurement Contracting Officers (PCO) and the Systems Program Offices (SPO).

DEMONSTRATION REVIEW (DR)—The formal review of a contractor's management control system to determine whether or not it satisfies the requirements of the 35 C/SCS Criteria.

DETERMINATION AND FINDINGS—A document signed by an authorized Government official justifying a decision to take a certain action, expressed in terms of meeting the regulatory requirements of the situation.

DIRECT COSTS—Those costs (labor, material, etc.) which can be reasonable and consistently related directly to service performed on a unit of work Charged directly and finally to the contract, without distribution to an overhead unit

DIRECT LABOR STANDARD—A specified output or a time allowance established for a direct labor operation.

DISCLOSURE STATEMENT—The official statement made by a contractor to the Government to formally describe their contract cost accounting practices in compliance with the Cost Accounting Standards (CAS).

DISCRETE EFFORT—Tasks which have a specific end product or end result.

DISCRETE MILESTONE—A milestone which has a definite, scheduled occurrence in time, signaling the finish of an activity, such as "release drawings," "pipe inspection complete," and/or signaling the start of a new activity. Synonymous with the term *objective indicator*.

DOD—Department of Defense.

DOE—Department of Energy.

DPRO—*See* Defense Plant Representative Office.

DR—*See* Demonstration Review.

DSMC—Defense Systems Management College.

DUAL SOURCE—Two contractors producing the same components or end items for the same program.

EAC—*See* Estimate at Completion.

EARNED HOURS—The time in standard hours credited to a workman or group of workmen as a result of their completion of a given task or group of tasks.

EARNED VALUE—What you got for what you spent; performance measurement; the Budgeted Cost of Work Performed (BCWP).

ECONOMIC LOT SIZE—That number of units of material or a manufactured item that can be purchased produced within the lowest unit cost range. Its determination involves reconciling the decreasing trend in preparation unit costs and the increasing trend in unit costs of storage, interest, insurance, depreciation, and other costs incident to ownership, as the size of the lot is increased.

EFFICIENCY FACTOR—The ratio of standard performance time is actual performance time, usually expressed as a percentage.

END-ITEM—The final production product when assembled, or completed, and ready for issue or deployment.

ENGINEERING COST ESTIMATE—An estimate derived by summing detailed cost estimates of the individual work packages and adding appropriate burdens. Usually determined by a contractor's industrial engineering, price analysis and cost accountants.

EQUITABLE ADJUSTMENT—The settlement between buyer and seller for the effects of a Change order.

ESAR—*See* Extended Subsequent Applications Review.

ESCALATION—Use of a price index to convert past to present prices or of converting present to future prices; increases due to inflation.

ESTABLISHED CATALOG PRICE—A price included in a catalog, price list, schedule, or other form that (1) is regularly maintained by a manufacturing vendor; (2) is published or made available for inspection by customers, and; (3) states prices at which sales are currently or were last made to a significant number of buyers constituting the general public.

ESTIMATE AT COMPLETION (EAC)—A value (expressed in dollars and/or hours) developed to represent a realistic appraisal of the final cost of tasks when accomplished. It is the sum of direct and indirect costs to date plus the estimate of costs for all authorized work remaining. The EAC = Cumulative Actuals + the Estimate-to-Completion.

ESTIMATE TO COMPLETE (ETC)—The value (expressed in dollar and/or hours) developed to represent a realistic appraisal of the cost of the work still required to be accomplished in completing a task.

ETC—*See* Estimate to Completion.

EVENT—Something that happens at a point or moment in time.

EXCESSIVE INVENTORY—Any inventory provided by a contractor or subcontractor in support of a given contract which exceeds the reasonable requirements of that contract, and which can be subject to some type of action by a buyer, for example, the suspension of further progress payments.

EXPENDITURE—A charge against available funds. It is evidenced by a voucher, claim, or other document approved by competent authority. Expenditure represents the actual payment of funds.

EXTENDED SUBSEQUENT APPLICATIONS REVIEW (ESAR)—A formal review performed in lieu of a full C/SCSC demonstration review when contractor conditions have changed: (1) when programs change from *one phase to another* (e.g., R & D into production); (2) when contractors move programs from *one facility to another;* (3) when contractors make significant *changes to their C/SCSC systems description.*

FAIR AND REASONABLE PRICE—A price that is fair to both parties, considering the agreed-upon conditions, promised quality, and timeliness of contract performance. Although generally a fair and reasonable price is a function of the law of supply and demand, there are statutory, regulatory, and judgmental limits on the concept.

FAR—*See* Federal Acquisition Regulation.

FEDERAL ACQUISITION REGULATION (FAR)—The regulations which govern all Federal procurements. Formerly referred to as Defense Acquisition Regulations (DAR) and earlier as the Armed Services Procurement Regulations (ASPR).

FEE—In specified cost-reimbursement contracts, fee represents an agreed-to amount beyond the initial estimate of costs. In most instances, fee reflects a variety of factors including risk, and is subject to statutory limitations. Fee may be fixed at the outset of performance, as in a cost-plus-fixed-fee arrangement, or may vary within a contractually specified minimum-maximum range, as in a cost-plus-incentive-fee arrangement. Fee is generally associated with cost reimbursable type contracts.

FENCES—Fences, or resource levels, established for a particular program provide a way by which the procuring activity can exert functional influence. Fences may just as appropriately be called ceilings and floors.

FFP—*See* Firm fixed-price (FFP) contracts.

FIRM FIXED-PRICE (FFP) CONTRACT—A contract which provides for a price that is not subject to adjustments on the basis of the seller's cost experience in performing the subcontract. This contract type places maximum cost risk, and full responsibility for all costs and profit or loss, on the subcontractor.

FISCAL YEAR—United States Government: 01 October to 30 September (12 months).

FIXED COSTS—Costs that do not vary with the volume of business, such as property taxes, insurance, depreciation, security, and minimum water and utility fees. Cost which does not fluctuate with variable outputs in the relevant range.

FIXED PRICE CONTRACTS—A category of contracts whose use is based on the establishment of a firm price to complete the required work. Includes: (1) firm-fixed price, (2) fixed price with escalation, (3) fixed price re-determinable, and (4) fixed price with incentive provisions contracts.

FIXED PRICE INCENTIVE (FPI) CONTRACT—A fixed price contract that provides for adjusting profit and establishing the final subcontract price according to a pre-established formula agreed to by the parties during negotiations. This type of subcontract will have a ceiling value beyond which the buyer will not reimburse the seller, but the seller is obligated to complete the subcontracted work.

FLEXIBLE PROGRESS PAYMENTS—A form of progress payments specifically authorized by the Defense FAR which takes into consideration the investment actually made by a contractor, and which generally exceeds the customary progress payment rate. Flexible progress payments must meet very precise requirements in order to be used.

FLYAWAY COSTS—The cost related to the production of a usable end item of military hardware. Flyaway cost includes the cost of procuring the basic unit (airframe, hull, chassis, etc.), a percentage of basic unit for changes allowance, propulsion equipment, electronics, armament, and other installed government-furnished equipment, and nonrecurring production costs. Flyaway costs equates to Rollaway and Sailaway costs.

FORWARD PRICING—Use of progressively escalated labor rates to convert direct labor hours to direct labor dollars and progressively escalated direct material and subcontract dollars to develop an escalated estimate. Contrasted with "constant dollar pricing", which uses a single un-escalated set of labor rates and does not escalate direct material and subcontract dollars to develop an un-escalated estimate.

FPI—*See* Fixed price incentive (FPI) contracts.

FUNCTIONAL DIVISION—Manufacturing, Engineering, Material, Business Management, Quality, etc.

FUNCTIONAL ORGANIZATION—An organization or group of organizations with a common operational orientation such as Quality Control, Engineering, or Turbine Area Engineer, Inspection, etc.

FUNDING PROFILE—An estimate of program funding requirements usually displayed in columnar spread sheet format by years, starting with previous year through the current year and out-years.

GANTT CHART—A simple graphical bar chart representation used as an aid in planning and scheduling, prepared by defining and drawing over a time scale when selected project tasks are to take place, updated as necessary to portray project status.

GENERAL AND ADMINISTRATIVE (G&A)—A form of indirect expenses incurred in the direction, control, and administration of the company (including selling expenses). These expenses are spread over the total direct and burden cost at a negotiated rate.

ICA—*See* the "Institute of Cost Analysis," or under the new organizational title of "Society of Cost Estimating and Analysis (SCEA)."

IDWA—*See* Interdivisional Work.

IMPLEMENTATION REVIEW/VISIT—An initial visit by selected members of the customer C/SCSC review team to a contractor's plant, to review the contractor's plans for implementing C/SCSC on a new contract. Such visits should take place within 30 days after contract award.

INCENTIVE TYPE CONTRACTS—Refer to a family of contracts which allow for recovery of costs and attainment of fee for the seller based on a negotiated formula. Incentive type subcontracts may be either fixed price with a ceiling, or cost reimbursable according to a formula, and are intended to reward the seller for outstanding performance.

INDEPENDENT COST ANALYSIS—An analysis of program cost estimates conducted by an impartial body disassociated from the management of the program.

INDEPENDENT COST ESTIMATE—An estimate of program cost developed outside normal advocacy channels by a team which generally includes representation from cost analysis, procurement, production management, engineering and program management.

INDEPENDENT GOVERNMENT COST ESTIMATE—An estimate of the cost for goods and/or estimate of services to be procured by contract. Such estimates are prepared by government personnel, i.e., independent of contractors.

INDIRECT COST—Resources expended which are not directly identified to any specific product or service.

INDIRECT COST POOLS—A grouping of indirect costs identified with two or more cost objectives but not specifically identified with any final cost objective.

INELIGIBLE—Means excluded from government contracting and subcontracting pursuant to statutory, executive order, or regulatory authority.

INSTITUTE OF COST ANALYSIS (ICA)—A professional organization dedicated to improving the effectiveness of cost and price analysis in government and industry. With the merger of the ICA with the National Estimating Society, the new title of Society of Cost Estimating and Analysis (SCEA) is appropriate.

INTERDIVISIONAL WORK—Any portion of a contract which is performed by another segment of the same company having overall responsibility for management of the prime contract. Commonly referred to as IDWA, Inter Divisional Work Authorization, and sometimes as IOTs, Inter-organizational Transfers.

INTERNAL REPLANNING—Replanning actions performed by the contractor for remaining effort within the scope of the budget that is remaining. The contractor is required to notify the government of all internal replanning actions.

IOT—*See* Interdivisional Work.

LABOR RATE VARIANCES—Difference between planned labor rates and actual labor rates. Labor rate variances are derived by subtracting from actual hours x planned rates, the actual hours x actual rates.

LABOR STANDARDS—A compilation of time study of standard time for each element of a given type of work.

LARGE BUSINESS—Any firm which is a significant contributor in its field and does not meet the definition of being a small business.

LATEST REVISED ESTIMATE (LRE)—*See* Estimate at Completion.

LETTER CONTRACT—A written preliminary contractual instrument that authorizes the immediate commencement of activity under its terms and conditions, pending definitization of a fixed-price or cost-reimbursement pricing arrangement for the work to be done. The contract must specify the maximum liability of the buyer and be superseded by a definitive contract within a specified period, not to exceed 180 days or 40% of authorized funds, whichever comes first. These agreements are not to be used except where a written determination is made that no other type of contract is suitable.

LEVEL OF EFFORT (LOE)—Work that does not result in a final product, e.g., liaison, coordination, follow-up, or other support activities, and which cannot be effectively associated with a definable end product process result. It is measured only in terms of resources actually consumed within a given time period.

LIQUIDATION OF PROGRESS PAYMENTS—The formal process of repaying a progress payment loan by the allocation of a specific percentage, as defined in the FAR, of the value of a contract line-item's unit price with each delivery. Contractors begin with an ordinary liquidation rate, and may go to a more attractive alternate liquidation rate if their performance so warrants the change.

LIQUIDATION RATE—The specific rate defined by the FAR for the repayment of progress payment loans by a supplier.

LOE—*See* Level of Effort.

LOSS CONTRACTS—Any contract or subcontract in which the costs incurred to date, plus the estimated costs to complete the effort will exceed either the contract price, or the contract ceiling on an incentive type contract, is considered a "loss contract."

LOSS RATIO FACTOR—The amount defined in the FAR by which the buyer is obligated to reduce progress payments made and to be made to a supplier. The loss ratio factor reduces the progress payment rate by the percentage value which the estimate at completion will exceed the value of the contract price, or ceiling on an incentive type contract.

MAKE OR BUY—The classification of components on a contract as to whether they will be produced by the contractor (Make) or obtained from an outside source (Buy).

MANAGEMENT CONTROL SYSTEMS—The planning, scheduling, budgeting, estimating, work authorization, cost accumulation, performance measuring, etc., systems used by a contractor to plan and to control the cost and scheduling of work.

MANAGEMENT RESERVE (MR)—A portion of the Contract Budget Base that is held for management control purposes by the contractor to cover the expense of unanticipated program requirements. It is not a part of the Performance Measurement Baseline.

MANAGEMENT RESERVE BUDGET—*See* Management Reserve (MR).

MANUFACTURING RESOURCE PLANNING (MRP II)—A method for the effective planning of all resources of a manufacturing company. Ideally, it addresses operational planning in units, financial planning in dollars, and has simulation capability to answer "what if" questions. It is made up of a variety of functions, each linked together: business planning, production planning, master production scheduling, material requirements planning (MRP), capacity requirements planning, and the execution support systems for capacity and material. Output from these systems would be integrated with financial reports such as the business plan, purchase commitment report, shipping budget, inventory projections in dollars, etc. Manufacturing Resource Planning (MRP II) is a direct outgrowth and extension of closed-loop MRP, Material Requirements Planning.

MASTER PROGRAM SCHEDULE (MPS)—The highest summary level schedule for a major program depicting overall program phasing and all major interfaces, contractual milestones, and program elements.

MATERIAL—Property which may be incorporated into or attached to an end item to be delivered under a contract or which may be consumed or expended in the performance of a contract. It includes, but is not limited to raw and processed material, parts, components, assemblies, fuels and lubricants and small tools and supplies which may be consumed in normal use in the performance of a contract.

MATERIAL REQUIREMENTS PLANNING (MRP)—A set of techniques which uses bills of material, inventory data and the master production schedule to calculate requirements for materials. It makes recommendations to release replenishment orders for material. Further, since it is time-phased, it makes recommendations to reschedule open orders when due dates and need dates are not in phase. Originally seen as merely a better way to order inventory, today it is thought of as primarily a scheduling technique, i.e., a method for establishing and maintaining valid due dates on orders.

MATERIAL REVIEW BOARD (MRB)—A joint contractor/government board established to review the disposition of nonconforming supplies that are referred to it for disposition.

MEMORANDUM OF AGREEMENT (MOA)—A document which establishes mutual agreement between the cognizant on-site agency and the government program offices in order to ensure adequate surveillance. The MOA delineates the responsibilities of both the procuring agency and the cognizant government office and should be explicit as to surveillance activities, frequency of audits and reports, depth and detail of analysis, notification of deficiencies and other special problems that may be unique to that contract.

MEMORANDUM OF UNDERSTANDING (MOU)—A document between the DOD procuring activity concerned and the contractor regarding the implementation and maintenance of its management control systems. The MOU clarifies the intent of the contractor and the DOD components relative to implantation of the criteria and its application on a plant-wide basis for all contractual activities in that facility.

METHODS OF PROCUREMENT—The procedures followed to translate requirements into contracts. The Government uses two major methods of procurement: competitive and other than competitive. Competitive procedures may be sealed bidding or competitive proposals. Other than competitive procedures are used in accordance with statutory authorities.

MIDPOINT PRICING—The use of a set of rates that are the average of a specific time period in lieu of progressively escalated rates to develop an escalated price estimate.

MILESTONE—An event, usually of particular importance, i.e., a big event.

MOA—*See* Memorandum of Agreement.

MOU—*See* Memorandum of Understanding.

MPS—*See* Master Program Schedule.

MR—*See* Management Reserve.

MRP—*See* Material Requirements Planning.

MRP II—*See* Manufacturing Resource Planning.

MULTIYEAR PROCUREMENT—A method of competitively purchasing up to five year's requirements in one contract which is funded annually as appropriations permit. If necessary to cancel the remaining quantities in any year, the contractor is paid an agreed-upon portion of the unamortized nonrecurring start-up costs.

NATIONAL ASSOCIATION OF PURCHASING MANAGEMENT—A professional/educational organization founded in 1915 to provide national and international leadership in purchasing and materials management research and education.

NATIONAL CONTRACT MANAGEMENT ASSOCIATION (NCMA)—A professional organization devoted to fostering the advancement of professionalism in contract management.

NCMA—*See* National Contract Management Association.

NEGOTIATED CONTRACT COST—The estimated cost negotiated in a Cost-Plus-Fixed-Fee Contract or the negotiated contract target cost in either a Fixed Price-Incentive Contract or a Cost-Plus-Incentive-Fee Contract. *See also* Contract Target Cost.

NEGOTIATION—Contracting through the use of either competitive or other-than-competitive proposals and discussions. Any contract awarded without using sealed bidding procedures is a negotiated contract.

NEGOTIATION OBJECTIVES—A range of goals, including desired costs or prices, which buyer analysis indicates as the limits within which fair and reasonable contract provisions can be negotiated. These objectives should summarize all buyer positions and assumptions relevant to price and other factors.

NETWORK—A logic flow diagram in a prescribed format consisting of the activities and events which must be accomplished to reach program objectives, which show their planned sequence and interrelationships.

NONRECURRING COSTS—Expenditures against specific tasks that are expected to occur only once on a given program. Examples are such items as preliminary design effort, qualification testing, initial tooling and planning, etc.

OBJECTIVE INDICATOR—*See* Discrete Milestone.

OBS—*See* Organizational Breakdown Structure.

ODC—*See* Other Direct Costs.

OFFER—A response to a solicitation that, if accepted, would bind the offeror to perform the resultant contract.

OFF THE SHELF—Procurement of existing systems or equipment without an RDT&E program or with minor development to make a system suitable for DOD or contractor needs. May be a commercial system/equipment or one already in inventory.

OPTION—A contract clause permitting an increase in the quantity of supplies beyond that originally stipulated or an extension in the time for which services on a time basis may be required.

ORDINARY LIQUIDATION RATE—The repayment or liquidation rate at which progress payment loans will be reduced through the delivery of contractual articles, and the allocation of some portion of the unit price for the abatement of the loan. The ordinary liquidation rate will be used to start all progress payment agreements and will match the customary progress payment rate as a percentage value.

ORGANIZATIONAL BREAKDOWN STRUCTURE (OBS)—A functionally oriented pyramid-like structure indicating organizational relationships and used as the framework for the assignment of work responsibilities. The highest level of the OBS is the top level of management for a weapon system. The organizational structure is progressively detailed downward to the lowest level of management. The OBS relates to the WBS in that compatible or corresponding levels of each structure normally have similar degrees of authority and work responsibility.

ORIGINAL BUDGET—The budget established at or near the time the contract was signed, based on the negotiated contract cost.

OTB—*See* Over Target Baseline.

OTHER DIRECT COSTS (ODC)—A group of accounting elements which can be isolated to specific tasks, other than labor and material. Included in ODC are such items as travel, computer time, and services.

OVER TARGET BASELINE (OTB)—A baseline which results from formal reprogramming with the approval of the customer.

OVERHEAD—Costs incurred in the operation of a business which cannot be directly related to the individual products or services being produced. *See also* Indirect Cost.

OVERRUN—Costs incurred in excess of the contract target cost on an incentive contract, or the estimated cost on a fixed fee contract.

PAR—*See* Problem Analysis Report.

PARAMETRIC COST ESTIMATE—A cost estimating methodology using statistical relationships between historical costs and other program variables such as system physical or performance characteristics, contractor output measures, manpower loading, etc. Also referred to as a "top-down" estimating approach.

PCO—Sometimes referring to the "Procurement Contracting Officer." *See also* Principal Contracting Officer.

PD—*See* Program Directive.

PERFORMANCE MANAGEMENT ASSOCIATION (PMA)—A professional organization dedicated to promoting high standards in performance measurement, with particular emphasis on C/SCSC.

PERFORMANCE MEASUREMENT BASELINE (PMB)—The time-phased budget plan against which project performance is measured. It is formed by the budgets assigned to scheduled cost accounts and the applicable indirect budgets. For future effort, not planned to the cost account level, the Performance Measurement Baseline also included budgets assigned to higher level CWBS elements. The PMB equals the total allocated budget less management reserve.

PERFORMING ORGANIZATION—The organizational element expending resources to accomplish a task.

PERIOD OF PERFORMANCE—The time interval of contract performance that includes the effort required to achieve all significant contractual schedule milestones.

PLANNING ACCOUNT—Tasks which have been detailed to the greatest extent practicable, but which cannot yet be subdivided into detailed tasks. Planning accounts can exist at any level above the task level.

PLANNING PACKAGE—A logical aggregation of far term work within a cost account that can be identified and budgeted but not yet defined into work packages. Planning packages are identified during the initial baseline planning to establish the time phasing of the major activities within a cost account and the quantity of the resources required for their performance. Planning packages are placed into work packages consistent with the rolling wave concept prior to the performance of the work.

PM—*See* Program/Project Manager.

PMA—*See* Performance Management Association.

PMB—*See* Performance Measurement Baseline.

PMI—*See* Project Management Institute.

PO—*See* Purchase Order.

PREPROPOSAL CONFERENCE—In negotiated procurements, a meeting held with potential contractors a few days after RFPs have been sent out, to promote uniform interpretation of work statements and specifications by all prospective contractors. *See also* Bidders Conference.

PRICE ANALYSIS—The process of examining and evaluating a prospective price without evaluation of the separate cost elements and profit of the individual offeror whose price is being evaluated. It may be accomplished by a comparison of submitted quotations, a comparison of quotations with market prices of the same or similar items, a comparison of price quotations and contract prices with past prices or current quotations for the same or similar items, the use of yardsticks (dollars per pound), or a comparison of proposed prices with independently developed buyer estimates.

PRICE NEGOTIATION MEMORANDUM—The document that defines the results of the negotiation. It is a permanent record of the decisions the negotiator made in settling a price for the work to be done.

PRICING—The process of establishing the amount or amounts to be received or paid in return for providing goods and performing services.

PRINCIPAL CONTRACTING OFFICER (PCO)—Sometimes referred to as the "Procuring Contracting Officer" or "Procurement Contracting Officer." The Government PCO is sole individual responsible for negotiation of the initial contract and the signing of the actual contractual document(s). Administration of the contract after award may be delegated to an ACO.

PRIVITY OF CONTRACT—The legal relationship between two parties of the same contract. The government has "privity of contract" with the prime contractor. The prime contractor has "privity of contract" with the subcontractor. Therefore, the government's relationship with subcontractors is indirect in nature. Government involvement with subcontractors is channeled through prime contractor directed activities: only the prime contractor is authorized to direct the subcontractor.

PROBLEM ANALYSIS REPORT (PAR)—A report made by the responsible manager to explain a significant cost/schedule variance, its probable impact on the program, and the corrective actions taken to resolve the problem.

PROCUREMENT—The process by which an organization acquires resources from which it will produce finished products.

PROCUREMENT OR PROCURING CONTRACTING OFFICER (PCO)—*See* Principal Contracting Officer.

PROCUREMENT PLAN—A description that sets the policy on dealing with subcontractors and details competitive bidding and management procedures at subcontractors' facilities.

PROCUREMENT REVIEW BOARD—A broad based management committee which approves major purchases of a certain value, prior to the placement of the subcontract.

PROFIT—Generally characterized as the basic motive of a business enterprise; on occasion referred to as the "wages of risk." In contract pricing, profit represents a projected or known monetary excess realized by a producer or performer after the deduction of cost incurred, direct and indirect, or to be incurred in the performance of a job, task, or a series of the same.

PROGRAM DIRECTIVE (PD)—A document which gives specific contract operational instructions. A PD may be issued to inform functional organizations of program requirements, selected control system options, place responsibilities, direct corrective actions, and to authorize or limit lines of authority. Often PDs are of a limited, short-term duration, but if they are of a permanent nature, are frequently superseded by regular company procedures.

PROGRAM (PROJECT) MANAGER (PM)—The person assigned the prime responsibility for overall management of a program.

PROGRAM RISK ANALYSIS—The system that provides a continuous analysis of identified risks, with respect to their impact on program cost, schedule, and technical performance.

PROGRESS PAYMENTS—Payments made to a contractor during the life of a fixed-price type contract on the basis of a percentage of total eligible costs incurred.

PROJECT—(1) Synonymous with the term "program" in general usage. (2) A planned undertaking having a finite beginning and ending, involving definition, development, production, and logistics support of a system or systems. A project may be the whole or part of a program. (3) Any series of homogenous tasks which have a specific objective, a definite start and stop date, and funding limitations which are consumed and may constrain project activities.

PROJECT MANAGEMENT INSTITUTE (PMI)—A nonprofit professional organization dedicated to advancing the state of the art in project management.

PROJECT MANAGER—An official who has been assigned responsibility for accomplishing a specifically designed unit of work effort or group of closely related efforts established to achieve stated or designated objectives, defined tasks, or other units of related effort on a schedule for performing the stated work funded as part of the project. The project manager is responsible for the planning, implementing, controlling, and reporting on a project.

PURCHASE ORDER (PO)—An order issued by a functional organization (usually material) to purchase any parts from a source outside the prime contractor.

PURCHASED LABOR—A type of labor used to relieve shop overload and/or to take advantage of special processing skills or fabricating facilities possessed by a supplier.

QUALITY—The composite of material attributes including performance features and characteristics of a product or service to satisfy a given need.

QUALITY PROGRAM—A program which is developed, planned, and managed to carry out, cost-effectively, all efforts to effect the quality of material and services from concept through validation, full-scale development, production, deployment, and disposal.

RATE COST CURVES—A mathematical way of explaining and measuring the impact of changing production rates on a program's total cost.

RAW MATERIALS—Includes raw and processed material in a form or state that requires further processing.

RDT&E—Research, Development, Test & Evaluation (also R&D).

READINESS ASSESSMENT—A meeting or series of meetings by selected members of the customer C/SCSC review team to a contractor's plant, to review contractor plans and progress in implementing C/SCSC in preparation for a full demonstration review. Such visits are expected to happen about 30 days after the initial implementation review/visit, or about 60 days after contract award.

REALIZATION FACTOR—The ratio of actual performance time to standard performance time, usually expressed as a decimal number.

REASONABLE COST—A cost is reasonable if, in its nature or amount, it does not exceed what would be incurred by an ordinarily prudent person in the conduct of competitive business.

RECURRING COSTS—Expenditures against specific tasks that would occur on a repetitive basis. Examples are sustaining engineering, production of operational equipment, tool maintenance, etc.

REPLANNING—A change in the original plan for accomplishing authorized contractual requirements; there are two types of replanning effort: (1) *Internal Replanning*. A change in the original plan that remains with in the scope of the authorized contract. It is caused by a need on the part of the contractor to compensate for cost, schedule, or technical problems which have made the original plan unrealistic. (2) *External Replanning*. Government directed changes to the contract can be in the form of a definitized change order or an unpriced change order that calls for a change in the original plan. While this change may remain within the scope of the original contract it most often exists as a change in the scope of the contract in terms of cost, schedule, technical parameter or a combination thereof.

REPROGRAMMING—A comprehensive replanning of the effort remaining in the contract resulting in a revised total allocated budget which may exceed the current contract budget base.

REQUEST FOR PROPOSAL (RFP)—An official procurement document that requests proposals from potential contractors.

REQUEST FOR QUOTE (RFQ)—An official document requesting a cost estimate for the performance of work.

RESPONSIBLE ORGANIZATION—A defined unit within the contractor's organization structure which is assigned responsibility for accomplishing specific tasks.

RFP—*See* Request for Proposal.

RFQ—*See* Request for Quote.

RISK—That level of uncertainty at which a decision maker knows the possible results of an action or no action, and can attach subjective probabilities to them.

RISK ANALYSIS—An examination of risk areas or tasks to determine options and the probable consequences for each task in the analysis.

RISK ASSESSMENT—The process of subjectively determining the probability that a specific interplay of technical performance, schedule, and costs as objectives, will or will not be attained along the planned course of action.

RISK MANAGEMENT—The process of identifying areas of risk that can affect the successful development of a system, and taking actions to close, or at least reduce the risk(s) to acceptable levels.

ROLLING WAVE CONCEPT—The progressive refinement of detailed of work definition by continuous subdivision of downstream activities into near-term tasks.

RUBBER BASELINING—An attempt by a contractor to take far-term budget baseline and move it into the current period in an attempt to disguise current cost problems. The attempt will be to move budget without a corresponding equal amount of work tasks, to cover current cost difficulties. It is an indicator of a likely overrun condition.

SAR—*See* Subsequent Application Review and/or "Selected Acquisition Report.

SCEA—*See* Society of Cost Estimating and Analysis.

SCHEDULE—A time plan of goals or targets which serve as the focal point for management actions.

SCHEDULE VARIANCE (SV)—The numerical difference between Earned Value (BCWP) and the Budget Plan (BCWS).

SCHEDULING—The act of preparing and/ or implementing schedules.

SEAC—*See* Statistical Estimate at Completion.

SEALED BID—A method of contracting that uses competitive bids, public opening of bids, and awards. A latter-day version of what used to be known as formal advertising, similar to but not the same as that method. Shares equal billing with competitive proposals.

SECOND SOURCE—Execution of established acquisition strategy to qualify two competitive producers for part or the entire system.

SELECTED ACQUISITION REPORTS (SAR)—Standard, comprehensive, summary status reports on DOD systems for management within the DOD. Required for periodic submission to the Congress, in accordance with DODI 7000.3.

SHOULD-COST ESTIMATE—An estimate of contract price which reflects reasonably achievable economy and efficiency. Its purpose is to develop a realistic price objective for negotiation purposes.

SHOW CAUSE LETTER—A written delinquency notice informing a contractor of a failure to perform within the terms of the contract and advising that the buyer is considering a termination for default, but affording the supplier the opportunity to show cause why the contract should not be terminated.

SIGNIFICANT VARIANCES—Those differences between planned and actual performance which require further review, analysis, or action. Appropriate thresholds should be established as to the magnitude of variances which will require variance analysis.

SMALL BUSINESS—A business, including its affiliates, which is independently owned and operated and is not dominant in its field of operation. Such firms typically receive preferred treatment in contracting matters.

SMALL DISADVANTAGED BUSINESS—A small business concern that is at least 51 percent unconditionally owned by one or more individuals who are both socially and economically disadvantaged, or a publicly owned business that has at least 51 percent of its stock unconditionally owned by one or more socially and economically disadvantaged individuals and that has its management and daily business controlled by one or more such individuals, which definition also includes economically disadvantaged Indian tribe or Native Hawaiian Organizations.

SOCIETY OF COST ESTIMATING AND ANALYSIS (SCEA)—A professional organization dedicated to improving the effectiveness of cost and price analysis in government and industry. SCEA represents a merger of the Institute of Cost Analysis (ICA) with the National Estimating Society.

SOLE SOURCE—Characterized as the one and only source regardless of the marketplace, possessing a unique and singularly available performance capability for the purpose of contract award. Sometimes also called "single source."

SOLICITATION—In contracting, the term means to go out to prospective bidders and request their response to a proposal.

SOURCE SELECTION—The process wherein the requirements, facts, recommendations and government policy relevant to an award decision in a competitive procurement of a system/project are examined and the decision made.

SOURCE SELECTION BOARD—A group of personnel representing various functional and technical areas involved in a procurement appointed by the source selection advisory council to direct, control, and perform the evaluation of proposals responsive to requirements, and to produce summary facts and findings required in the source selection process.

SOW—*See* Statement of Work.

SPECIAL TOOLING—All jigs, dies, fixtures, molds, patterns, tapes, gauges, other equipment and manufacturing aids, and replacements thereof, which are of such a specialized nature that, without substantial modification or alteration, their use is limited to the development of production of particular supplies or parts thereof, or the performance of particular services. The term includes all components of such items but does not include: (1) consumable property; (2) special test equipment; or (3) buildings, nonseverable structures, general or special machine tools, or similar capital items.

SPO—*See* System Program Office.

STANDARD—A term applied in work measurement to any established or accepted rule, model, or criterion against which comparisons are made.

STANDARD COST—The normal expected cost of an operation, process, or product including labor, material, and overhead charges, computed on the basis of past performance costs, estimates, or work measurement.

STANDARD TIME—The amount of time allowed for the performance of a specific unit of work.

STATEMENT OF WORK (SOW)—A description of a product or services to be procured under a contract; a statement of requirements.

STATISTICAL ESTIMATE AT COMPLETION (SEAC)—A statistically computed forecast based on performance to date and the mathematical projection of this performance to derive the estimated contract cost value by the BCWP cost performance index.

SUBCONTRACT—A contractual document which defines the effort of providing hardware, software, services, data, parts, components, assemblies or other items which one company (supplier) commits to perform for another company (buyer).

SUBCONTRACT MANAGEMENT—The process of issuing, managing, controlling and administering subcontracts between a prime and a next tier subcontractor.

SUBCONTRACT AND PURCHASING MANAGEMENT—The process of planning, directing, monitoring, and controlling the source selection with requests by the program manager. Included in the process of planning, directing, and controlling of subcontract activities are also RFP transmittal, proposal evaluation, and subcontract negotiation and administration.

SUBSEQUENT APPLICATION REVIEW (SAR)—A visit by government personnel (and/or prime contractor and/or both) to a contractor's facility to determine whether the contractor has properly applied the management control system which had been previously accepted as meeting the requirements of C/SCSC, to a *new contract*.

SUPPLEMENTAL AGREEMENT—Bilateral written amendment to a contract by which the parties settle price and/or performance adjustments to the basic contract.

SURVEILLANCE—A term used in C/SCSC to mean the monitoring of continued compliance with an approved/validated management control system.

SURVEILLANCE MONITOR—The individual in the CAO who is responsible for coordinating C/SCSC surveillance functions with other members of the CAO organization and with the auditor to assure that the surveillance objectives are accomplished.

SUSPENSION—Actions taken to disqualify a contractor temporarily from Government contracting and Government approved subcontracting. A contractor so designated is termed "suspended."

SUSPENSION OF PROGRESS PAYMENTS—The act of halting the further processing of progress payments to a contractor. Such actions may be temporary or permanent, or may also require the repayment of prior funds, or the increase in the liquidation rate of prior payments.

SV—*See* Schedule Variance.

SYSTEM PROGRAM OFFICE (SPO)—A term used by the Department of Defense to designate the office of the program manager, comprised of technical, business, and administrative personnel assigned full-time to support the program manager. It is the single point of contact with industry, Government agencies and other activities participating in the system acquisition process.

TARGET COST—*See* Contract Target Cost and/or Contract Budget Base.

TCPI—*See* To Complete Performance Index.

THRESHOLDS—Monetary, time, or resource points, placed on something, which are used as a guideline, which if breached, cause some type of management review to happen.

TO COMPLETE PERFORMANCE INDEX (TCPI)—The projected value to be earned for every measurable unit to be expended in the future.

TOTAL ALLOCATED BUDGET (TAB)—The sum of all budgets allocated to a contract. Total allocated budget consists of the performance measurement baseline and all management reserve. The total allocated budget will reconcile directly to the contract budget base.

TRUTH IN NEGOTIATIONS—The law which created the requirement for the submission and certification in writing of cost or pricing data as to its accuracy, completeness, and currency for the award of any negotiated contract expected to exceed $100,000. Certain exemptions apply that are tied to adequate price competition or other conditions which reflect a competitive marketplace.

UB—*See* Undistributed Budget.

UNDISTRIBUTED BUDGET (UB)—Budget applicable to contract effort which has not yet been identified to CWBS elements at or below the lowest level of reporting to the government.

UNIT COST—Total labor, material, and overhead cost for one unit of production, i.e., one part, one gallon, one pound, etc.

UNPRICED CHANGES—Authorized but unnegotiated changes to the contract.

UNSOLICITED PROPOSALS—A proposal that is made to a buyer by a contractor without prior formal or informal solicitation from the buyer.

UNUSUAL PROGRESS PAYMENTS—Any progress payments in which the rate differs from the rates authorized by the FAR. Such unusual progress payments require the specific approval of the Government Contracting Officer in order to be reimbursed by the Government.

USAGE—The number of units or dollars of an inventory item consumed over a period of time.

VALIDATION—A term used in C/SCSC to mean "approval" or compliance with the criteria.

VALUE ANALYSIS—A systematic and objective evaluation of the function of a product and its related cost. The analysis evaluates the product characteristics in terms of aesthetics, utility, and demand. As a pricing tool, value analysis provides insight into inherent worth of a product.

VARIABLE COST—A cost that changes with the production quantity or the performance of services. This contrasts with fixed costs that do not change with production quantity or services performed.

VARIANCE—The difference between the expected/budgeted/planned and the actual results.

VARIANCE AT COMPLETION (VAC)—Variance at Completion is the algebraic difference between Budget at Completion and Estimate at Completion (VAC = BAC – EAC).

VARIANCE THRESHOLD—The amount of variance beyond which a Problem Analysis Report is required, as agreed to between the contractor and the customer. Variance parameters will differ depending on the function, level and stage of the project.

WAIVER—(1) Specifications: a written authorization to accept a configuration item of other designated items, which during production or after having been submitted for inspection, are found to depart from specified requirements, but nevertheless are considered suitable "as is" or after rework by an approved method. (2) Decision not to require certain criteria to be met for certain reasons.

WBS—*See* Work Breakdown Structure.

WEIGHTED GUIDELINES—A technique for developing fee and profit negotiation objectives, within percentage ranges established by regulation.

WHAT IF ANALYSIS—The process of evaluating alternative strategies.

WORK BREAKDOWN STRUCTURE (WBS)—The WBS is a product-oriented family tree division of hardware, software, services and program unique tasks which organizes, defines, and graphically displays the product to be produced, as well as the work to be accomplished to achieve the specified product. There are several types of WBSs, including these two major categories: (1) *Project Summary WBS (PSWBS)*. A summary WBS tailored to a specific defense material item by selecting applicable elements from one or more summary WBSs or by adding equivalent elements unique to the project in accordance with government defined WBS requirements. (2) *Contract WBS (CWBS)*. The complete WBS for a contract, developed and used by a contractor within the guidelines of government defined WBS requirements and the contract statement of work.

WORK BREAKDOWN STRUCTURE DICTIONARY—A document which describes the tasks of WBS elements in product-oriented terms, and relates each element to the direct cost charging practices of the program.

WORK BREAKDOWN STRUCTURE ELEMENT—A discrete portion of a WBS. A WBS element may be an identifiable product, a set of data, or a service.

WORK PACKAGE BUDGETS—Resources which are formally assigned by the contractor to accomplish a work package, expressed in dollars, hours, standards, or other definitive units.

WORK PACKAGES (WP)—Detailed short-span jobs, or material items, identified by the contractor for accomplishing work required to complete a contract.

WP—*See* Work Packages.

Appendix B

An Unofficial Restatement of the FAR & DOD-FAR Covering Progress Payments

FAR SUBPART 32.5, PROGRESS PAYMENTS BASED ON COSTS

This section contains the Government's broad policy and procedural statement on the use of progress payments.

32.500 Scope of subject: exclusions from this subpart section are payments made under cost reimbursement contracts, and contracts for construction or shipbuilding or ship conversion which often provide for progress payments based on a percentage or on the stage of construction of the project.

32.501 General: progress payments may be of two types, customary or unusual, as defined below.

32.501-1 Customary progress payment rates: the customary progress payment rate under FAR is currently set at 80 percent for a large business and 85 percent for small businesses. The DOD is authorized to establish their own customary rates for foreign military sales and flexible progress payments, which may differ from the FAR rates. (Note of caution: progress payment rates will differ from period to period, and only the current rate authorized under a specific contract should be used.)

Any rates set higher than the current authorized customary rate is considered an "unusual progress payment," and is covered in the next section. Contractors, prime and subordinate, may not exceed the authorized customary progress payment rate without first obtaining specific approval of the Government. (Note of caution: the unauthorized issuance of an unusual progress payment could cause a major disruption in the cash-flow of a contractor, and should never be allowed under any circumstances, without first obtaining approval from the Government.)

Sometimes a combination of advance payments and progress payments are authorized under the same contract, in which case the customary progress payment rate may not be exceeded.

Under the Defense Procurement Improvement Act of 1986, progress payments are limited to 80 percent of work accomplished for undefinitized work. A higher rate for unusual progress payments or flexible progress payments is not allowed for undefinitized work.

32.501-2 Unusual progress payments: prime contractors have no authority to authorize unusual progress payments on their own, and must obtain prior approval from the Government contracting officer, who will insist on three requirements being met.

First, the supplier must demonstrate that it will experience large pre-delivery expenditures in relation to their total contract price, and such expenditures will impact their working capital and credits. Second, the supplier must document their actual need to supplement their private financing with unusual progress payments. Lastly, the contractor request must be approved by both the head of the Government contracting activity, and the Government finance office, per 32.502-2.

Additionally, the excess of unusual rates over customary rates must be kept to a minimum, and progress payments are not to be considered unusual, merely because they are issued on letter contracts, or definitive contracts superseding letter contracts.

32.501-3 Contract price: for the purpose of making progress payments and determining the limitation of progress payments, the following rules apply in establishing the subcontract price.

	The Subcontract Type:	The Subcontract Price:
(1)	Firm-fixed price contracts	is the current contract price, plus authorized but unpriced modifications, which have been funded by the buyer.
(2)	Fixed-price redeterminable or economic price adjustment	is the initial price until modified.
(3)	Fixed-price incentive	is the target price plus unpriced modifications; however, the buyer may provisionally increase the price up to the ceiling or maximum price if the supplier properly incurred such costs.
(4)	Letter subcontracts	is the maximum amount obligated by the contract as modified.
(5)	Unpriced orders under basic ordering agreements	is the maximum amount obligated by the contract as modified.
(6)	Any portion of a contract which allows reimbursement of costs only (a cost type)	is excluded from the subcontract price for purposes of progress payment billings.

The Government contracting officer, and therefore the prime contractor's buyer, may not make progress payments or increase the subcontract price beyond that which has been obligated for the prime contract, as amended.

32.501-4 Consideration for progress payments: the Government does not require a separate consideration for the granting of progress payments, provided that the resulting initial contract or subcontract anticipated the incorporation of such provisions at the time of award. If however, the contract was consummated, and then as an after thought, the supplier requests that progress payments be incorporated into the contract, then the buyer must obtain adequate new consideration from the seller. (Note: DOD subcontracts which are initially negotiated with a customary progress payment rate, which are later requested for flexible progress payments, are now required to provide a new consideration in order to go to flexible rates per a DOD-FAR change in December, 1990).

Adequate new consideration can be either monetary or nonmonetary in form. Monetary means is simply a reduction in the original contract price, to compensate for the new progress payment provisions. Nonmonetary means is the incorporation of more favorable contract terms to the buyer. The Government is clear that it expects any nonmonetary consideration to approximate to the extent practicable, the dollar value that the original contract price would have been less, had progress payments been included into the initial award.

Criteria for determining the adequacy of new consideration is the dollar value of benefits to the seller, from reduced financial costs on its equivalent working capital. Also acceptable as consideration, is the estimated profit rates that the seller will experience through the use of the new progress payments. However, the Government will not allow for the costs of interest to be a part of any such consideration estimates.

32.501-5 Other protective terms: the Government reserves the right to require sellers to provide additional protective terms, in addition to those protections covered in progress payment provisions. These terms may take any of the following forms:

(a) Personal or corporate guarantees.

(b) Subordinations or standbys of indebtedness.

(c) Special bank accounts.

(d) Protective covenants of the type required for the protection of advanced payments, which are covered under FAR 52.232.12, (p), which restricts the seller from altering its assets, without specific advance approval of the Government.

32.502 Preaward matters: these sections contain those matters which typically will concern the buyers prior to subcontract award.

32.502-1 Use of customary progress payments: the Government requires the inclusion of a progress payment clause in both the solicitation and any resulting award of contracts which contain progress payments. If a seller responds to a solicitation which did not contain a provision for progress payments, and their response was conditional upon receiving progress payments, then that supplier's response shall be rejected as non-responsive.

Buyers may provide for customary progress payments if: (1) the period of performance from contract award and work begins to first delivery is in excess of 4 months for a small business, and 6 months for all others, (2) such seller expenditures prior to delivery will have a significant impact of their working capital. Sellers may demonstrate a special circumstance to justify progress payments, particularly for a small business.

To reduce the administrative burden, progress payments should generally only be included in contracts which exceed $1,000,000 in value for a large business, or $100,000 for a small business.

Buyers may combine multiple orders running concurrently from the same supplier to meet the minimum dollar threshold. Normally, progress payments are not to be used on commercially available items, where adverse impacts on the seller's working capital cannot be demonstrated.

A single liquidation rate should be established for multiple orders combining to qualify for progress payments.

32.502-2 Contract finance office clearance: the Government's contracting officer (and therefore the private contractor's buyer) may not take any the following actions without first obtaining the approval of the Government's finance office:

(a) Providing progress payments at a rate higher than the current authorized customary rate.

(b) Deviating from the progress payment terms contained in this FAR section.

(c) Giving progress payments to a supplier whose financial condition is in doubt; who has had a request for advance payment or loan guarantee denied for financial reasons; or who is on the Government's "Hold-up List."

32.502-3 Solicitation provisions: the buyer shall insert the FAR clause 52.232-13, "Notice of Progress Payments" in all requests for proposals and invitations for bids, in which a progress payment clause is expected to be included in any resulting award.

However, the buyer may restrict progress payments to small business concerns only, under authority of FAR 32.101. In such cases the buyer will reference FAR clause 52.232-14, "Notice of Availability of Progress Payments Exclusively for Small Business Concerns." This would restrict progress payments to small business concerns only, although both large and small business firms would be expected to respond to the solicitation.

If no progress payments are anticipated, then the buyer will reference FAR clause 52.232-15, "Progress Payments Not Included."

32.502-4 Contract clauses: the buyer will incorporate FAR clause 52.232-16, "Progress Payments," in any solicitation and resulting contract in which progress payments are included.

In those cases where the supplier is a small business concern, the buyer will incorporate 52.232-16, and also include the Alternate I sections, intended for small business firms only. (Note: DOD-FAR may have different rules covering small business and small minority businesses, so one should always refer to the DOD-FAR when dealing with defense subcontracts).

Should the use of progress payments be started prior to definitization, the buyer will incorporate 52.232-16, and include Alternate II sections, which apply to progress payments under letter contract conditions.

In those situations in which it may be advisable to allow for a separate progress payment rate for various sections of a given contract, in which the contract may be severable and accounted for separately, the terms of such agreements must be clearly described in the language of the contractual document. In these situations, separate progress payment requests and invoices must be submitted to maintain segregated accounting for the various rates.

32.503 Postaward matters: these sections contain those matters which typically will concern the buyers subsequent to the subcontract award. Certain issues however, such as the review of the supplier's accounting system and controls, as required by FAR section 32.503-3, would likely occur prior to the contract award.

32.503-1 Contractor requests: all requests for progress payments shall be submitted on FAR Standard Form 1443, "Contractor Request for Progress Payment." The form must be completed in accordance with the instructions on the reverse side of SF 1443, and all related terms of the contract. The supplier must include any related supplemental information as reasonable requested by the buyer.

32.503-2 Supervision of progress payments: progress payments must be supervised by the buyer, either by a "prepayment review or periodic review," depending upon the circumstances of a particular contract and the financial conditions of a given supplier. Several factors must be considered by the buyer, with an overall view of protecting the best interests of the prime contractor and ultimately the Government.

Issues to be considered are the past experience with the supplier, their performance record, reliability, quality of work, quality of management, financial condition, accounting methods and controls, etc. Circumstances external to a given contract must be included in any evaluation, including indirect cost problems, since external factors can frequently affect the supplier's ability to fully liquidate progress payment loans.

The degree of required supervision will vary by contract, depending upon the particular conditions at the time.

32.503-3 Initiation of progress payments and review of accounting system: before making an award which will include progress payments, the buyer is obligated to determine prior to subcontract award that the supplier will be capable of fully liquidating such progress payment loans, and has an adequate accounting system and controls in place.

This determination is typically done by having recent experience with the supplier, and/or by a pre-award audit, performed by the buyer's firm, or by the Government, within the previous 12 months. Use of Government audit branches and recent reports is encouraged to the greatest extent practicable.

32.503-4 Approval of progress payment requests: if it has been established through a recent audit or other reliable means, that the supplier has an adequate accounting system and financial controls in place, the buyer *may* approve the progress payment requests based on the "certification" given by the supplier on the face of the SF 1443. Thus a buyer may pay a given invoice first, including the initial request, and then review the invoice after payment.

However, two conditions must be met: there should have been a prior recent audit/verification of the firm, and there will be no known adverse conditions which could affect the ability of the supplier to fully liquidate the progress payment loans.

The buyer should not routinely request audits of a supplier, unless there is reason to question the certified amounts, or there is some reason to have concern that a loss is probable.

If a given supplier has submitted an invoice, in which part of it appears to be proper, but another part may be in question, the buyer should approve for payment that portion of the request which appears to be proper. A full invoice should not be withheld pending a resolution of the amounts in question, when some portion is appropriate for payment, and some portion may be in question.

32.503-5 Administration of progress payments: regardless of the fact that the buyer is permitted to process progress payments for approval based on the certification of the supplier, the buyer is nevertheless obligated to periodically review progress payments already made, and to be made, to determine the validity of such payment requests.

Such post-payment reviews shall determine at a minimum that the unliquidated progress payments are supported by the value of work already accomplished, the unpaid balance of the contract appears adequate to cover the cost of completion, the supplier has adequate resources to complete the job, and there is no reason to question the validity of the accounting system, or controls, or certifications so made.

As a general rule, multiple contracts which are combined to meet the minimum threshold value should be administered separately. However, if the supplier so requests it, the buyer may allow the supplier to combine such progress payment invoices for ease of administration, as long as the orders are subject to a uniform liquidation rate, are under the jurisdiction of the same buyer, and a detail schedule is available to provide performance information on each order.

32.503-6 Suspension or reduction of progress payments: the progress payment clause contained in FAR 52.232-16, paragraph (c), gives the Government (and therefore the prime contractor's buyer) the right to reduce or suspend progress payments, or to increase the liquidation rates under certain specific conditions.

In all such cases the buyer is expected to act objectively, and to take such extreme actions only after notifying the supplier that such actions are planned, and thus giving the seller the opportunity to discuss the issues with the buyer. The overall impact of the action on the supplier should be considered, such as its existing financial condition, credit arrangements, cash requirements, and the particular equities involved. All such actions taken and the basis for them should be documented for the record.

There are generally six conditions which will warrant the action of suspension or reduction of supplier progress payments. They are:

1. *Subcontractor noncompliance.* A supplier must comply with all material (substantive) requirements of the subcontract. This requirement as it pertains to progress payments deals with the issue of having in place an adequate accounting system and financial controls, in order to be able to account for all progress payments requested, certified, and received by the supplier.

   An inadequate supplier accounting system and questionable financial controls are valid reasons to suspend progress payments.

2. *Unsatisfactory financial condition.* If a buyer finds that subcontract performance has become endangered by the supplier's financial condition, or by its failure to make progress under the existing subcontract, to the degree that full liquidation of payments already paid are in question, or that further payments would only increase the potential loss, the suspension of additional payments would be in order.

3. *Excessive inventory.* When a buyer finds that the inventory allocated to the particular subcontract, which has been used to justify progress payments, exceeds the reasonable requirements to support it, either in total requirements or in advance of the time frame to support smooth operations, then action to halt payments is in order. Requests should be made to transfer the excess inventory to another account, and for the return of any over-payment values made.

4. *Delinquency in payment of costs of performance.* When it becomes apparent that the subcontractor is delinquent in payments to its lower level suppliers, an evaluation of the condition is in order. If it is determined that the situation reflects an unsatisfactory financial condition, then a suspension of further payments is appropriate under item # 2 above.

If the financial condition of the subcontractor is found to be adequate, and the supplier agrees to cure all such delinquencies, to avoid further delinquencies, and to make arrangements to reduce further financial risks to the subcontract, then continued payments may be made.

If there are disputed costs between the supplier and lower level suppliers, such disputed costs must be excluded from progress payment invoices, until they are settled. All payments to the subcontractor's employee profit sharing plans must be made strictly in accordance with such agreements.

5. *Fair value of undelivered work.* For purposes of interpreting this issue, the fair value of undelivered work is considered to be the lesser of: (1) the subcontract price of undelivered items, less the estimated costs required to complete the subcontract, or, (2) the incurred costs related to the undelivered items.

The buyer is obligated to monitor the fair value of undelivered items, as defined above, as it relates to the unliquidated progress payment loan. If the unliquidated loan exceeds the fair market value of the undelivered work, then the buyer is obligated to take action to eliminate the excessive payments.

This action is typically accomplished by invoking the "loss ratio adjustment," to be discussed below. When taking such action the buyer should consider the degree of subcontract completion, the quality and quantity of subcontractor effort on the undelivered work, the amount of effort and estimated costs to complete the effort, and the amount of funds remaining to be paid for the subcontract.

6. *Loss contracts.* Subcontractors are required to submit a monthly progress payment invoice in order to be paid progress payments. In this form, FAR Standard Form SF1443, there are specific lines which report: the total costs incurred to date (line 12a), and the total estimated costs to complete the order (line 12b). When the sum of these two lines exceeds the subcontract price, note *price* not *costs,* then it is presumed that the supplier will lose money on the order and the buyer is then obligated to take corrective action in order to protect the progress payment loans made.

The obligation of the buyer is to invoke what is called the "loss ratio factor," which will exclude that value of any loss the supplier is expected to incur on this order from future progress payments, and the estimated value of all delivered work.

The first action which must be taken is to make sure that the subcontract price reflects all work which has been authorized by the buyer. All pending change orders and unpriced orders must be included in the estimated value of the subcontract price, to the extent that these orders have been authorized by the buyer. The formula used to calculate the loss ratio factor (LRF) is as follows:

$$\text{LRF} = \frac{\text{SUBCONTRACT PRICE (CURRENT PRICE + UNPRICED)}}{\text{TOTAL COSTS TO COMPLETE (LINES 12A + 12B)}}$$

The loss ratio factor is then multiplied by the values in line 11 of the invoice, which specify the costs eligible for progress payments. The effect of invoking the loss ratio adjustment is to provide a revised (downward) rate which will be used to authorize all future progress payments to this supplier on a specific order. Thus, if the loss ratio factor results in a value of 83.3 percent (which would be the case with a 20 percent overrun from price), then this value is multiplied by the authorized progress payment rate (assume 80 percent), to provide a revised progress payment rate of 66.64 percent, a revised rate substantially below the current customary rate of 80 percent.

The new rate adjustment would be applied to all future progress payment requests, until the supplier's estimate to complete is changed, as well as used in assessing the value of delivered units. The buyer in such cases is expected to enlist the support from all available sources, example, quality, technical, internal audit, and/or the Government's audit. The buyer should contact the supplier and advise them in writing prior to taking an action of reducing the progress payment rate.

32.503-7 Limitation on general and administrative expenses (G&A) for progress payments: this item deals with the allocation of G&A type expenses to progress payments, and limitations of such allocations.

The limitation is the amount of $5 million or more, and applies to those contractors who use a suspense account under Appendix A of Cost Accounting Standard (CAS) 410. G&A expenses shall not be eligible for inclusion in progress payments until the value of work in process inventories under new contracts, a new contract is that which was received subsequent to CAS 410 being implemented at the contractor, exceeds the value of their old contracts. Contractors must pro rate the value of any G&A expenses allocated to progress payments.

With the passage of time since CAS 410 became effective, in 1976, the importance of this FAR provision becomes moot.

32.503-8 Liquidation rates—ordinary method: progress payment loans are repaid by the supplier by making deliveries of contract line items. At the point of delivery the supplier is paid the unit price of the article being delivered, less a portion of the unit price which is used to liquidate the progress payment loan.

The ordinary method of liquidating such loans is to deduct an amount from the unit price of the article being delivered, an amount which is identical to the authorized progress payment rate. Thus, a customary progress payment rate of say 80 percent of "costs," would liquidate at 80 percent of the unit "price," using the ordinary method of liquidation. (Note the distinction between costs and price.)

32.503-9 Liquidation rates—alternate method: the ordinary liquidation rate will continue throughout the subcontract term, unless the buyer authorizes a change in the liquidation rate allowed under this FAR paragraph.

This paragraph provides for an alternate liquidation rate to be applied, which allows the supplier to retain the progress payment loans for a longer period of time, prior to repayment through liquidations. The alternate liquidation rate provision may also allow for the supplier to retain some portion of their profits earned under delivered articles.

Nine conditions must be met in order for a supplier to be allowed the use of the alternate liquidation rate:

(1) The subcontractor requests a reduction in liquidation rates, i.e., the alternate liquidation rate.

(2) The rate has not been changed in the prior 12 months.

(3) The subcontract delivery schedule spans a period of 18 months from the subcontract award.

(4) Actual cost data is made available to the buyer on items delivered, or for a performance period of 12 months if no deliveries have been made.

(5) The reduced liquidation rates will still allow the buyer to recoup under each invoice the full amount of the progress payments applicable to costs allocated to each invoice.

(6) The subcontractor will not be paid for more than the costs of items delivered, together with earned profits on such items.

(7) The unliquidated progress payments may not exceed the limits of either: the progress payments made against incomplete work, including unliquidated next tier subcontractor payments; or, the value of incomplete work, which is defined as supplies and services required by the effort, for which delivery and invoicing are incomplete.

(8) The buyer and subcontractor agree on a new rate.

(9) The subcontractor agrees to certify annually or more frequently if required by the buyer, that the alternate rate continues to meet the conditions of items (5), (6), and (7) above.

Once a rate has been changed to the alternate liquidation rate, the buyer must reverse such action if the subcontractor starts to experience a lower profit rate than was anticipated when the rates were changed. Such changes will be made to payments paid, and to be paid. Also, these rates must be kept current with any changes, upward or downward, in the subcontract target price or profit.

When a liquidation rate is changed, the buyer will issue a subcontract change modification which specifies the new rate. No additional consideration is required for the change in liquidation rates beyond that which was initially required.

32.503-10 Establishing alternate liquidation rates: the buyer is obligated to assure that any changes to the liquidation rate will maintain a rate high enough to recoup progress payments on each billing. All such actions adjusting these rates must be supported by documentation explaining the reasons in the procurement file. As a minimum the liquidation rate must be at least the value of progress payments anticipated, divided by the subcontract price.

The liquidation rate must consider the estimated value of authorized work which may not have been priced, plus any anticipated economic adjustments. Minimum liquidation rates will be expressed in tenths of a percentage point, rounded upward to the next highest tenth.

32.503.11 Adjustments for price reduction: the buyer must be alert to all proactive and retroactive adjustments in a price redeterminable subcontract which contains progress payments. A buyer must obtain a rebate from the supplier for any excessive payments made for delivered items, based on the recomputed rate, and adjust the unliquidated progress payment amounts as appropriate.

32.503-12 Maximum unliquidated amount: the buyer must be alert to excesses in unliquidated progress payments, and if so discovered must promptly made adjustments by: increasing the liquidation rate, or reducing the progress payment rate, or by suspending further progress payments.

Excesses typically will occur when: the costs to perform exceeds the subcontract price; the alternate liquidation rate was authorized and the subsequent actual costs exceed the estimated costs; the rate of progress or the quality of performance is unsatisfactory; and, hardware rejections, or wastage, or spoilage is excessive.

When these conditions appear, the buyer will enlist the support of the cost analysts, engineers, and audit personnel until the problems are resolved.

32.503-13 Quarterly statements for price revision contracts: this paragraph pertains only to those subcontracts which contain progress payments and are of either a price revision, or price renegotiation type, as covered in FAR 52.216-5, -6, -16, -17.

The buyer must occasionally compare the quarterly statements submitted by the supplier, and ensure to the extent possible that the costs of delivered items as stated in such statements are excluded from the costs of undelivered items. This action is necessary to allow for the orderly liquidation of progress payment loans where the actual price of delivered articles is subject to possible changes.

32.503-14 Protection of Government title: under progress payments arrangements, the Government holds title to all materials, work-in-process, finished goods and other items of property defined in paragraph (d) of FAR clause 52.232-16. Occasionally, the buyer (acting for the Government's ACO) must ensure that such title of the Government is not encumbered by liens or other devices which would prevent a free title to all materials covered by progress payment loans. Under ordinary circumstances, the certification contained on progress payment invoices would be sufficient to provide such assurances.

Should the buyer become aware of any arrangements or conditions at the subcontractor which would impair the Government's right to a free title to such goods, the buyer must, acting for the ACO, require additional protective provisions as described in FAR 32.501-5 covered above.

The very existence of such encumbrances constitutes a violation of the obligations of the supplier under the progress payment provisions, and the buyer is authorized to suspend or reduce progress payments so made. Also, if the supplier had failed to disclose an existing encumbrance in the progress payment invoice certification as submitted, the buyer should consult with legal counsel for a possible violation of Federal law, specifically the False Claims Act.

32.503-15 Application of Government title terms: a supplier's materials which are covered by progress payments and therefore title to such property rests with the Government, shall not be considered as Government Furnished Property, GFP. The rules covering the acquisition, handling, and disposition of certain types of such property is covered elsewhere in FAR: special tooling is covered under FAR 52.245-17; and the termination clause of FAR 52.249 covers termination inventory.

A subcontractor may sell or otherwise dispose of production scrap materials covered by progress payments in the normal course of doing business, provided that the proceeds of such sales go to reduce the costs of contract performance, and progress payments made.

A supplier may transfer material inventory covered by progress payments only if: the transaction is approved by the prime contractor's buyer and the Government ACO; the proceeds go to reduce the costs of contract performance; and an amount equal to the unliquidated progress payments shall be credited to the subcontract.

If at the end of the subcontract performance period all of the progress payments have been fully liquidated, and all contract obligations have been met, and there remains excess property procured on the contract, title to such materials will rest with the performing subcontractor.

32.503-16 Risk of loss: although under progress payments the title rests with the Government, except for normal spoilage, the risk of loss, theft, destruction, or damage to such property will remain with the supplier receiving progress payments. This is always the case, except in those instances where the Government has expressly assumed the risk for such materials. And the Government does not assume the risk for loss of materials under a termination or default action.

Should a loss of materials happen under a subcontract in which progress payments have been provided, the supplier is obligated to repay the contract in an amount which will liquidate the loans for the materials lost. Supplier's are not obligated to repay for materials lost, for which the Government has assumed the risk of loss.

32.504 Subcontracts: the Government encourages prime contractors to provide customary progress payments to their subcontractors in accordance with FAR 32-502-1.

Prime contractor payments of progress payments to their next tier subcontractors are recoverable in the full amount (100 percent) of such payments paid to a supplier. A prime contractor considering the granting of unusual progress payments will be guided by FAR 32.501-2. All such payment arrangements must be approved by the Government, and a contract modification will be issued to specify the new rate in the progress payment clause paragraph (j)(4) of FAR 52.232-16.

The prime contractor (the buyer) has a duty to assure that a subcontractor's progress payments conform to the same rules and standards as that contained in the prime contract, as defined in paragraph (j) of FAR 52.232-16. The Government must be assured that the prime contractor has installed the necessary management control systems and internal audit procedures.

The terms of the subcontractors progress payment clause shall allow for the inclusion of the following safeguards to protect the interests of the Government: the prime contractor not the Government will administer the subcontractor progress payments; title in the property covered by progress payments will vest with the Government; the Government will retain the right to have access to a supplier's records; language of the subcontract may add the term "prime contractor" to any reference to the Government's "Contracting Officer" or simply the "Government". The terms of FAR 52.232-16, paragraph (h) covering defaults will be included in the subcontract clause.

If a prime contractor with a cost reimbursable type contract allows for progress payments to its next tier fixed-price subcontractors, such payments to its suppliers will be reimbursable only to the extent that they comply with the requirements of FAR 32.502-1 covering customary progress payments.

Any unusual payments must be approved by the Government in accordance with FAR 32.501-2. All liquidations of supplier progress payments must be in accordance with FAR 32.503-8, -9, and -10. All subcontractor terms must comply with the terms of the FAR section.

FAR 52.232-13/16,
PROGRESS PAYMENT CONTRACT CLAUSES

This section of the FAR contains a series of contract/subcontract clauses covering the subject of progress payments, some of which are intended to work in conjunction with other clauses in the same series.

52.232-13 Notice of Progress Payments: as was specified in FAR 32.502-3(a) above, a prime contractor when soliciting bids from suppliers will make reference to this clause to indicate that progress payments are intended to be included in any resulting procurement.

52.232-14 Notice of Availability of Progress Payments Exclusively for Small Business Concerns: this solicitation clause should be used when a response is invited from both large and small businesses, but progress payments will be restricted to only small businesses in any resulting procurements. This approach is allowed under FAR 32.502-3(b)(2).

52.232-15 Progress Payments Not Included: this clause is to be used in solicitations in which progress payments will not be included as a part of any resulting procurement.

52.232-16 Progress Payments: this clause is used by the Government in all contracts in which progress payments are included. Prime contractors authorizing the use of progress payments are wise to incorporate this clause into the prime contract document by reference, or to closely paraphrase all of the provisions of this standard contract clause.

Alternate I: this clause is used when the supplier is a small business concern, and substitutes paragraphs (a)(1) and (a)(2) with new language allowing for different rates to be used.

Alternate II: this clause is used on letter subcontracts, and adds two new paragraphs: (l) which covers the liquidation of progress payments made under the letter subcontract at the point of definitization; and (m) in which a specific dollar ceiling is to be specified, which will not exceed 80 percent of the dollar value of the letter subcontract.

DOD-FAR PART 232.5,
PROGRESS PAYMENTS BASED ON COSTS

This is the Department of Defence (DOD) policy statement on progress payments, some of which is redundant to the FAR, and other sections are unique to only DOD procurements.

232.501 General

232.501-1 Customary progress payment rates: this section sets the customary rate for progress payments for DOD contracting. These rates will vary from period to period, and are currently set at 80 percent for large businesses; 85 percent to small businesses; and (as of 12-19-90) 90 percent to small disadvantaged businesses.

Foreign Military Sales (FMS) progress payment rates are the same as those for DOD rates.

The customary rates set for flexible progress payments is set by use of either the CASH II, CASH III, CASH IV or CASH V computer models, as defined in DOD-FAR 232.502-1 (S-71).

232.501-2 Unusual progress payments: sets the limits of contracting officers to authorize unusual progress payments at $25,000,000 without prior approval of the Office of the Assistant Secretary of Defense (Production and Logistics). All other unusual progress payments shall be coordinated by the DOD Contract Finance Committee.

232.501-3 Contract price: the contract price for making progress payments may exceed the funds authorized under a contract if a contract includes an appropriate limitation of funds clause. Progress payments will be limited to the lesser of either the appropriate percentage of contract price, or 100 percent of the funds authorized.

232.502 Preaward Matters

232.502-1 Use of customary progress payments

(S-70) *Customary FMS Progress Payments:* progress payments may be used by the DOD on acquisitions on behalf of foreign governments and international organizations, in accordance with Section 22 of the Arms Export Control Act (FMS). FMS progress payments are not to be used to replenish U.S. inventories or DOD cooperative logistics support arrangements.

(S-71) *Customary Flexible Progress Payments:* the Government acknowledges the fact that contractor/subcontractor investment of their cash in contract performance is influenced by a number of factors such as delivery schedules, company cash management practices, and the Government's payment practices. Normal progress payment practices are typically insensitive to these factors, and as a result, often require investments of contractor cash which vary by firm and by contract. Flexible progress payments are designed to overcome these cash requirement disparities.

Under a flexible progress payment arrangement, cash needs are determined and projected in relation to a firm's cash investment in work-in-process inventory over the entire life of a contract. Total cash investment is measured by a weighted average of costs incurred by a contractor to perform on the contract. The DOD has set a policy of requiring a contractor investment of between 5 percent to 25 percent of work-in-process inventory over the life of a given contract, depending on the fiscal year which provides the funds.

The actual flexible progress payment rate will be determined by use of one of the four DOD Cash Flow models which will consider the contract cost profile, delivery schedules, subcontractor progress payments, liquidation rates, and payment/reimbursement cycles. Upper limits of flexible rates will be 100 percent, and the lower limit the current authorized progress payment rate.

Government Contracting Officers may authorize the use of flexible progress payment rates if: the contractor requests them; the contractor agrees to satisfy all the conditions of this DOD-FAR section; the contractor agrees to submit certified cost or pricing data in accordance with FAR 15.804-2; and the contract value is in excess of $1 million for negotiated fixed-price contracts. A new requirement which was added in 1990 is the obligation for a buyer to obtain some form of consideration for flexible progress payments if they are requested after the contract was definitized, and were not considered during the negotiations.

Flexible progress payments are not available to formally advertised/sealed bids contracts, or for undefinitized contract actions. Also new in 1990 is the restriction on the use of flexible progress payments where 100 percent of the contract performance is outside of the United States.

Contractors desiring flexible progress payments must submit to the Contracting Officer (or prime contractor buyer) cash flow data as specified by the DOD Cash Flow model which reflects: actual and projected incurred costs broken out by element of cost, by month, for the duration of contract performance; float times for each element of cost; progress payment receipts and delivery payment receipts with associated contract unit prices and profit percentages. Contracting Officers (and buyers) are obligated to verify these data using normal procedures to validate cost and pricing data. Administrative Contracting Officers (buyers) are encouraged to establish, when administratively practical, advanced agreements at supplier locations for cash investment float and payment lags which are common to multiple contracts.

Flexible progress payment rates will be redetermined when requested by either the Government or contractor, when the contractor's investment in work-in-process inventory is expected to vary by a value greater than plus or minus 2 percent from the DOD investment policy requiring a specific investment value range of between 5 percent to 25 percent (currently set at 20 percent), depending upon the fiscal year funding. Rates once agreed, are expected to last until such time as the conditions change, such as progress payment lag times, additional new effort on a contract.

The standards for customary flexible progress payments to subcontractors are the same as those for prime contractors, and are governed by the requirements in FAR 32.504. Subcontractors wishing flexible progress payments must first request them, and independently satisfy all of the same conditions of this DOD-FAR section. The subcontractor's flexible progress payment rate will be determined on its own merits, without regard to the established rates of the prime contractor.

Flexible progress payments intended to be used on a contract or subcontract after definitization, and will follow the rules of FAR clause 52.232-16 until definitization.

232.502-2 Contract finance office clearance: any deviations from progress payment policy or procedures as stated in FAR subpart 32, or this DOD-FAR section must be authorized by the Office of the Assistant Secretary of Defense (Production and Logistics), in accordance with DOD-FAR 232.171.

232.502-4 Contract clauses: the Contracting Officer (buyer) will insert the appropriate contract clauses covering progress payments as specified in DOD-FAR 252.232-700X, as defined below.

232.503 Postaward Matter

232.503-1 Contractor requests: unless otherwise stated by specific agency requirements, contractor requests for progress payments may be made on a computer generated equivalent of FAR Standard Form 1443.

232.503-6 Suspension or reduction of payments: loss contracts will require a loss ratio adjustment calculation by the Contracting Officer (buyer) in accordance with FAR 32.503-6 (g), by preparation of a supplementary analysis to accompany the contractor's request for progress payments.

A contractor/subcontractor may be requested to prepare the supplementary analysis to accompany their progress payment request when it is determined by the Contracting officer (buyer) that the supplier, after review, has reliable and accurate methods to estimate its Costs to Complete the effort. The review of the supplier's ability to estimate such costs must be alert to improper influences, which could be prejudicial to the Government's (prime contractor's) best interests.

There must be an auditable trail which will permit the verification of such calculations, which requires that the loss ratio adjustments be made to a supplier's original SF1443 invoice, without alteration or replacement of such data.

DOD-FAR 252.232-7003 to 7007, PROGRESS PAYMENT CLAUSES

This section contains subcontract clauses on progress payments, some of which is redundant to the FAR, but some new and unique DOD clauses are incorporated.

252.232-7003 Progress Payments for Foreign Military Sales Acquisitions: to be used when progress payments are applied to FMS applications, described in DOD-FAR 232.502-1 (S-70).

252.232-7004 Flexible Progress Payments: used when flexible progress payments are substituted for customary progress payments, as described in DOD-FAR 232.502-1 (S-71, new Nov. 1990)

252.232-7005 Payments Under Fixed-Price Construction Contracts: as prescribed in DOD-FAR 232.111 (S-71).

252.232-7006 Payments Under Fixed-Price Architect-Engineer Contracts: as prescribed in DOD-FAR 232.111 (S-72).

252.232-7007 Progress Payments: used in DOD progress payment applications for both the solicitation and contract clauses. It is approximately equivalent to FAR 52.232-13 Notice of Progress Payments, and FAR 52.232-16 Progress Payments.

Alternate I: to be used when the supplier is a small business concern, and substitutes the payment rate and two clauses, (a)(1) and (a)(2). In 1990 the DOD-FAR changed to eliminate this clause for small businesses requesting flexible progress payments.

Alternate II: used under progress payments on letter contracts, and adds two additional paragraphs, (l) and (m).

Appendix C

An Index of Progress Payment Subjects in the FAR / DOD-FAR / DCAA Manual

This appendix provides a subject index of progress payment subjects contained in three important United States Government documents. The KEY to the letter prefix for each reference indicates the source document and referenced numerical section:

F = Federal Acquisition Regulation (FAR)

D = Department of Defense FAR Supplement (DFAR)

A = Defense Contract Audit Agency Contract Audit Manual (DCAA)

Underlining indicates a primary section on a given subject.

A
Accounting system survey form: F53.301-1408
Acquisition of major systems: F34.0
Acquisition planning: F7.0; D207.0
Advance agreements: F31.109; F42.10; D242.10

Appendix D

Cost/Schedule Control Systems Criteria from DODI 5000.2 and DOD 5000.2-M

Department of Defense
INSTRUCTION

February 23, 1991
NUMBER 5000.2

USD(A)

SUBJECT: Defense Acquisition Management Policies and Procedures

References: (a) DoD Instruction 5000.2, "Defense Acquisition Program
                  Procedures," September 1, 1987 (hereby canceled)
              (b) DoD 5025.1-M, "Department of Defense Directives System
                  Procedures," December 1990, authorized by DoD Directive
                  5025.1, "Department of Defense Directives System,"
                  December 23, 1988
              (c) DoD Directive 5000.1, "Defense Acquisition,"
                  February 23, 1991
              (d) DoD Directive 3150.1, "Joint Nuclear Weapon Development
                  Studies and Engineering Projects," December 27, 1983
              (e) DoD 5200.1-R, "Information Security Program Regulation,"
                  June 1986, with Change No. 1, June 27, 1988, authorized by
                  DoD Directive 5200.1, "DoD Information Security Program,"
                  June 7, 1982
              (f) DoD Directive O-5205.7, "Special Access Program (SAP)
                  Policy," January 4, 1989
              (g) Title 10, United States Code, Section 2430, "Major defense
                  acquisition program defined"
              (h) DoD Directive 5134.1, "Under Secretary of Defense
                  (Acquisition)," August 8, 1989
              (i) Title 10, United States Code, Section 2302(5),
                  "Definitions: major system"
              (j) Office of Management and Budget Circular A-109, "Major
                  System Acquisitions," April 5, 1976
              (k) DoD Directive 7750.5, "Management and Control of
                  Information Requirements," August 7, 1986

A. REISSUANCE AND PURPOSE

    This Instruction and its enclosures:

    1. Reissue DoD Instruction 5000.2, "Defense Acquisition Program
        Procedures" (reference (a)).

    2. Authorize the Under Secretary of Defense for Acquisition to publish
        DoD 5000.2-M, "Defense Acquisition Management Documentation and
        Reports" in accordance with DoD 5025.1-M, "Department of Defense
        Directive System Procedures" (reference (b)).

3. Establish:

   a. An integrated framework for translating broadly stated mission needs into stable, affordable acquisition programs that meet the operational user's needs and can be sustained, given projected resource constraints; and

   b. A rigorous, event-oriented management process for acquiring quality products that emphasizes effective acquisition planning, improved communications with users, and aggressive risk management by both Government and industry.

B. APPLICABILITY AND PRECEDENCE

1. This Instruction applies to:

   a. The Office of the Secretary of Defense; the Military Departments; the Chairman, Joint Chiefs of Staff and Joint Staff; the Unified and Specified Commands; the Defense Agencies; and DoD Field Activities (hereafter referred to collectively as "DoD Components").

   b. The management of major and nonmajor defense acquisition programs and highly sensitive classified programs.

2. DoD Directive 5000.1, "Defense Acquisition" (reference (c)) and this Instruction rank first and second in order of precedence for providing policies and procedures for managing acquisition programs, except when statutory requirements override. If there is any conflicting guidance pertaining to contracting, the Federal Acquisition Regulation/Defense Federal Acquisition Regulation Supplement shall take precedence over DoD Directive 5000.1 and this Instruction.

3. The acquisition of nuclear and nuclear capable weapon systems are additionally governed by DoD Directive 3150.1, "Joint Nuclear Weapon Development Studies and Engineering Projects" (reference (d)).

C. DEFINITIONS

1. Acquisition Program. A directed, funded effort that is designed to provide a new or improved materiel capability in response to a validated need.

2. Highly Sensitive Classified Program. An acquisition special access program established in accordance with DoD 5200.1-R, "Information Security Program Regulation" (reference (e)), and managed in accordance with DoD Directive O-5205.7, "Special Access Program Policy" (reference (f)).

3. Implementation. The publication of directives, instructions, regulations, and related documents that define responsibilities and authorities and establish the internal management processes necessary to implement the policies or procedures of a higher authority.

4. Major Defense Acquisition Program. An acquisition program that is
    not a highly sensitive classified program (as determined by the
    Secretary of Defense) and that is:

    a. Designated by the Under Secretary of Defense for Acquisition as a
        major defense acquisition program, or

    b. Estimated by the Under Secretary of Defense for Acquisition to
        require:

        (1) An eventual total expenditure for research, development,
            test, and evaluation of more than $200 million in fiscal
            year 1980 constant dollars (approximately $300 million in
            fiscal year 1990 constant dollars), or

        (2) An eventual total expenditure for procurement of more than
            $1 billion in fiscal year 1980 constant dollars
            (approximately $1.8 billion in fiscal year 1990 constant
            dollars).

    NOTE: This definition is based on the criteria established in
            Title 10, United States Code, Section 2430,"Major defense
            acquisition program defined" (reference (g)) and reflects
            authorities delegated in DoD Directive 5134.1, "Under
            Secretary of Defense for Acquisition" (reference (h)).

5. Major System. A combination of elements that will function together
    to produce the capabilities required to fulfill a mission need,
    including hardware, equipment, software, or any combination thereof,
    but excluding construction or other improvements to real property. A
    system shall be considered a major system if it is estimated by the
    Under Secretary of Defense for Acquisition to require:

    a. An eventual total expenditure for research, development, test,
        and evaluation of more than $75,000,000 in fiscal year 1980
        constant dollars (approximately $115,000,000 in fiscal year 1990
        constant dollars), or

    b. An eventual total expenditure for procurement of more than
        $300,000,000 in fiscal year 1980 constant dollars (approximately
        $540,000,000 in fiscal year 1990 constant dollars).

    NOTE: This definition is based on the criteria established in
            Title 10, United States Code, Section 2302(5) "Definitions:
            major system" (reference (i)).

6. Nonmajor Defense Acquisition Program. A program other than a major
    defense acquisition program or a highly sensitive classified program.

7. Performance. Those operational and support characteristics of the
    system that allow it to effectively and efficiently perform its
    assigned mission over time. The support characteristics of the

system include both supportability aspects of the design and the support elements necessary for system operation.

8. Supplementation. The publication of directives, instructions, regulations, and related documents that add to, restrict, or otherwise modify the policies or procedures of a higher authority.

9. Additional definitions are contained in Part 15 of this Instruction.

D. **POLICY AND PROCEDURES**

The policies and procedures of this Instruction implement:

1. DoD Directive 5000.1, "Defense Acquisition" (reference (c)),

2. The guidelines of Office and Management and Budget Circular A-109, "Major System Acquisitions" (reference (j)), and

3. Current statutes.

E. RESPONSIBILITIES

1. Heads of DoD Components shall ensure that the policies and procedures in this Instruction and its enclosures are followed by their respective Components.

2. Offices proposing changes to individual sections of this Instruction shall coordinate proposed changes with the Director, Acquisition Policy and Program Integration, Office of the Under Secretary of Defense for Acquisition prior to DoD-wide staffing of the change.

F. INFORMATION REQUIREMENTS

The reporting requirements contained in this Instruction have been licensed in accordance with DoD Directive 7750.5, "Management and Control of Information Requirements" (reference (k)). See Section 11-D, attachment 1, for the correct report titles, Report Control Symbols, and Office of Management and Budget Control Numbers.

G. SUPPLEMENTATION AND IMPLEMENTATION

1. Unless prescribed by statute or specifically authorized herein, the policies and procedures set out in this Instruction shall not be supplemented without the prior approval of the Under Secretary of Defense for Acquisition.

2. DoD Component Heads shall distribute this Instruction and DoD 5000.2-M, "Defense Acquisition Management Documentation and Reports" to the Program Manager and appropriate field operating command level within 60 days of receipt.

3. Implementing directives, instructions, regulations, and related issuances shall be kept to the essential minimum as deemed appropriate by the DoD Component Acquisition Executive. Copies of

all such issuances shall be provided to the Director of Acquisition
Policy and Program Integration, Office of the Under Secretary of
Defense for Acquisition within 10 days of publication.

H. WAIVERS

Requests for exceptions or waivers to any of the mandatory provisions of
this Instruction must be submitted to the Under Secretary of Defense for
Acquisition via the DoD Component Acquisition Executive unless specific
waiver authority has been granted below the Under Secretary level by this
Instruction. Statutory requirements may not be waived.

I. EFFECTIVE DATE

1. This Instruction is effective immediately for planning purposes.

2. Defense acquisition programs scheduled for milestone reviews 6 months
    after the date of publication of this Instruction are subject to the
    new review procedures and documentation requirements identified in
    this Instruction.

For all matters in this   For all matters in this
Instruction relating to   Instruction except operational
operational test and evaluation.   test and evaluation.

Robert C. Duncan   Donald J. Yockey
Director, Operational   Acting Under Secretary of
Test and Evaluation   Defense for Acquisition

Enclosures - 16

1.   Part 1 - Document Background and Table of Contents
2.   Part 2 - General Policies and Procedures
3.   Part 3 - Acquisition Process and Procedures
4.   Part 4 - Requirements Evolution and Affordability
5.   Part 5 - Acquisition Planning and Risk Management
6.   Part 6 - Engineering and Manufacturing
7.   Part 7 - Logistics and Other Infrastructure
8.   Part 8 - Test and Evaluation
9.   Part 9 - Configuration and Data Management
10. Part 10 - Business Management and Contracts
11. Part 11 - Program Control and Review ◄━━━
12. Part 12 - Special Situations
13. Part 13 - Defense Acquisition Board Process
14. Part 14 - Office Symbols and Titles
15. Part 15 - Definitions
16. Part 16 - Major Subject Index

PART 1

DOCUMENT BACKGROUND AND TABLE OF CONTENTS

DoD acquisition management policies and procedures have traditionally been published in numerous separate Directives and Instructions. These documents were typically supplemented by the DoD Components. Over time, this practice resulted in a heavily cross-referenced maze of guidance that stifled creativity and individual judgment and defied practical use.

This Instruction seeks to remedy that problem by establishing a core of fundamental policies and procedures that can be implemented down to the Program Manager and field operating command level without supplementation. The subject matter information in this Instruction was condensed from over 45 separate DoD issuances that have been canceled and countless DoD Component publications that are being canceled.

The contents of this Instruction must meet the diverse needs of Program Managers, milestone decision authorities, and their respective supporting staffs. Accordingly, the policies and procedures are organized along functional and organizational lines.

Individual sections within subsequent parts of this Instruction identify references appropriate to the subject matter being addressed and are structured to be self-contained. Cross-references to subject matter in other sections are provided to facilitate the effective integration of effort that is essential to success.

When appropriate, references to other sections of this Instruction are shown in the text as "(see Section 4-F)." This reference would be to Section F of Part 4.

TABLE OF CONTENTS

PART 11

SECTION B

CONTRACT PERFORMANCE MEASUREMENT

References: (a) DoD Instruction 7000.2, "Performance Measurement for
                   Selected Acquisitions," June 10, 1977 (canceled)
              (b) DoD 5000.2-M, "Defense Acquisition Management Documentation
                   and Reports," February 1991, authorized by this Instruction
              (c) Cost/Schedule Control Systems Criteria Joint Implementation
                   Guide (AFSCP 173-5, AFCCP 173-5, AFLCP 173-5, AMC-P 715-5,
                   NAVSOP 3627, DLA H 8400.2, DCAA P 7641.47), October 1, 1987
              (d) Cost/Schedule Control Systems Criteria Joint Surveillance
                   Guide (AFSCP 173-6, AFLCP 173-6, AMC-P 715-10, NAVMAT P
                   5243, DSA H 8315.1, DCAA P 7641.46) July 1, 1974
              (e) Defense Federal Acquisition Regulation Supplement (DFARS),
                   Subpart 234.005-71, "Contract Clauses for Major Systems
                   Acquisition," and Contract Clause 252.234-7001,
                   "Cost/Schedule Control Systems"
              (f) Federal Acquisition Regulation (FAR), Subpart 31.202,
                   "Direct Costs," and Subpart 31.203, "Indirect Costs,"
                   current edition

1. PURPOSE

   a. This section replaces DoD Instruction 7000.2, "Performance
      Measurement for Selected Acquisitions" (reference (a)), which has
      been canceled.

   b. These policies and procedures establish the basis for applying
      cost/schedule control systems criteria (C/SCSC) to significant
      defense contracts.

   c. The purpose of cost/schedule control systems criteria is to provide
      contractor and the Government program managers with accurate data to
      monitor execution of their program and to:

      (1) Preclude the imposition of specific cost and schedule management
          control systems by providing uniform evaluation criteria to
          ensure contractor cost and schedule management control systems
          are adequate;

      (2) Provide an adequate basis for responsible decisionmaking by both
          contractor management and DoD Component personnel by requiring
          that contractors' internal management control systems produce
          data that:

          (a) Indicate work progress;

(b)   Properly relate cost, schedule, and technical
      accomplishment;

(c)   Are valid, timely, and able to be audited; and

(d)   Provide DoD Component managers with information at a
      practical level of summarization; and

(3)   Bring to the attention of DoD contractors, and encourage them to
      accept and install, management control systems and procedures
      that are most effective in meeting requirements and controlling
      contract performance.

2. POLICIES

a. When applicable, the contract shall require that any system used by
    the contractor in planning and controlling the performance of the
    contract shall meet the criteria set forth in this section.

    (1)   Nothing in these criteria is intended to affect the basis on
          which costs are reimbursed and progress payments made, and
          nothing herein shall be construed as requiring the use of any
          single system, or specific method of management control or
          evaluation of performance.

    (2)   The contractor's internal systems need not be changed, provided
          they satisfy these criteria.

    (3)   The contractors' management control systems shall include
          policies, procedures, and methods which are designed to ensure
          that they shall accomplish the considerations highlighted in
          attachment 1.

b. Unless waived by the milestone decision authority or a designated
    representative, compliance with the cost/schedule control systems
    criteria shall be required on significant contracts and subcontracts
    within all acquisition programs, including highly sensitive
    classified programs and major construction programs.

    (1)   This also includes significant contracts executed for foreign
          governments and for specialized organizations such as the
          Defense Advanced Research Projects Agency, and significant
          acquisition effort performed by Government activities.

    (2)   Significant contracts are research, development, test, and
          evaluation contracts with a value of $60 million or more or
          procurement contracts with a value of $250 million or more (in
          fiscal year 1990 constant dollars).

c. Compliance with the cost/schedule control systems criteria shall not
    be required on firm fixed price contracts (including firm fixed price
    contracts with economic price adjustment provisions), time and
    materials contracts, and contracts which consist mostly of level-of-

effort work. Exceptions may be made by the milestone decision
authority for individual contracts.

    d. On contracts that are determined to be not significant enough for
cost/schedule control systems criteria application, the cost/schedule
status report (C/SSR) shall be required unless excluded under
paragraph 2.c., above. The cost/schedule status report is described
in DoD 5000.2-M, "Defense Acquisition Management Documentation and
Reports" (reference (b)).

3. PROCEDURES

    a. General. Cost and schedule performance data provided to the
Government will be summarized directly from the same systems used for
internal contractor management.

        (1) The policies and procedures contained herein will not be
construed as requiring the use of specific systems or changes in
accounting systems which will adversely affect the equitable
distribution of costs to all contracts, or compliance with cost
accounting standards, rules, and regulations.

        (2) No changes will be required in contractors' existing cost and
schedule control systems except those changes minimally
necessary to meet the cost/schedule control systems criteria.

    b. Subcontracts. Subcontracts within applicable programs, excluding
those that are firm fixed price, may be selected for application of
cost/schedule control systems criteria by mutual agreement between
prime contractor and the contracting DoD Component, according to the
criticality of the subcontract to the program.

        (1) Coverage of certain critical subcontracts may be directed by the
Program Manager, subject to the changes clause of the contracts.

        (2) In those cases where a subcontractor is not required to comply
with the criteria, the cost/schedule status report approach to
performance measurement will normally be used. (See DoD
5000.2-M, "Defense Acquisition Management Documentation and
Reports" (reference (b)).)

    c. Milestone Decision Review. The applicability of cost/schedule
control systems criteria and provisions concerning the acceptability
and use of contractor's cost/schedule control systems will be:

        (1) Included in the Integrated Program Summary (IPS) developed in
support of a Milestone II or Milestone III decision review (see
Section 11-C);

        (2) Addressed in acquisition plans; and

        (3) Set forth in solicitations and made a contractual requirement in
appropriate procurements (see Subparts 234.005-71 and

252.234-7001 of the Defense Federal Acquisition Regulation
Supplement (reference (e)).

d. Reviews of Systems. To ensure compliance with cost/schedule control
    systems criteria, contractors' systems will be reviewed during
    various phases of the contracting process as follows:

    (1) Where the cost/schedule control systems criteria are included as
         a requirement in the request for proposal, an evaluation review
         will be performed as an integral part of the source selection
         process.

    (2) After contract award, an in-plant demonstration review will be
         made to verify that the contractor is operating systems that
         meet the criteria.

    (3) Upon successful completion of the demonstration review,
         contractors will not be subjected to another demonstration
         review unless there are positive indications that the
         contractors' systems no longer operate so as to meet the
         criteria.

    (4) Subsequent contracts may require a review of shorter duration
         and less depth to ensure proper and effective application of the
         accepted systems to the new contract.

    (5) Detailed procedures relating to contractual application,
         interpretive guidance, inter-Service relationships, and conduct
         of systems reviews are in the Cost/Schedule Control Systems
         Criteria Joint Implementation Guide (reference (c)).

e. Advance Agreement. After determination that a management system
    meets the cost/schedule control systems criteria, an advance
    agreement may be established between the Department of Defense and
    the contractor to be incorporated by reference into future contracts.

    (1) The use of the advance agreement contemplates the execution of a
         written instrument that references the cost/schedule control
         systems criteria and negotiated provisions, which:

         (a) Reflect an understanding between the contractor and the DoD
              of the cost/schedule control systems criteria requirements.

         (b) Identify the specific cost/schedule control systems
              criteria compliant system(s) that the contractor intends to
              use on applicable contracts with DoD Components.

    (2) The advance agreement will include or reference a written
         description of the accepted system(s).

         (a) The system description should be in sufficient detail to
              permit adequate surveillance by responsible parties.

(b) The use of the advance agreement is preferred where a
     number of separate contracts between one or more DoD
     Components and the contractor may be entered into during
     the term of the advance agreement.

(c) The DoD Component negotiating the advance agreement with
     the contractor will make the agreement for all prospective
     contracting DoD Components.

(3) Action to develop an advance agreement may be started by either
     the contractor or the DoD Component, normally in connection with
     a contractual requirement.

     (a) Reference to an advance agreement satisfies the
          cost/schedule control systems criteria requirement in
          requests for proposal.

     (b) Procedures for executing advance agreements are included in
          the Cost/Schedule Control Systems Criteria Joint
          Implementation Guide (reference (c)).

f. Surveillance. Recurring evaluations of the effectiveness of the
    contractor's policies and procedures will be performed to ensure that
    the contractor's system continues to meet the cost/schedule control
    systems criteria and provides valid data consistent with the intent
    of this section.

    (1) Surveillance reviews will be based on selective tests of
         reported data and periodic evaluations of internal practices
         during the life of the contract.

    (2) Guidance for surveillance is contained in the Cost/Schedule
         Control Systems Criteria Joint Surveillance Guide
         (reference (d)).

4. RESPONSIBILITIES AND POINTS OF CONTACT

    a. Each DoD Component will designate a component performance measurement
        cost/schedule control systems criteria focal point.

        (1) The Component focal points will constitute the Performance
             Measurement Joint Executive Group (PMJEG).

        (2) The Performance Measurement Joint Executive Group will provide
             uniform joint policy and procedure recommendations for DoD
             Component Head approval.

        (3) The Performance Measurement Joint Executive Group will provide
             uniform cost/schedule control systems criteria interpretation,
             arbitration, and coordination with industry.

    b. The Defense Contract Audit Agency and applicable contract
        administration offices will participate in reviews of contractors'
        systems under their cognizance, perform surveillance, and collaborate

with each other and with the procuring DoD Component in reviewing areas of joint interest.

c. The matrix below identifies the offices to be contacted for additional information on this section. The full titles of these offices may be found in Part 14 of this Instruction.

DoD Component	Points of Contact	
	General	Specific
OSD	Dir, AP&PI	DepDir, CM
Dept of Army	ASA(RDA)	SARD-ZP
Dept of Navy	ASN(RDA)	Dir, APIA
Dept of Air Force	ASAF(FM)	SAF/FMC

Attachments - 2

1. Cost/Schedule Control Systems Criteria
2. Cost/Schedule Control Systems Definitions

COST/SCHEDULE CONTROL SYSTEMS CRITERIA

The contractors' management control systems shall include policies,
procedures and methods that are designed to ensure that they will accomplish
the considerations reflected herein.

1. Organization

    a. Define all authorized work and related resources to meet the
       requirements of the contract, using the contract work breakdown
       structure (WBS).

    b. Identify the internal organizational elements and the major
       subcontractors responsible for accomplishing the authorized work.

    c. Provide for the integration of the contractor's planning, scheduling,
       budgeting, work authorization and cost accumulation systems with each
       other, the contract work breakdown structure, and the organizational
       structure.

    d. Identify the managerial positions responsible for controlling
       overhead (indirect costs).

    e. Provide for integration of the contract work breakdown structure with
       the contractor's functional organizational structure in a manner that
       permits cost and schedule performance measurement for contract work
       breakdown structure and organizational elements.

2. Planning and Budgeting

    a. Schedule the authorized work in a manner which describes the sequence
       of work and identifies the significant task interdependencies
       required to meet the development, production, and delivery
       requirements of the contract.

    b. Identify physical products, milestones, technical performance goals,
       or other indicators that will be used to measure output.

    c. Establish and maintain a time-phased budget baseline at the cost
       account level against which contract performance can be measured.
       Initial budgets established for this purpose will be based on the
       negotiated target cost. Any other amount used for performance
       measurement purposes must be formally recognized by both the
       contractor and the Government.

    d. Establish budgets for all authorized work with separate
       identification of cost elements (labor, material, etc.).

e. To the extent the authorized work can be identified in discrete,
    short span work packages, establish budgets for this work in terms of
    dollars, hours, or other measurable units. Where the entire cost
    account can not be subdivided into detailed work packages, identify
    far term effort in larger planning packages for budget and scheduling
    purposes.

f. Provide that the sum of all work package budgets, plus planning
    package budgets within a cost account equals the cost account budget.

g. Identify relationships of budgets or standards in work authorization
    systems to budgets for work packages.

h. Identify and control level-of-effort activity by time-phased budgets
    established for this purpose. Only that effort which cannot be
    identified as discrete, short span work packages or as apportioned
    effort may be classed as level-of-effort.

i. Establish overhead budgets for the total costs of each significant
    organizational component whose expenses will become indirect costs.
    Reflect in the contract budgets at the appropriate level the amounts
    in overhead pools that are planned to be allocated to the contract as
    indirect costs.

j. Identify management reserves and undistributed budget.

k. Provide that the contract target cost plus the estimated cost of
    authorized but unpriced work is reconciled with the sum of all
    internal contract budgets and management reserves.

3. Accounting

a. Record direct costs on an applied or other acceptable basis in a
    manner consistent with the budgets in a formal system that is
    controlled by the general books of account.

b. Summarize direct costs from cost accounts into the work breakdown
    structure without allocation of a single cost account to two or more
    work breakdown structure elements.

c. Summarize direct costs from the cost accounts into the contractor's
    functional organizational elements without allocation of a single
    cost account to two or more organizational elements.

d. Record all indirect costs which will be allocated to the contract.

e. Identify the bases for allocating the cost of apportioned effort.

f. Identify unit costs, equivalent unit costs, or lot costs as
    applicable.

g. The contractor's material accounting system will provide for:

    (1) Accurate cost accumulation and assignment of costs to cost accounts in a manner consistent with the budgets using recognized, acceptable costing techniques.

    (2) Determination of price variances by comparing planned versus actual commitments.

    (3) Cost performance measurement at the point in time most suitable for the category of material involved, but no earlier than the time of actual receipt of material.

    (4) Determination of cost variances attributable to the excess usage of material.

    (5) Determination of unit or lot costs when applicable.

    (6) Full accountability for all material purchased for the contract, including the residual inventory.

4. <u>Analysis</u>

    a. Identify at the cost account level on a monthly basis using data from, or reconcilable with, the accounting system:

        (1) Comparison of budgeted cost for work scheduled and budgeted cost of work performed;

        (2) Comparison of budgeted cost for work performed and actual (applied where appropriate) direct costs for the same work; and

        (3) Variances resulting from the comparisons between the budgeted cost for work scheduled and the budgeted cost for work performed and between the budgeted cost for work performed and actual or applied direct costs, classified in terms of labor, material, or other appropriate elements together with the reasons for significant variances.

    b. Identify on a monthly basis, in the detail needed by management for effective control, budgeted indirect costs, actual indirect costs, and cost variances with the reasons for significant variances.

    c. Summarize the data elements and associated variances listed in subparagraphs 4.a.(1) and (2), above, through the contractor organization and work breakdown structure to the reporting level specified in the contract.

    d. Identify significant differences on a monthly basis between planned and actual schedule accomplishment and the reasons.

    e. Identify managerial actions taken as a result of criteria items in paragraphs 4.a. through 4.d., above.

    f. Based on performance to date, on commitment values for material, and on estimates of future conditions, develop revised estimates of cost at completion for work breakdown structure elements identified in the contract and compare these with the contract budget base and the latest statement of funds requirements reported to the Government.

5. <u>Revisions and Access to Data</u>

    a. Incorporate contractual changes expeditiously, recording the effects of such changes in budgets and schedules. In the directed effort prior to negotiation of a change, base such revisions on the amount estimated and budgeted to the functional organizations.

    b. Reconcile original budgets for those elements of the work breakdown structure identified as priced line items in the contract, and for those elements at the lowest level in the program work breakdown structure, with current performance measurement budgets in terms of changes to the authorized work and internal replanning in the detail needed by management for effective control.

    c. Prohibit retroactive changes to records pertaining to work performed that would change previously reported amounts for direct costs, indirect costs, or budgets, except for correction of errors and routine accounting adjustments.

    d. Prevent revisions to the contract budget base except for Government directed changes to contractual effort.

    e. Document internally the changes to the performance measurement baseline and notify expeditiously the procuring activity through prescribed procedures.

    f. Provide the Contracting Officer and the Contracting Officer's authorized representatives with access to the information and supporting documentation necessary to demonstrate compliance with the cost/schedule control systems criteria.

COST/SCHEDULE CONTROL SYSTEMS DEFINITIONS

1. Actual Cost of Work Performed (ACWP). The cost incurred and recorded in accomplishing the work performed within a given time period.

2. Actual Direct Costs. Those costs identified specifically with a contract, based upon the contractor's cost identification and accumulation system as accepted by the cognizant Defense Contract Audit Agency representatives. (See definition 14, below.)

3. Allocated Budget. (See definition 32, below.)

4. Applied Direct Cost. The amount recognized in the time period associated with the consumption of labor, material, and other direct resources, without regard to the date of commitment or the date of payment. These amounts are to be charged to work-in-progress in the time period that any one of the following occurs:

    a. When labor, material, and other direct resources are actually consumed.

    b. When material resources are withdrawn from inventory for use.

    c. When material resources are received that are identified uniquely to the contract and scheduled for use within 60 days.

    d. When major components or assemblies are received on a line flow basis that are identified specifically and uniquely to a single serially numbered end item.

5. Apportioned Effort. Effort that is not readily divisible into work packages, but is related proportionately to measured effort.

6. Authorized Work. Effort that has been definitized and is on contract, plus that for which definitized contract costs have not been agreed to, but for which written authorization has been received.

7. Baseline. (See definition 24, below.)

8. Budgeted Cost for Work Performed (BCWP). The sum of the budgets for completed work packages and completed portions of open work packages, plus the applicable portion of the budgets for level of effort and apportioned effort.

9. Budgeted Cost for Work Scheduled (BCWS). The sum of budgets for all work packages, planning packages, etc., scheduled to be accomplished (including in-process work packages), plus the amount of level-of-effort

and apportioned effort scheduled to be accomplished within a given time period.

10. Budgets for Work Packages. (See definition 36, below.)

11. Contract Budget Base. The negotiated contract cost plus the estimated cost of authorized unpriced work.

12. Contractor. An entity in private industry which enters into contracts with the Government. In this Instruction, the word also may apply to Government-owned, Government-operated activities that perform work on defense programs.

13. Cost Account. A management control point at which actual costs may be accumulated and compared to the budgeted cost of the work performed. A cost account is a natural control point for cost/schedule planning and control, since it represents the work assigned to one responsible organizational element on one contract work breakdown structure element.

14. Direct Costs. Any costs that may be identified specifically with a particular final cost objective. This term is explained in the Federal Acquisition Regulation (reference (f)).

15. Estimate at Completion (EAC). Actual direct costs, plus indirect costs allocable to the contract, plus estimate of costs (direct and indirect) for authorized work remaining.

16. Indirect costs. Costs, which because of their incurrence for common or joint objectives, are not subject readily to treatment as direct costs. This term is further defined in the Federal Acquisition Regulation (reference (f)).

17. Initial Budget. (See definition 22, below.)

18. Internal Replanning. Replanning actions performed by the contractor for remaining effort within the recognized total allocated budget.

19. Level-of-Effort (LOE). Effort of a general or supportive nature that does not produce definite end products.

20. Management Reserve or Management Reserve Budget. An amount of the total allocated budget withheld for management control purposes, rather than designated for the accomplishment of a specific task or set of tasks. It is not a part of the performance measurement baseline.

21. Negotiated Contract Cost. The estimated cost negotiated in a cost plus fixed fee contract, or the negotiated contract target cost in either a fixed price incentive contract or a cost plus incentive fee contract.

22. Original Budget. The budget established at, or near, the time that the contract was signed and based on the negotiated contract cost.

23. Overhead. (See definition 16, above.)

24. <u>Performance Measurement Baseline</u>. The time phased budget plan against which contract performance is measured. It is formed by the budgets assigned to scheduled cost accounts and the applicable indirect budgets. For future effort, not planned to the cost account level, the performance measurement baseline also includes budgets assigned to higher level contract work breakdown structure elements and undistributed budgets. It equals the total allocated budget less management reserve.

25. <u>Performing Organization</u>. A defined unit within the contractor's organizational structure, which applies the resources to perform the work.

26. <u>Planning Package</u>. A logical aggregation of far term work within a cost account which may be identified and budgeted in early baseline planning, but is not yet defined into work packages.

27. <u>Procuring Activity</u>. The subordinate command in which the Procurement Contracting Officer is located. It may include the program office, related functional support offices, and procurement offices. Examples of procuring activities are the Army Missile Command, Naval Sea Systems Command, and Air Force Electronic Systems Division.

28. <u>Replanning</u>. (See definition 18, above.)

29. <u>Reprogramming</u>. Replanning of the effort remaining in the contract, resulting in a new budget allocation that exceeds the contract budget base.

30. <u>Responsible Organization</u>. A defined unit within the contractor's organizational structure that is assigned responsibility for accomplishing specific tasks.

31. <u>Significant Variances</u>. Those differences between planned and actual performance requiring further review, analysis, or action. Thresholds should be established as to the magnitude of variances that will require variance analysis, and the thresholds should be revised as needed to provide meaningful analysis during execution of the contract.

32. <u>Total Allocated Budget</u>. The sum of all budgets allocated to the contract. Total allocated budget consists of the performance measurement baseline and all management reserve. The total allocated budget will reconcile directly to the contract budget base. Any differences will be documented as to quantity and cause.

33. <u>Undistributed Budget</u>. Budget applicable to contract effort that has not yet been identified to contract work breakdown structure elements at, or below, the lowest level of reporting to the Government.

34. <u>Variances</u>. (See definition 31, above.)

35. <u>Work Breakdown Structure (WBS)</u>. (See Section 6-B.)

36. <u>Work Package Budgets</u>. Resources that are assigned formally by the contractor to accomplish a work package, expressed in dollars, hours, standards, or other definitive units.

37. <u>Work Packages</u>. Detailed tasks or material items identified by the contractor for accomplishing work required to complete the contract. A work package has the following characteristics:

   a. It represents units of work at levels where work is performed.

   b. It is clearly distinguishable from all other work packages.

   c. It is assignable to a single organizational element.

   d. It has scheduled start and completion dates and, as applicable, interim milestones; all of which are representative of physical accomplishment.

   e. It has a budget or assigned value expressed in terms of dollars, manhours, or other measurable units.

   f. Its duration is limited to a relatively short time span or it is subdivided by discrete value milestones to ease the objective measurement of work performed.

   g. It is integrated with detailed engineering, manufacturing, or other schedules.

DEPARTMENT OF DEFENSE MANUAL

DEFENSE ACQUISITION MANAGEMENT DOCUMENTATION AND REPORTS

February 1991
UNDER SECRETARY OF DEFENSE FOR ACQUISITION

OFFICE OF THE SECRETARY OF DEFENSE

WASHINGTON, D.C. 20301

February 23, 1991

FOREWORD

This Manual is issued under authority of DoD Instruction 5000.2, "Defense Acquisition Management Policies and Procedures," January 1, 1991. It contains procedures and formats to be used to prepare various milestone documentation, periodic in-phase status reports, and statutory certifications.

This Manual applies to the Office of the Secretary of Defense; the Military Departments; the Chairman, Joint Chiefs of Staff and Joint Staff; the Unified and Specified Commands; the Defense Agencies; and DoD Field Activities (hereafter referred to collectively as "DoD Components").

It is the policy of the Department of Defense that Department of Defense acquisition documentation and reports, as defined herein, shall be:

1. Authorized by statute or Department of Defense policy;

2. Necessary for the conduct of official business; and

3. Properly planned, coordinated, produced, and distributed in accordance with this Manual.

Specific responsibilities pertaining to major areas of this Manual are provided in each individual part, as appropriate. The Under Secretary of Defense for Acquisition has the responsibility for preparation, maintenance, distribution, and update of this Manual.

This Manual is effective immediately for periodic reports and required certifications. However, the milestone documentation formats in this Manual shall first apply to programs coming to a milestone review 6 months after the date of publication of DoD Instruction 5000.2, "Defense Acquisition Management Polices and Procedures." This Manual is mandatory for use by all DoD Components, and DoD Component Heads shall distribute this Manual to the Program Manager and appropriate field operating command level within 60 days of receipt.

This Manual is intended for DIRECT implementation. There shall be no supplementation by DoD Components. Implementation necessary to establish the internal management processes required to comply with this Manual is permitted.

Send recommended changes to the Manual through proper channels to:

Under Secretary of Defense for Acquisition
ATTN: Office of Acquisition Policy and Program Integration
Pentagon, Room 3E1034
Washington, DC 20301

DoD Components may obtain copies of this Manual through their own
publications channels. Other Federal Agencies and the public may obtain
copies from the U.S. Department of Commerce, National Technical Information
Service, 5285 Port Royal Road, Springfield, VA 22161.

For all matters in this   For all matters in this
Manual relating to operational   Manual except operational
test and evaluation.   test and evaluation.

Robert C. Duncan   Donald J. Yockey
Director, Operational   Acting Under Secretary of
Test and Evaluation   Defense for Acquisition

TABLE OF CONTENTS

PART 16

SECTION H

SUPPLEMENTAL CONTRACT COST INFORMATION

DEFENSE ACQUISITION EXECUTIVE SUMMARY SECTION 7

PURPOSE:

    This section displays, in tabular form, summary-level contract
identification, schedule, and performance information.

PROCEDURES:

1. The "contract identification data" and "contract schedule data"
    sections apply to all large contracts identified in Defense
    Acquisition Executive Summary Section 6, (Program Background Data).

2. The "contract performance data" section applies primarily to those
    contracts requiring a Cost Performance Report (CPR) or a
    Cost/Schedule Status Report (C/SSR), (see Part 20), or other report
    containing cost performance data (identify the source).

    a. Items 3; 4.a.and 4.b.; 6 through 8; 15 through 16; 18 through 24;
        and 27 are taken directly from the Cost Performance Report or a
        Cost/Schedule Status Report without change.

    b. The remaining items are based on information available in other
        program documents or program cost estimates.

    c. Data should be no more than 60 days old. If the data is more
        than 60 days old, an explanation will be provided under the
        comments section (item 26).

    d. Reported data should be consistent with the contract effort. For
        example, when a Cost Performance Report or a Cost/Schedule Status
        Report is being received on a contract option, relevant dates and
        values associated only with the option, not the basic contract,
        should be shown.

    e. When a Cost Performance Report or a Cost/Schedule Status Report
        is not required, the Program Manager should provide the best
        estimate of contract cost at completion (item 25 below) and
        identify in the comments section (item 26) the source. This
        includes firm fixed price (FFP) contracts.

    f. For firm fixed price contracts, entries should be provided for
        items 1 through 5; 8a; 9 through 14; and 25.

g. Blanks, such as "not applicable (N/A)" and "to be determined (TBD)" should be avoided. If the Program Manager believes the contractor reported data is in error, the correct data and appropriate comments should be provided in the comments section (item 26).

3. When a contract is more than 90 percent complete (Cumulative Budgeted Cost for Work Performed (BCWP) divided by Total Allocated Budget), significant effort is complete (see item 13 below), and no additional modifications are anticipated, state in Section 26, "This is the Final Report". This section may be deleted from the next Defense Acquisition Executive Summary submission and the contract included in Defense Acquisition Executive Summary Section 6 (Program Background Data), part 4, line 1 (Completed Contracts), unless otherwise directed.

PREPARATION INSTRUCTIONS:

CONTRACT IDENTIFICATION DATA:

1. Program Name. Enter the preferred name of the program being reported. This name is the same as that reported in Section 6 (Program Background Data), part 4.

2. Contract Name. Enter a descriptive contract title which distinguishes this contract from others being reported for this program. This title is the same as that reported in Section 6 (Program Background Data), part 4.

3. Contractor Data

   a. Enter the name of the prime or associate contractor.

   b. Enter the division identification when appropriate (such as Rockwell International (Collins) or Boeing (Vertol)).

   c. Enter the city of the contractor's main facility performing the work.

   d. Enter the state of the contractor's main facility performing the work.

4a. Contract Number. Enter the assigned contract number (e.g., N00007-90-C-0001).

4b. Change Order Nr. Enter the latest change order number, including those that are not definitized.

4c. Contract Type. Enter the type of contract as defined in subchapter 3, part 16 of the Federal Acquisition Regulation (reference (g)), such as cost-plus-incentive-fee (CPIF), cost-plus-fixed-fee (CPFF), cost-plus-incentive-fee/award fee (CPIF/AF), fixed-price incentive firm target (FPIF), or firm fixed price (FFP). For incentive

contracts, enter in the comments section (item 26) the share ratio
(for example, 50/50 or 60/40).

4d. Contract Deliveries. Enter the total contract major end item
      delivery quantity, the cumulative quantity planned for delivery to
      date, and the actual quantity delivered to date.

5.   Program Phase. Identify the program phase for which work is being
      done on this contract (i.e., DEV for engineering and manufacturing
      development or PROD for production or ship construction).

6.   Negotiated Cost. Enter the current cost (excluding fee or profit)
      for all contract effort on which agreement has been reached as of the
      report date shown in item 15. For a cost-type contract, enter the
      estimated cost negotiated for the authorized contract effort,
      excluding amounts negotiated for cost growth. For a fixed price type
      or cost plus incentive fee type contract, enter the definitized
      contract target cost. No entry is required for a firm fixed price
      contract.

7.   Cost of Authorized, Unpriced Work. Enter the contractor's estimated
      cost (excluding fee or profit) for all work where written
      authorization has been received, but definitized contract prices have
      not been negotiated. No entry is required for firm fixed price
      contracts.

8a.   Target Price. Enter the contractor's current estimated contract
      target price. For a cost-type contract, enter the current estimated
      price, including the estimated cost for authorized effort, any
      estimated cost growth, and applicable fee.

8b.   Ceiling Price. Enter the contractor's current estimated contract
      ceiling price, if applicable. For example, no entry is required for
      a firm fixed price contract.

CONTRACT SCHEDULE DATA:

9.   Contract Definitization Date: Enter the initial contract
      definitization date (MON YY) (e.g., JUN 86 for June 1986).

10.   Work Start Date. Enter the date (MON YY) work started on the
      contract, whether or not the contract is definitized. For a contract
      option or modification being reported separately, show the date work
      started on the reported effort, not the basic contract start date.

11.   Critical Milestone 1 - Name and Completion Date. Enter the name and
      current estimate of the completion date (MON YY) for the first of two
      contract critical milestones as defined by the Program Manager. For
      engineering and manufacturing development contracts, this may be the
      preliminary design review (PDR), or equivalent. For production
      contracts, this may be first production item delivery or equivalent.
      The event selected should be consistent from report to report. Once
      the event is completed, a different, more current and active,
      contract milestone should be entered in item 11.

12. <u>Critical Milestone 2 - Name and Completion Date</u>. Enter the name and current estimate of the completion date (MON YY) for the second of two contract critical milestones defined by the Program Manager. For engineering and manufacturing development contracts, this may be the critical design review (CDR), or equivalent. For production contracts, this may be full rate production capability or equivalent. The event selected should be consistent from report to report. Once the event is completed, a different, more current and active, contract milestone should be entered in item 12.

13. <u>Significant Effort Completion Date</u>. Enter the Program Manager's current estimated completion date (MON YY) for the significant effort on the contract. It should represent that point in the contract when the major portion of the contract work is expected to be completed. After this date, the expenditure rate is expected to decrease significantly as the contractor reassigns personnel. For engineering and manufacturing development contracts, this may be the date when the last major testing is expected to be completed. For production contracts, this may be the date that the last major item of equipment is expected to be delivered to the Government.

14. <u>Estimated Completion Date</u>. Enter the Program Manager's current estimate of the date (MON YY) that the contract effort actually will be completed. For contracts with a Cost Performance Report or Cost/Schedule Status Report, this is when cumulative Budgeted Cost for Work Performed for all practical purposes equals the contract budget base.

<u>CONTRACT PERFORMANCE DATA</u>:

15. <u>Report Date</u>. Enter the accounting period cutoff date (MM/DD/YY) for the data covered by the contractor's report (Cost Performance Report or Cost/Schedule Status Report) that is being used to prepare this section.

16. <u>Source Document</u>. Enter the source document (Cost Performance Report, Cost/Schedule Status Report, or ·Other) that is being used to prepare this format. If "Other" is entered, specify the source of the cost performance data.

17. <u>Verification of Data</u>. Enter the review type and date the review was conducted (or is planned to be conducted) on the contractor's cost and schedule management control system (e.g., (a.) "Subsequent application review (SAR)," (b.) "April 1988", or (a.) "walk-through-talk-through (WTTT), " (b.) "April 1990"). Identify in the comments section (item 26) any problems or inconsistencies in the performance data, any known problems in the contractor's cost and schedule management control system, and any waivers granted from Cost/Schedule Control System Criteria (C/SCSC) review requirements (see Part 11-B, DoD Instruction 5000.2, "Defense Acquisition Management Policies and Procedures" (reference (e))).

16-H-4

18. Budgeted Cost for Work Scheduled (BCWS). Enter the cumulative Budgeted Cost for Work Scheduled from the performance report (column 7 on the Cost Performance Report and column 2 on the Cost/Schedule Status Report).

19. Budgeted Cost for Work Performed (BCWP). Enter the cumulative Budgeted Cost of Work Performed from the performance report (column 8 on the Cost Performance Report and column 3 on the Cost/Schedule Status Report).

20. Actual Cost of Work Performed (ACWP). Enter the cumulative Actual Cost of Work Performed from the performance report (column 9 on the Cost Performance Report and column 4 on the Cost/Schedule Status Report).

21. Management Reserve (Mgt Res). Enter the total amount of contractor management reserve remaining from the performance report (column 14 on the Cost Performance Report and column 7 on the Cost/Schedule Status Report).

22. Contract Budget Base (CBB). Enter the sum of negotiated cost (item 6) plus the estimated cost for the authorized, unpriced work (item 7) from the performance report (block 5 on the Cost Performance Report format 3 and block 5 on the Cost/Schedule Status Report). If the contract is not definitized, explain in the comments section (item 26) what the contract budget base represents and when contract definitization is anticipated. For cost-type contracts, include in the contract budget base only the estimate for authorized effort, not the estimates for cost growth.

23. Total Allocated Budget. Enter the sum of all budgets allocated to the contract from the performance report (block 6 on the Cost Performance Report format 3). This amount normally equals the contract budget base (item 22). If this amount differs from the contract budget base, an explanation is required in the comments section (item 26). (See paragraph 27 below.)

24. Contractor's Estimated Cost. Enter the contractor's latest revised estimate of contract cost at completion (excluding fee or profit) for the period covered by the performance report. It includes only authorized effort.

25. Program Manager's (PM's) Estimated Cost. Enter the Program Manager's best estimate of contract cost at completion (excluding fee or profit) for the period covered by the performance report (see item 26 below). It includes only authorized effort. Cost estimates in excess of the Government's liability must be reported. The Program Manager's best estimate and its source should be provided for contracts (including firm fixed price contracts) that do not require contract cost reporting.

26. Comments. This section is designed to provide concise information on contract performance, including any effect of contract performance on overall program execution.

16-H-5

a. Address the Program Manager's estimate of contract cost at
    completion as follows:

    (1) Enter the range of estimates at completion, reflecting best
        and worst cases.

    (2) Provide the estimate at completion reflecting the best
        professional judgment of the servicing cost analysis
        organization. If the contract is at least 15 per cent
        complete and the estimate is lower than that calculated
        using the cumulative cost performance index, provide an
        explanation.

    (3) Justify the Program Manager's best estimate (item 25) if the
        contract is at least 15 per cent complete and the estimate
        is lower than that calculated using the cumulative cost
        performance index.

b. Display in rank order the top five challenges to meeting contract
    objectives. Indicate for each challenge the best case, worst
    case, and best estimate regarding the effect on cost, schedule
    and performance. Describe action being taken to achieve the best
    estimate.

c. If a contractor's cost at completion is estimated to exceed the
    Government's liability (e.g., ceiling price, firm fixed price
    amount, contract "cap"), discuss actions being taken to ensure
    contractor compliance with the contract requirements and how
    increases in future program cost will be avoided.

d. Address the primary reasons for "significant" changes since the
    last report period for contract milestone completion dates (items
    11 through 14), contract budget base (item 22), problems on cost
    and schedule management control system reviews (item 17), and the
    reasons for authorizing over target baselines (item 27).

e. Keeping with the intent of the Defense Acquisition Executive
    Summary as an early warning report of both potential and actual
    problems, the Program Manager is expected to exercise sound
    judgment in providing comment in item 26. All aspects of
    contract performance, in addition to cost, should be reviewed
    including the potential for contract adjustments and the ability
    to execute the contract properly. Also all significant aspects
    of the contract award schedule, including definitization dates,
    should be assessed. Consideration should be given to the effect
    of delays that threaten to extend major contract award dates that
    are on the critical path of program master schedule activities or
    that threaten to expose the Government to unnecessary cost risk.
    These provisions are applicable for all types of contracts
    including fixed-price contracts, those with a "cost" cap, and
    those that may, for any reason, have waived Cost/Schedule Control
    Systems Criteria requirements.

16-H-6

27. <u>Over Target Baseline</u>. If the total allocated budget (item 23) exceeds the contract budget base (item 22), provide the date the change was authorized and the amount of any adjustments made to past cost and schedule variances.

28. <u>Unit Cost Report Requirements</u>. If the contract is a "major contract" as defined in Part 18, this block must be completed.

   a. <u>Contract Cost Baseline Established</u>. Enter the date that the contract cost baseline was established (MMDDYY).

   b. <u>Statement</u>. State either "There have been no breaches of the contract cost baseline," or state "There has been a breach of the contract cost baseline." (item 28.a).

   c. <u>Comments Since the Baseline Report</u>. This section provides information on the cost variance and schedule variance from the time of the baseline report to the current reporting period. The baseline report is defined in Part 18, Attachment 2.

<u>Attachments - 2</u>

1. Supplemental Contract Cost Information
2. Supplemental Contract Cost Information Continuation Page

DAES FORMAT 7
SUPPLEMENTAL CONTRACT COST INFORMATION

CONTRACT IDENTIFICATION DATA

1. PROGRAM NAME	2. CONTRACT NAME	3. CONTRACTOR DATA
		A NAME ____
4a. CONTRACT NUMBER / 4b. CHANGE ORDER NR	4c CONTRACT TYPE / 4d CONTRACT DELIVERIES: TOTAL QTY ____ PLANNED DELIV ____ ACTUAL DELIVERY ____	B DIVISION ____ C CITY ____ D STATE ____
5. PROGRAM PHASE DEV ____ PROD ____	6 NEGOTIATED COST	7 COST OF AUTHORIZED, UNPRICED WORK / 8a TARGET PRICE / 8b CEILING PRICE

CONTRACT SCHEDULE DATA

9. CONTRACT DEFINITIZATION DATE (MON YY)	11 CRITICAL MILESTONE 1 NAME: COMPLETION DATE (MON YY)	13 SIGNIFICANT EFFORT COMPLETION DATE (MON YY)
10. WORK START DATE (MON YY)	12 CRITICAL MILESTONE 2 NAME: COMPLETION DATE (MON YY)	14 ESTIMATED COMPLETION DATE (MON YY)

CONTRACT PERFORMANCE DATA

LEAVE BLANK	15 REPORT DATE (MM/DD/YY)	16 SOURCE DOCUMENT CPR ____ CSSR ____ OTHER ____	17 VERIFICATION OF DATA a REVIEW TYPE b REVIEW DATA (MON YY)

18 BCWS	19 BCWP	20 ACWP	21 MGT RES	22 CONTRACT BUDGET BASE	23 TOTAL ALLOCATED BUDGET	24 CONTR'S EST COST	25 PM'S EST COST

26 COMMENTS

27. OVER TARGET BASELINE

IF AMOUNT IN 23 EXCEEDS AMOUNT IN 22 PROVIDE THE FOLLOWING:

DATE AUTHORIZED (MON YY) ____   COST VARIANCE ADJUSTMENT ____   SCHEDULE VARIANCE ADJUSTMENT ____

DEFENSE ACQUISITION EXECUTIVE SUMMARY SECTION 7

SUPPLEMENTAL CONTRACT COST INFORMATION CONTINUATION PAGE

28. Unit Cost Report Requirements.   CLASS

   a. Contract Cost Baseline Established On:

   b. Statement:
       There have been no breaches of the contract cost baseline
       or
       There has been a breach of the contract cost baseline

   c. Comments since baseline report:

Baseline SAR Values as of DEC 31, 19XX	Values as of Last Unit Cost Breach	Current Values	Change Since Baseline SAR	Changes Since Last Unit Cost Breach
Cost Variance:				
$ _____	N/A*	_____	_____	N/A*
% _____	N/A*	_____	_____	N/A*
Schedule Variance:				
$ _____	N/A*	_____	_____	N/A*
% _____	N/A*	_____	_____	N/A*

*   If the program has submitted a Selected Acquisition Report (SAR) to
     reflect a unit cost breach, the appropriate fields will contain data.
     If the program has not had a unit cost breach, reflect this with "N/A"
     in the appropriate fields. The example above assumes there has been no
     unit cost breach.

Index

About the Authors

Quentin W. Fleming is with MicroFrame Technologies, Inc., a firm specializing in program management software systems.

Previously he was with Northrop Corporation from 1968 to 1991. In 1980 he wrote the management controls section for the B-2 Bomber proposal; in 1987 he was Cost Account Manager (CAM) for the principal subcontractor on the Advanced Tactical Fighter (ATF); in 1990 he developed a multi-functional subcontract management training program.

He has authored four published hardbound business books:

A Guide To Doing Business On The Arabian Peninsula, AMACOM-American Management Association, 1981.

Put Earned Value (C/SCSC) Into Your Management Control System, Publishing Horizons, Inc., 1983.

Project and Production Scheduling, Probus Publishing Company, 1987, with Bronn and Humphreys.

Cost/Schedule Control Systems Criteria: The Management Guide To C/SCSC, Probus Publishing Company, 1988.

He holds a Master of Arts degree in management from the University of Redlands.

Quentin J. Fleming is a management consultant with expertise in organizational assessment, managerial effectiveness and strategic planning.

Previously he was with IBM and Northrop in the areas of administration, finance and contract management. He holds a Master of Business Administration degree from the University of Southern California.

This book may be kept